The Third Line

The Third Line

—— ❧ ——

The Opera Performer as Interpreter

DANIEL HELFGOT
with
WILLIAM O. BEEMAN

Schirmer Books
An Imprint of Macmillan Publishing Company
New York

Maxwell Macmillan Canada
Toronto

Maxwell Macmillan International
New York   Oxford   Singapore   Sydney

Schirmer Books
An Imprint of Macmillan Publishing Company
866 Third Avenue
New York, NY 10022

Maxwell Macmillan Canada, Inc.
1200 Eglinton Avenue East, Suite 200
Don Mills, Ontario M3C 3N1

Macmillan Publishing Company is part of the Maxwell
Communication Group of Companies

Library of Congress Catalog Card Number: 93–12311

Printed in the United States of America

printing number
1 2 3 4 5 6 7 8 9 10

Library of Congress Cataloging-in-Publication Data

Helfgot, Daniel
    The third line : the opera performer as interpreter / Daniel
  Helfgot with William O. Beeman.
       p.   cm.
    Includes bibliographical references and index.
    ISBN 0–02–871036–3 (alk. paper)
    1. Singing—Interpretation (Phrasing, dynamics, etc.)   2. Acting
  in opera.   I. Beeman, William O.   II. Title
MT892.H44   1993
782.1'146—dc20
                                        93–12311
                                           CIP
                                           MN

The paper used in this publication meets the minimum requirements of American National Standard for Information Sciences—Permanence of Paper for Printed Library Materials. ANSI
Z39.48-1984. ⊚™

Contents

— ❧ —

Preface   ix
Acknowledgments   xi

CHAPTER 1   *Why We Need the Third Line*   *1*

Modern Opera Performance   1
Singing as a Career: A Special Note to Singers   4
The Plan of This Book   6

CHAPTER 2   *Preparation for the Third Line: A
                     Capable Mind in a Capable Body*   *9*

The Illiterate Parrot versus the Intellectual Singer   9
Meaningless Sounds   11
Imbuing Performance with Meaning   12
A Capable Body   14
Fach   18
Relaxation   19
The "Look"   22

CHAPTER 3   *Third Line Skills I: The Opera
                     Performer as Actor*   *25*

The Singer as Stage Actor   26
The Negative Valuation of Acting Skills   27
Preparing for Singing/Acting   29
Stage Directors versus Music Directors   30

v

Despairing the Passing of the Golden Age   31
Backstage Savvy   33
Making Visual Music: The Composer as Dramatist   34
Librettists and Composers   40
Finding an Interpretation: Text versus Music   42

CHAPTER 4 *Third Line Skills II: The Opera Performer as Musician*   45

Understanding the Score   46
Approaching the Score for the First Time   48
Enjoying Musical Preparation   50
Understanding Musical Style   52
Conclusion   61

CHAPTER 5 *Third Line Skills III: Movement and Expression*   63

The Opera Performer on Stage   63
Movement   65
Expression   65
Fusing Movement and Expression   67
Training for Today   68
Natural Life, Gesture, and Movement   69
How Much Movement   71
Telling Stories   74
Focus   75
Focus and Facial Expression   83
Entanglements   86
Look at People!   87

CHAPTER 6 *Writing the Third Line*   89

The Marriage of Text and Music   90
The Third Line   91
The Performer as Third Creative Partner   93
Balance and Taste   101

CHAPTER 7 *Practicing the Third Line*   105

Repeated Text   112
Interpreting Large Contours   119
Interpreting Sparse Text   124
Using the Third Line When Others Sing   128

CHAPTER 8 *Accomplishing the Third Line* 131

Less is More: Economy in Performance 131
Hang-Ups and Gestures 134
The Third Line and the Rehearsal Process 136
The Third Line and the Study of Arias 138
The Third Line as Career Investment 139
The Fourth (and Fifth) Line 140

CHAPTER 9 *Help in Writing the Third Line:*
Coaches and Other Aids in Learning 143

Coaching as Learning 143
Finding a Coach 145
The Acting Coach 147
Vocal Color and Style 148
The Language Coach 152
The Style Coach 158
A Lifetime of Learning 160
Coaching and the Third Line 164

CHAPTER 10 *Balancing the Third Line: The Singer*
and the Voice Teacher 167

Technicians and Guides 169
The Sanctity of Vocalism 171
Vocal Instruction and Vocal Performance Education 173
Managing Vocal Instruction 175
Financing Instruction 178
Making the Most of Lessons 179
Gurus and Mother Hens 180

CHAPTER 11 *Using the Third Line: The Audition* 183

What Is an Audition? 184
Preparing for an Audition 186
Preparation and the Soul of the Singer 188
The Accompanist 191
Repertoire and Self-Classification 193
Résumés 197
Management and Auditions 200
Doing the Audition 201

CHAPTER 12 *Performing with the Third Line:*
Competitions and Recitals 205

Clothing for Competitions 208
Repertoire 209

The Résumé   210
Using the Third Line in Competitions   211
Recitals   211
The Third Line and Musical Practice in the Recital   214
The Third Line and the Recital as Theater   215

CHAPTER 13   *Expanding the Third Line: Opera
                        as an Art Form*   *219*

Practical Realities   222
What Can You Offer Opera?   225
Revolutionize, with No Apologies!   225

APPENDIX   *Resources for Opera:
                     An Annotated Bibliography*   *229*

Index   239

Preface

———————— 〜🙙 ————————

Opera may be the most misunderstood theatrical art. Its supporters are wildly enthusiastic, while its detractors are derisive. It is hailed as the most sublime of experiences, and vilified as the silliest and most absurd of entertainments. Both these views, although contradictory, depict opera quite accurately. At its best, opera is indeed sublime. At its worst, it is ridiculous.

Opera becomes ridiculous when it is allowed to be less than it can or should be. Although composers and librettists conceived of opera as a total art fusing theatrical and musical skills, in the twentieth century, it has often become a lopsided beast, at times dominated by vocalism to the exclusion of all other skills. In doing so, it loses touch with the kinship it has with the other lively forms of theater-plus-music with which it has close affinities: musical comedy, operetta, light opera, and musical theater. These forms have changed and evolved continuously, developing new and exciting artistic possibilities on a regular basis. In the meantime opera must fight to avoid becoming frozen, rigid, and pompous. Rigidity in opera is championed by defenders of "tradition," but "tradition" often means fear of evolutionary change.

Most opera performers receive the message that they are on stage primarily to sing instead of perform. Whatever else they are able to do by way of acting is icing on the cake. The result is that opera singers in training receive instruction in little other than vocal technique. When called upon to act, they hide behind their need to produce sound. This retards the development of opera and cheats composers, librettists, and audiences of complete realization of the audiovisual nature of the art.

Personalities from diverse backgrounds in the opera profession, by proclaiming the supremacy of the voice over the ideal of the total integrated performance, have frequently slowed the progress of training complete performers. These same persons have attacked creative staging as detrimental to the "purity" of opera. Producers, directors, and designers today find themselves engaged in a continual war in trying to keep the form updated, fresh, and provocative in spite of ill-equipped performers and conservative management.

The dilemma facing those who love opera as an evolving art, rather than as a museum art, is how to maintain it as a contemporary form of entertainment. It is hard to see how this can be done when most singers are not trained to move, jump, run, walk, or even use their speaking voices onstage.

We take the position in this book that the masters who gave us opera—both those in the past, and those writing today—deserve a total singer for a total art. No halfway measures should be satisfactory. No compromises should be made. Yes, of course, opera should always have the best possible singing. But that is not enough. Opera lovers should not be satisfied to see marvelous scores receive pale, half-baked, fossilized stage renderings where the poetry of the libretto is lost and the performers' actions and attitudes make no sense. The idea that opera should be stuffed and placed in a gilded cage while other musical theater forms thrive—because performers in these other forms benefit from a much different and richer form of training—must be put aside.

Opera has been the ultimate artistic goal of master creators in the arts for four centuries. Writers, composers, artists, designers, choreographers, theater directors, movie makers, actors, and dancers have looked at it as the *non plus ultra* of the creative mind. Singers are at the center of this cosmic picture. It is up to the operatic performers to make sure that opera will grow and thrive, for all of the hopes and dreams of the creators of operatic works and productions are dashed if there are no performers capable of carrying out their visions. Operatic activity cannot be transformed from performance to preservation—to become a stiff, stilted, withdrawn myth. That is not the way Gluck, Mozart, Rossini, Bizet, Verdi, Wagner, Puccini, Prokofiev, Stravinsky, Berg, or Britten intended it to be.

We have written this book in order to emphasize that singers can and should become fully empowered performers. As we point out, it is not easy for someone who aspires to a career in opera to get proper training and guidance. Much of the education of a singer today must be self-education. This education can and should last a lifetime, and it should be a joyous process. For singers it is a fabulous journey of exploration of their own body and mind, of languages, culture, history, philosophy, and, yes, music. A career in opera is admittedly an extremely difficult thing to achieve. For those singers who love the art in the vibrant growing form it should be, not in the mummified form in which it is most often seen, the process of self-development holds rich rewards.

The formula for realizing one's full potential as an operatic performer is simple, but not simplistic. The source of all understanding is the score and its two parallel "lines": text and music. We look at the performance as a result of the first two lines—a "third line" that emerges with equal respect to both of them. A score is not a vocalise, but rather the words of a writer shaped by a composer. Opera never should lose sight of the fact that the matrimony of text and music is permanent. So "opera interpretation," not "opera singing," is the third line—the artists' response to the work of the creators.

Acknowledgments

———————— ?? ————————

Thanks are due to The National Endowment for the Humanities and the Stanford Humanities Center for support leading to the completion of this book. Support was also provided by Brown University, Opera San José, Des Moines Metro Opera and the California State University Summer Arts Program at Humboldt State University, Arcata, California where this book had its initial genesis.

Among the singers and opera professionals who have read and commented on parts of the manuscript are Andrew Bird, James Bailey, Melissa Coyne, Harold Evans, Frank Farris, Victoria Hart, William Livingston, Charlene Marcino, Roger Staples, Marcie Stapp, and Reed Woodhouse. Not all of the above agreed with our ideas, so they should not be held in any way responsible for the content of the book. Nevertheless their commentary was invaluable in shaping the manuscript.

CHAPTER 1

———————— 𝓮𝓮 ————————

Why We Need the Third Line

MODERN OPERA PERFORMANCE

Most readers of this book are in the process either of becoming performers in opera, or of guiding performers toward a career in opera. Not only is an opera career one of the most physically demanding in the world, it is also mentally exhausting, expensive, and full of heartaches. It is extraordinarily competitive as well, with chances of real success—or even of making a living at it—very slim.

Yet as all who love opera know in their hearts, opera has the possibility of being a wonderful profession in terms of personal fulfillment. Music takes on a special significance for the singer of opera—it is no longer abstract sound, but rather sound filled with meaning. Opera performers use their musical gifts to make the figures of fantasy come to life, catching audiences in a magical spell that is elevated beyond the spoken word as well. To opera performers, *nothing* matches the deep satisfaction of a successful performance. It makes them feel good in every way.

The demands of opera today are changing rapidly. Interpreters will be expected to command more performance skills than their immediate predecessors ever imagined. Singers must find a way to train and equip themselves adequately for the increasing challenges of the profession.

The conflict between vocalism and more complete performance has been a central problem for composers and librettists, producers and audiences since the beginning of opera. Tastes, attitudes, and solutions have shifted back and forth over the years. Composers during some periods gave up the desire for drama. They used poor libretti and created music as a vehicle for simple vocal exhibitionism. Composers in other periods have done the opposite.

The great change in modern opera performance is the slow shift from opera as a purely musical art celebrating vocalism, to opera as a total performing art where theatrical and musical values exist in equal strength. There are many reasons for this shift. One is the example set by a number of modern singers: that a singer can indeed be a lively and vital actor as well as a musician. Directors discovered the artistic power inherent in the skilled singing actor. They demanded that productions be carefully staged and rehearsed for a longer period than had been customary in order to make opera productions real theater rather than costumed recitals. Scholars added to the shift by increasing research into the dramatic intentions of opera composers and librettists from Gluck and Mozart, through Verdi, and down to modern times.

The advent of new technology began to cause a tremendous change in the expectations of the opera audience. Among the most important changes are supertitles and television and, to some extent, movies. With supertitles the opera audience could suddenly understand the meaning of the action onstage. Performers could not sing arias embodying love or rage with a deadpan expression and semaphoric gestures without seeming ridiculous. Their actions now more than ever had to match a story line and a dramatic text.

Opera on television with subtitles exposes performers to audience scrutiny in an intimate way. What works on stage simply does not work on television. An aging, overweight soprano still may find approval as Mimi in *La Bohème* at a few opera houses. The same singer appears absurd on the television screen in the same role. We cannot turn back the clock! Opera on television and video-cassette will continue to be an important avenue for the spread of the art as it widens the opera audience. When the opera audience returns to the theater having seen television or film, it is impossible for them not to compare the two production modes.

These changes are much bemoaned by a small group of opera administrators and fans who complain that the great vocal stars of yesteryear have no modern counterparts—that people emerging in careers on the opera stage are people who don't duplicate the feats of the singers of some mythical Golden Age of Opera.

To this we say, "Nonsense!" The best (but not all, by any means) of today's emerging singers not only have all the vocal strength of their predecessors, but are also able to engage their audiences with their acting and interpretation. They are trained (or should be trained) as musicians and as linguists in as many as five languages. Moreover, they are easy and comfortable to work with. In the hands of a few capable and imaginative directors, these singers have made it possible for opera to move forward, develop, and become a total entertainment—not something that must continually apologize for itself because of its artificiality. Even in this emerging new Golden Age, opera is still the laughingstock of many related professions and potential patrons. Jokes about fat ladies in helmets persist as an important reminder.

It is fortunate that many people have gotten the message that opera is now better than ever. The result is an unprecedented boom at the box office. According to the Central Opera Service, the American opera audience increased by 20 percent, from 17.7 million in the 1987–88 season to 21.4 million in the 1988–89 season. This makes opera the fastest-growing entertainment form in the United States. Since 1964 both audiences and the total number of performances have tripled. The demographics are also good. Audiences are increasingly younger and more eclectic in their entertainment tastes than they were ten years ago.

The opera administration establishment of the past consisted largely of European émigrés from the World War I and World War II era. They generally sought to preserve the art in the way they remembered it in the old country.[1] However, opera has evolved since then; it has changed under the influence of other arts.

In the United States, vocal music is no longer produced only for the ear. Popular music becomes more like opera every day. In the fifties and sixties, pop songs were meant to be heard or danced to. Today popular music is made to be watched as well. Most hit songs are now being produced with an accompanying video which is in effect a miniopera. The majority of songs aired on MTV tell a story. Rock concerts are complex productions with elaborate visual effects and are choreographed from beginning to end. Tickets to these concerts are costly, but no more expensive than tickets to operas. Opera may thus be far less alienating to a younger generation used to seeing music presented visually and to paying lots of money for it.

Opera and rock videos may remain totally separate as musical forms. Nevertheless, cross-pollination between popular idioms and opera has been a feature of the art since the days of Handel. He built popular tunes into his works, just as modern composers like Henry Mollicone use jazz and rock idioms in their work. The second act of Mollicone's *Hotel Eden* (premiere, Opera San José, 1989) features a rock trio used to great dramatic effect.

Opera is also growing because of the decentralization of the arts in America. The nation is losing its fixation on New York as the center of all cultural events. Opera is following the trend established twenty years ago in regional theater—most of the growth is taking place in medium-sized and small cities. Cities such as Reno, Nevada, and Richmond, Indiana, have established professional opera companies. Smaller companies can take greater financial and artistic risks. Adventuresome new works can be seen premiering in unexpected places such as Omaha, San José, Minneapolis, and Houston.

This is a tremendously exciting time for aspiring singers. Opportunities are available as they never were before—but there are also more singers than ever before. The question remains: can singers acquire the skills that they need to have successful and fulfilling careers?

SINGING AS A CAREER: A SPECIAL NOTE
TO SINGERS

We all know the romantic view of an opera career: The singer appears on stage before an adoring audience of thousands, in a fabulous costume, accompanied by a full orchestra, portraying a figure of legend and romance, his or her voice cascading to the farthest walls of the opera hall, creating a sensation in the audience, all ending with dozens of curtain calls amid showers of roses. The artist becomes a sacred being whose every whim must be satisfied. As an international star, he or she lives on an estate in Switzerland or a Fifth Avenue New York apartment, and is whisked from world capital to world capital on a pink cloud of luxury.

This scenario is a fantasy that keeps many aspiring singers going during their darkest days, but it is very far from the reality experienced by all but a handful of international superstars. Scores of opera singers are either unemployed, have only occasional opportunities to sing, sing only smaller roles which earn few accolades, or sing only in small regional companies where they receive no national or international attention.

In many ways the international superstar singers are engaged in a kind of art that is completely different from the workaday world of opera singing. Many of these artists have become sacred monsters—not because they are unpleasant people, but because they are caught up in a whirlwind of promotion and publicity that often compromises their art. There are still many large opera houses that will fly one of these singers in for a performance with only one dress rehearsal, if any. The opera then becomes a kind of recital for the star with support from some other singers and an orchestra. Many audience members come only to hear the famous singer, caring little about the opera itself.

To those reading this book who are singers, we stress that, if they want to work in opera because their dream is to become superstars, chances are they will be deeply disappointed. If, however, fledgling singers want to work in opera because they love the art more than anything else and cannot imagine being happy unless they are able to sing—even if only once in a while, or in small roles or small houses, or as public employees singing in a small-town theater in Central Europe—they have a fighting chance for a career. If they do become superstars—congratulations! But if they don't, they will have been privileged to do the thing they love the most—certainly no small achievement in life.

As we will suggest below and throughout this book, even if singers fall short of the bright lights and glamor, they can derive deep satisfaction from the process of training and equipping themselves for performing. Preparing roles for performance is an intellectual adventure which will use all of their physical, mental, and emotional skills. It is a fascinating process which they can be engaged in throughout their life.

The rigors, heartaches, and competition of an opera career are not the only obstacles singers must face. It is also difficult to know where to get proper training and career advice. Most formal training for opera still centers on the training of the vocal instrument. It is centered on the vocal studio and on the voice teacher. The voice teacher is, of course, absolutely indispensable in opera training. If a person cannot sing very well, he or she cannot work as a performer in the field. But today vocal training is simply not enough. As we will maintain throughout this book, singers need to learn acting, physical movement and dance, languages, music history, cultural history, literature, and musicology, to mention just a few essential skills. Moreover, they need to develop a method for bringing all of these skills to bear on the material they will be required to perform on stage. The purpose of this book is to help singers develop a strategy for accomplishing this massively complicated training, and for using it effectively.

Singers must do most of the work in designing and executing training themselves. This may be a surprise to many who are already in training, or who plan on entering school for the purpose of learning to perform in opera. Opera training programs are, with few exceptions, inadequate to the task of training performers in all of the things they must be able to do. These programs are typically centered in music-teaching institutions and focus almost exclusively on vocal training.

In 1984 the National Association of Schools of Music published a survey of university- or conservatory-based opera training programs entitled "The Education and Training of the Singer-Actor." This survey revealed the deep bias toward exclusive training of vocal skills in the development of opera performers. Although virtually every program claimed to require training in languages, acting, dance, martial arts, and other skills, students were rarely required to demonstrate actual competence in these areas before receiving their degrees. Too often, students were thrust into full student productions of operas with no stage background except voice instruction. They were expected to learn stage movement and acting on the fly.

We were sad to note that even vocal instruction in many programs appeared to be inadequate, consisting typically of a single voice lesson each week—or approximately 26 lessons in a school year. Formal coaching, if offered at all, was also generally once a week for an hour. Moreover, students usually had to take the "luck of the draw" for vocal instructors, with little chance to switch.

Things have changed for the better since 1984, and there are some programs that have made concerted efforts to balance training, but many opera programs still suffer from the same gap between the ideal and the real. This is the basis for our conclusion that aspiring performers in opera today, even those who attend a formal opera training program, must design and execute their own course of study. We are not saying, "Don't go to a conservatory," or "Don't major in opera performance at college." Such programs can be an efficient way to begin. But singers themselves will have to look hard at what they are learning and find the additional people and resources to draw on to help them train and reach their goals. They will get a great deal of help from their fellow singers, from the people they find as teachers, and from books and publications, but singing is not like medical school where someone tracks students onto an automatic career path. It is up to singers to train themselves to become powerful interpreters of the operatic literature and jealous guardians of their own dreams and goals.

THE PLAN OF THIS BOOK

We hope this book will serve as a guide for singers, and for those who have an interest in singers and singing, to the many things performers must learn in order to establish themselves in an opera career. It does have a central focus, however. That focus is a technique for interpretation which we call "the third line."

The third line is, briefly, the interpretive line a singer adds to the other two lines in an operatic score. The first line is the text of the libretto. The second is the musical line. The third line is one the *singer* adds and consists of the body movement, eye focus, facial expression, and inflection that make the score leap off the page and into reality on the stage. The third line is the singers' considered conclusion as performers—their visual, physical, mental, and vocal answer to the tasks set for them by the composer and librettist.

Singers must command all three lines in order to be successful performers. Teachers and coaches will help them master the first two lines, but only the singers can write the third line. It is the part of their performance that will be uniquely theirs: the culminating result of their study, experience, imagination, and hard work.

We begin Chapter 2 with a discussion of the two pieces of raw material a singer must bring to the act of creating the third line: a capable mind and a capable body. Singers must develop an open, free set of attitudes to performance, and they must train their bodies to respond with flexibility if they hope to be successful.

In Chapter 3, as an introduction to the concept of the third line, we deal with the opera performer as an actor. This is the area of opera performance that has been most neglected in the near past, and that singers will have to fill in most rigorously if they are involved in a typical opera training program.

Chapter 4 addresses the second skill necessary for creating the third line: the opera performer as musician. In this chapter we try to emphasize that opera performers are more than just singers. They are total musicians and need a great many musicological skills in order to work with other singers and with an orchestra.

In Chapter 5 we take up the question of movement and expression. It is important to have a capable body, but it is also important to know how to use those physical skills to best advantage onstage and in coordination with singing.

How to construct the third line is the topic of Chapter 6. In this chapter, we talk about the marriage of text and music, and the ways performers can add a clear interpretive dimension, including movement and expression, to the operatic score. Here we provide numerous examples of the third line added to standard opera excerpts.

Chapter 7 deals with special interpretive problems encountered by singers and the way they can be dealt with using third line techniques. In particular, singers' problems in finding interpretive solutions to repetitive texts, situations with little dramatic motivation, and the interpretation of broad melodic contours are treated here.

In Chapter 8 we discuss polishing performance through the use of the third line. The principal focus is on achieving balance in interpretation by practicing and rehearsing opera performance through the third line.

Singers can rarely obtain all the information and feedback they need by themselves for effective performance. Chapter 9 addresses the subject of coaching and other methods for obtaining information that will help in writing the third line. We provide a description of the many kinds of coaching that singers are likely to need throughout their training. We then suggest avenues that singers may pursue to receive that coaching, along with some observations about the complementary roles of coach and voice teacher.

In Chapter 10 we deal with the voice teacher and his or her role in the development of a singing career. We try to emphasize the development of a healthy relationship with the voice teacher, along with suggestions about how that relationship can be kept in balance with other career development needs.

Auditions, competitions, and recitals are central to career advancement in the opera profession. They are often the most difficult ordeals faced by any singer. In Chapters 11 and 12, we discuss these three difficult circumstances and make practical suggestions for getting through them unscathed using the third line.

Finally, in Chapter 13 we return to the question of opera as an art form. We hope to help all readers to see opera as an integrated activity involving many different forms of training and many different skills. If opera is to be an art form, however, we believe it must be an evolving form. We hope to provide a few suggestions for readers to add their own artistry to the pool of creativity that is helping opera change and mature.

This book was written because we, like the readers, love opera and all it stands for. Throughout the text we point to many other useful books that have been written by those who also love opera and want performers to succeed. We hope readers will take the time to study these books as well and thereby enrich both their performance and their life.

NOTES

1. Ben Krywosz of the New Music-Theatre Ensemble in Minneapolis feels that the United States is now emerging with its own artistic tradition. "Every culture on earth has a musical theater impulse," he claims. "Opera is the European response to this impulse. America is now developing its own traditions and American opera will bear a relationship to European opera roughly analogous to the relationship between American culture and European culture."

CHAPTER 2

———— 🐦 ————

Preparation for the Third Line:
A Capable Mind in a Capable Body

THE ILLITERATE PARROT VERSUS THE
INTELLECTUAL SINGER

In order to become a performer in opera, and to construct the third line as a plan for interpretation of operatic material, it is necessary to have a mind and a spirit capable for the task. Singers who want to perform in opera today must cease thinking of themselves as vocalists cranking out sounds, and begin to think of themselves as interpretive artists conveying meaning to the audience via thorough preparation and exercise of musical and theatrical skills.

Too many singers have no aspirations in performing beyond making beautiful sounds. Whereas it is absolutely necessary for anyone who has a hope of making a career to be able to do that, it is not enough merely to sing well. The authors of the score provided *two* lines to deal with—text and music—singers cannot ignore the first in favor of the second. The text of an opera and the things it narrates—the plot and the meaning of the story—were good enough to inspire the composer's music. They should therefore be good enough to inspire singers to immerse themselves in comprehending the literary and cultural aspects of the work in order to develop their interpretation of it. This is the essence of the creation of the third line.

If a singer's conception of performing in opera is limited to vocalism, he or she runs the risk of becoming an "illiterate parrot" capable of reproducing sounds, but with little understanding of the deeper meaning of what is being sung. Singers need to understand why the composer designated particular sounds to accompany particular words, creating expression with meaning greater than the words or the music alone. Being an illiterate parrot is not, or should not be, acceptable in the opera profession today.

As we have pointed out in the introduction to this book, there are still a few mature stars who manage to hold a major position in the field without much in the way of acting abilities. They also have little insight into the music they perform or the text that the music shapes. They have spectacular voices and sell lots of tickets. However, they have had their music spoon-fed to them, have been coached incessantly by imitation or rote learning, and have been indulged on stage for years. They are "sacred monsters" in the profession. No one in opera management wants more singers with the same liabilities in the future if it can be helped.

Illiterate parrots create problems in any opera company, no matter how great or famous they are. They use up valuable rehearsal time, are difficult to deal with on stage, and are liable to make unreasonable demands when unable to perform what is asked by a conductor or stage director. In the end, they are unlikely to please an audience beyond the level of infatuation on the part of celebrity hounds.

How do such people get hired in the first place? First, the audition system is admittedly flawed: it is difficult to judge the full capabilities of any artist within a few minutes. Second, some companies, especially at the regional level, may not have much choice for certain roles. A production of *Tosca* requires three powerful singers: Tosca, Cavaradossi, and Scarpia. The vocal requirements of these roles may force a company to look less carefully at singers' other skills, and an illiterate parrot may be hired solely to fill a given role's vocal requirements. The staff then spends a frantic, stressful rehearsal period trying to equip the inadequate performer for the part. Third, groups of singers may be "packaged" by artist managers. In order for a company to have one excellent performer, the singer's manager may compel it to hire several lesser talents. The manager then gets paid for several artists rather than just one. Finally, singers may be fine in certain roles where they do not have to do much interpretation or acting, but, when engaged for others that require them to really communicate on stage, they fall flat.

The fault may also lie with the company. Some companies are still in the business of producing operatic "museum pieces" where singers are stick figures against a backdrop. For such companies the ability of a performer to breathe life into the drama of the words and music of the work is unimportant. Vocalism reigns absolutely in these companies, and it is perpetrated on the public in the name of *bel canto* aesthetics, or in the name of "tradition." In truth, audiences are shortchanged by organizations where the art form is not fully served.

The opposite of the illiterate parrots are the sensitive intellectual singers, who have a full knowledge of literature, musical style, acting, and interpretation. These singers also have lively, inquisitive minds. They are willing to put in the time and the effort to research the roles they sing, and learn the things necessary to create a believable performance. In short, they are singers capable of creating the third line to the score.

Intellectual singers are prepared for the task of performing opera because they have acquired the experience to be flexible when asked to undertake new interpretations. Rather than knowing just one way to interpret a role, they are able to conceive of many possibilities.

Opera companies love intellectual singers, because they are co-workers in the production. They come to rehearsal fully prepared, not just musically, but with interpretive ideas of their own, and with a flexibility that allows them to try new things onstage without being afraid or argumentative. They are secure in their vocalism, and they know in advance exactly where stage action is likely to occur in the score. They have prepared their roles with these things in mind, so that, when challenging things are asked of them by the stage director, they do not become flustered, shaken, resentful, or suspicious.

Most of all, intellectual singers are committed to the communication of meaning through music, not just to the production of sounds. They realize that opera tells stories through characters. Every character conveys meaning onstage with every word and every gesture. Even though words are sung on the opera stage, the audience must receive their full meaning.

We assume that many reading this book aspire to a career in opera, or are interested in helping others develop a career. We hope these readers will take to heart the distinction between illiterate parrots and intellectual singers and work with us to stamp out the former. If opera is to flourish and develop the kind of public support it deserves, it must have the best-prepared performers possible—who express ideas through music with the most beautiful instrument possible, one that is used as an interpretive tool.

It is interesting to note that some of today's opera performers got their start in musical comedy and operetta, where better stage skills are traditionally demanded. Nevertheless, it is a fallacy to think that performers in these other musical theater forms are necessarily better total performers simply because they are better actors. The vocal demands on these singer-actors are much less than in opera. Today's performers-in-training should aim for the best of both worlds: the highest standards in both vocal and stage artistry.

MEANINGLESS SOUNDS

How do singers become illiterate parrots? Part of the difficulty sometimes begins with the preeminence of the vocal studio in opera training. Most performers get the bulk of their instruction from voice teachers who do all they can to make the voice a reliable instrument. In the short time each week they have with their teachers, singers may not be able to receive adequate instruction in all areas of performing.

Moreover, vocal instruction requires a good deal of mechanized learning. Scales and vocalises are necessary for the physical training of the vocal musculature. When singers move on to practice interpretation through songs and arias, memorization is necessary. Oftentimes singers are learning vocal material in languages they neither read, speak, nor understand. Therefore much of the memorization becomes rote repetition. The result is that vocal interpretation is replaced by vocal mechanization.

Singers may never break the pattern of mechanized learning, even when professionally employed—the habit is too ingrained. It is surprising how many performers have only the vaguest idea of the meaning of the words they are singing. Fewer still have a clear notion of the historical contexts or the musicological significance of the composition of the operas in which they are performing.

We believe that it is very difficult, if not impossible, to give a satisfying performance based even partially on rote memorization. Such a performance is stripped of meaning. *The moment singers emit sounds rather than meanings, they are not performing opera, they are doing something else—something parrots can do.* Even if merely emitting sounds works for a time, when singers fail to express meanings, they are cheating their audiences. They are also cheating themselves of most of the pleasure of performing, and shortchanging the librettist and the composer. In effect, they are betraying opera itself.

IMBUING PERFORMANCE
WITH MEANING

Part of the task of becoming an opera performer is to develop a set of mental habits whereby both the process of learning and the process of performing become humanized. Having a capable mind means learning to think of everything one sings as having a meaning, even vocalises. Being able to do this is not the result of some esoteric talent. It is a matter of mental habit—allowing imagination and visualization skills to come into play at every turn.

Of course, imagination is not much good if it is limited in scope—so singers must develop the additional habit of pursuing continual research and discovery for everything they sing. The material to enrich the imagination comes from all possible sources: from study; from teachers, coaches, and other knowledgeable people; from travel; from life experience; and from one's own analysis of the musical text. A singer's life in the art of opera should be a continual search for meaning and the best way to communicate it.

Meaning arises from context. This includes the historical and musical background of the works and also the *subtext*—the underlying meaning—of the text being sung. The immediate context of the performance is also vital in helping a singer gain an understanding of the proper approach to the material being presented. The historical and musical background can be discovered through study and research. The subtext is something that the singer as a creative artist supplies in cooperation with the artistic staff, especially the stage director and conductor, of any production. The immediate context in performance includes an understanding of the performance space, co-artists, and the audience.

We will take a production of *Rigoletto* as an example. In preparing for the performance, singers need to know about the original work: *Le Roi S'Amuse* by Victor Hugo. It is essential to know why it was written, and what the social and critical commentary surrounding the work meant for its reception. It is then important to know why Verdi chose to write this work, and where this fell in his own musical biography. It is also important to understand why Verdi and his librettist changed certain critical aspects of the original Hugo work for the opera, why the government censors gave Verdi such a hard time, and why the opera's title was *Rigoletto* and not *La Maledizione* ("the curse"), as Verdi had originally wished, or why Hugo's *roi* (king) became a duke in Verdi's treatment.

These factors will be important in understanding what the stage director will require of performers in the opera. It will also provide important clues for musical preparation. In one production of *Rigoletto,* the performer playing the title role was asked to enter from the side of the stage. He objected, claiming that, since he was the title character, he *had* to enter from center stage. He was gently reminded that he is being called *cane* (dog) by Count Monterone who eventually curses him. Moreover, for Verdi the curse *(La Maledizione)* was in many ways more important than the character Rigoletto. In reality, the singer's entrance from the side of the stage was more powerful in terms of the drama than a center-stage entrance. This was a clear case where egocentrism on the part of the performer got in the way of an understanding of the basic concepts of the work. Valuable rehearsal time and a good working mood were sacrificed in the interchange.

In developing a subtext for Rigoletto, the performer needs to develop an idea about deformed people and their reception in society. As a singer prepares to play Rigoletto, his perspective will be intensely personal. The singer portraying Gilda will have to develop a sense of what it means to be the protected daughter of such a person. Father-daughter relations are extremely important in the opera, as well as parental overprotectiveness.

In understanding the immediate context of the performance, it is important for singers to know for whom they are performing, where, and why. Is the performance an excerpt for an audition or contest, or a full production with complete staging, makeup, and costumes? Will there be one person present or 4,000? Is the performance staged in a proscenium arch theater, in the round, in a recital hall, or in a classroom? Are the other performers seasoned veterans or young artists? Is the performance being televised or broadcast? How full is the house? How well is the audience likely to know the opera? Is the work being done with full orchestra or piano accompaniment? Will it be performed with supertitles or without? Will it be sung in the original language or in translation?

All of the above are factors that must be considered before singing a note. Singers who do not allow their performance to be informed by these factors are not fulfilling their duty as artists and interpreters of the authors' work.

Some singers reading this may be thinking: "That is too much to think about! Here I am desperately worrying about hitting my high notes and I'm expected to think about Victor Hugo!" Of course singers cannot concentrate on all contextual factors at once while singing, but it is part of training and developing a capable mind for opera performance to work all of these factors into their preparation. Those who truly love opera work to develop a performing spirit. As they mature and gain experience, they find this process richly rewarding—even fun. Each new artistic assignment becomes something akin to a treasure hunt with new delights at every turn.

A CAPABLE BODY

Having a capable body for opera involves two separate but integrated kinds of knowledge:

1. Knowing one's own body and what it is suitable for in performance
2. Knowing how to handle that body to good effect when performing

Neither of these is necessarily an inherent knowledge, but both can be developed over time as part of the equipment for performing.

Physique du rôle—Operatic Roles and Physical Suitability

All singers must first understand what their body is like, and what physical advantages and limitations exist for performing. Then they must be realistic about the kinds of things that can be performed with that body. Opera is a visual art. Singers will rarely, one hopes never, be allowed to sing a given role just because they "have the notes," without also being able to portray the role convincingly. When the curtain goes up, the singer's effectiveness onstage will be to a great degree determined by how close to the character he or she is able to look and act. Directors know this and will not consider singers who are obviously physically inappropriate. Therefore singers should make it easy on themselves, capitalize on their strengths, and choose to put their energy into developing those roles for which they are physically suited.

The one thing that cannot easily be changed about physical appearance is height. If singers are very tall or very short, it can limit the roles they can aspire to, depending on voice type. In general, lower voices have an advantage in casting if they are tall. Very tall basses and baritones are quite suited for most of the roles they might be expected to play. However, a six-foot soprano may have some difficulty in being cast for many of the traditional soprano roles. Even for a six-foot soprano, however, all is not lost. She may make a stunning Queen of the Night for *Die Zauberflöte*, or an imposing Brünnhilde in *Die Walküre*. A very short bass or baritone will find many opportunities in comic or character roles. A tall tenor is nearly always welcome as a romantic figure, and short tenors may be able to be cast opposite short women, or in character parts.

The above are, of course, stereotypes and not universal truths. There are ways to get around the physical unsuitability of a particular singer through clever casting and staging, but even the cleverest director can only push a concept so far. Porgy is definitely black, and Desdemona is white. Cio-cio-san is 15 years old, and the Grand Inquisitor is 90 (unless one tampers drastically with the original concept of the operas).

Weight is a very important reality in opera, just as it is in all of the entertainment field. To be frank, if singers are overweight, they are greatly limited today in their professional opportunities in opera. Some readers may point to the famous international stars who are clearly overweight and wonder about this statement. The requirements of the opera stage are very different today from the way they were even ten years ago. Today's audiences are not as forgiving as they were in the recent past. Much has occurred in the last several decades in the visual media which is causing audiences to insist that performers in opera be believable in their roles. In addition, performers must now assume that they will have opportunities to be featured on television or film—media that are much less forgiving than is the stage. This has, to be sure, drawn complaints from some opera patrons who claim that today's performers are chosen only to look good and not to sound good. There is a grain of truth in this, in that the convincing performer now has a definite edge in casting. This should alert singers to the fact that, with a stunning voice, excellent musical and stage skills, and an appropriate appearance, nothing will stand in the way of a successful career!

Some readers may insist that the voice is still the dominant factor in performing opera. To this we say that, if this is so, we despair for the future of the art form. Opera will then be doomed to a role as a ridiculous and ridiculed entertainment which always requires excuses, justification, and defense from smirks and jokes in the world at large. We would never deny the importance of the voice in opera performance. However, it is a waste of talent and resources to let voices alone eclipse the possibility for a fulfilling total theatrical experience.

One other area relating to physical appearance is also changing. Racial or physical characteristics are no longer the limitations they once were in casting. Black and Asian singers were at one time limited to certain roles on the opera stage. The range of characters now portrayed by these singers has widened greatly, and race-blind casting is slowly becoming standard for many companies. Yet concepts in this area vary from director to director. In the meantime, it would be foolish for dramatic sopranos with an Asian background to exclude Butterfly from their repertoire in favor of the very Roman Floria Tosca, or for black "Verdi" tenors to avoid Otello in favor of the duke of Mantua. Realism in movies or theater is often a prime consideration. In some cases, unless makeup can do the trick, a singer may be required to look the part to be considered for it.

Flexibility

A singer's body must be capable of doing a great many things onstage for the singer to be a viable performer in opera. We repeat once more a central message of this book: *Opera composers and librettists did not just write for great voices—they wrote for total performers.*

There are three other principal areas of physical training that singers must work on to accompany a great voice: eye focus, facial expression, and body movement. We will address the first two areas briefly below and all three again in Chapter 5. Becoming flexible enough with body position and movement to perform gracefully and effectively on stage usually requires special training.

The singer must find the best way to make the body flexible and capable. There are many useful methods. Each singer should try the ones that work best for him or her. Some methods that have been effective are:

1. *Dance Training.* Dance is wonderful for singers. It gives the body strength, grace, and suppleness. It keeps the muscles toned without adding unnecessary bulk. It teaches one to move easily on stage and to maintain balance in almost any circumstance. Ballet teaches one to choreograph body movements with music as a matter of habit, helping to develop an ingrained sense of rhythm. Other dance training—acrobatic, modern, or even folk dancing—is also beneficial. It is important to remember that movement and music are two elements constantly present in opera. A singer must be able to handle both together without exceptions or excuses. One point to keep in mind when considering ballet training is that body carriage and breath support for ballet dancers are different from those for singers. If singers know this in advance and can keep the physical differences distinct in their mind, they can benefit greatly from this training.

2. *Martial arts.* Fencing, karate, jujitsu, tae kwon do, and other martial arts provide many of the benefits of ballet and help coordinate movements with others. Fencing is a practical skill for occasional use on the stage as well as a physical training exercise.

3. *Tai Chi.* This Chinese discipline is one of the best available for total body balance, control, and flexibility.

4. *Gymnastics.* A singer may never have to do handstands on the Roman rings on stage, but gymnastics training will provide the physical strength and ability to handle singing under any circumstances.

5. *The Alexander technique.* This technique for overall body balance and alignment has been a tremendous help to people in all areas of the

performing arts. It has proved particularly beneficial to singers in increasing the efficiency of the use of the voice. It also aids in promoting smooth and balanced action on stage.

6. *Overall physical conditioning.* Singers must remain healthy all the time if they want to work regularly. Regular exercise—swimming, running, cycling, calisthenics, and other aerobic activity—lowers the heart rate, and it may help to control unwanted adrenalin flow (reducing the effects of stage fright) and to improve breathing efficiency.

Flexibility also requires the development of a mental attitude. Singers should expect to use their bodies in a variety of ways when performing. The Japanese director Tadashi Suzuki makes an important point when he states: "A word is an act of the body." When one is singing, the whole body is engaged—not just the vocal apparatus. And remember, a singer's body is engaged in *expressing* that word in its totality, including subtext, and not just its sound.

Readiness

Extensive body training emphasizing strength and flexibility is important, but it is not enough by itself. Singers must also be prepared to use their bodies in a variety of ways when singing.

The difficulty with vocal training is that it usually takes place under highly restricted circumstances. Work in the vocal studio usually involves singing in one position with one fixed facial expression (which Wesley Balk calls "SAD"—Serious, Anxious, and Deadpan). Worse yet, some teachers encourage the production of sound with abnormal facial contortions, reflecting an almost total disregard for the face as the best tool a singer has to express a role and its emotions.

Singers rarely practice using facial expressions to reflect the emotions of the material they are working on. Nor do they practice one of the most important acting techniques available for the stage: controlled eye focus, which for the audience means conveying the meaning of a thought through a focus.

Very few singers will have ever vocalized on their backs, while sitting, or while running around the room. And yet any performer may well be called upon to do just those things onstage as part of a performance. Otherwise, how do the Mimis and Violettas die if not on their backs? How does the secretary in *The Consul* sing if not seated at her desk? How does Nemorino play his drunk scene without skipping, jumping, or juggling a bottle? Of course, it is possible to avoid all this and bend to singers' limitations, but the price will always be a sacrifice of quality in the overall production, turning opera into a costumed recital.

Be assured, singers who have not prepared themselves for stage movement suffer vocally when called upon to perform unexpected stage actions while singing. The vocal poise of the protected studio setting is never replicated in performance.

The only way to avoid this difficulty is to prepare far in advance. Singers should practice vocalises and arias in a variety of physical situations using different facial expressions and a range of eye focus. They should create imaginary stage contexts during practice sessions which require movement and many body positions and postures. Anyone who can sound wonderful and express meaning and emotion under these circumstances will be able to do anything a director asks, or that the operatic literature demands.

Wesley Balk's writings, *The Complete Singer-Actor,*[1] *Performing Power,*[2] and *The Radiant Performer,*[3] prescribe a whole range of exercises singers can follow to train the body and face in flexibility and readiness. We recommend these books highly as a guide to practice. As Balk points out, there is an added benefit to this kind of training. Singers find that as they become comfortable rehearsing in different body positions and with a variety of facial expressions and focuses, their singing usually improves. Why? Because as they concentrate on integrating their vocal performance with their whole body, they invariably "get out of the way of their voice." In other words, in concentrating on the voice as an emanation of the whole body, singers "forget" to make those many small adjustments which they use to attempt to help themselves sound "better" during the course of singing, but which always seem to interfere with uniform sound production. Eloise Ristad documents this phenomenon very well in her book *A Soprano on her Head,*[4] and Barry Green and W. Timothy Gallwey provide many exercises for achieving this effect in *The Inner Game of Music.*[5]

FACH

The word *Fach* is a German term used officially to classify singers into specific categories for role placement. The categories are employment categories. Each opera house uses a number of singers in each Fach for their season's productions. The "nearly" official categories (with examples) are shown in Tables 2-1 and 2-2.

In the description of these categories provided by the German system (detailed in Rudolf Kloiber's *Handbuch der Oper*[6]), it is clear that these categories are not just vocal categories—they are also "body" and "acting" categories. A singer is suitable for one set of roles or another based on singing voice, body type, and particular acting talents. In general, the categories of the Fach system range between serious/romantic and character/humorous roles, but the individual Fach categories tend to overlap each other.

As a system for employment, as we discuss in a later chapter, the Fach system does not work very well in practical terms. We are mentioning it here, however, because it is a very useful system for thinking about physical and temperamental characteristics and the way they will fit into the needs of an opera company. The Fach categories are a helpful tool for singers in assessing their

Table 2-1. Female Repertoire

Soubrette (soubrette)
  Zerlina (*Don Giovanni*)
Lyrischer Koloratursopran (lyric coloratura)
  Zerbinetta (*Ariadne auf Naxos*)
Lyrischer Sopran (lyric soprano)
  Mimi (*La Bohème*)
Dramatischer Koloratursopran (dramatic coloratura)
  Queen of the Night (*Die Zauberflöte*)
Jugendlich-dramatischer Sopran (young dramatic soprano)
  Butterfly (*Madama Butterfly*)
Dramatischer Sopran (dramatic soprano)
  Aïda (*Aïda*)
Hochdramatischer Sopran ("high" dramatic soprano)
  Brünnhilde (*Die Walküre*)
Lyrischer Mezzosopran (lyric mezzosoprano)
  Cherubino (*Le Nozze di Figaro*)
Dramatischer Mezzosopran (dramatic mezzosoprano)
  Carmen (*Carmen*)
Alt (contralto)
  Azucena (*Il Trovatore*)

own strengths. Every singer should know in which roles his or her talent is best displayed on stage, and develop those characters first; these roles are calling cards. One must remember, however, that even the German opera houses ignore the Fach once a singer is under contract. If a singer under contract has the notes and looks the part, a German opera house administration would much rather give the role to that singer than to pay a guest artist an extra fee to do the part.

Table 2-2. Male Repertoire

Spieltenor (character tenor)
  Pedrillo (*Die Entführung aus dem Serail*)
Lyrischer Tenor (lyric tenor)
  Alfredo (*La Traviata*)
Italienischer Tenor (spinto tenor)
  Rodolfo (*La Bohème*)
Jugendlicher Heldentenor (young heldentenor)
  Calaf (*Turandot*)
Heldentenor (heldentenor)
  Siegfried (*Siegfried*)
Lyrischer Bariton (lyric baritone)
  Figaro (*Il Barbiere di Siviglia*)

(continued)

Table 2-2. (continued)

Kavalierbariton ("romantic" baritone)
  Valentin (*Faust*)
Charakterbariton (character baritone)
  Iago (*Otello*)
Heldenbariton (heldenbariton)
  Wotan (*Der Ring der Niebelungen*)
Bassbariton (bass-baritone)
  Figaro (*Le Nozze di Figaro*)
Bass-buffo (buffo bass)
  Leporello (*Don Giovanni*)
Seriöser Bass (serious bass)
  Sarastro (*Die Zauberflöte*)

RELAXATION

The most important aspect of body preparation for performance of any kind—musical, acting, athletic, public speaking—is learning how to relax. *Nothing will inhibit performance more than excess body tension.* This is easy to say, but the ability to relax at will is a difficult skill to develop. Most readers know this all too well. The pressures of audition or performance can often throw voice and acting completely out of kilter. Because an artist, in performing in opera, is using his or her body as a form of communication, anything that inhibits that function must be eliminated.

Since singing is an athletic exercise, it is useful to read the sports press and note what famous athletes say about tension and relaxation. Jackie Joyner, the world-record–holding Olympic runner, said in 1988 before her record-shattering 100-meter run: "I will be able to do my best if only I can relax enough while running." Of course she did not mean *total* relaxation—that would make it impossible to run. She meant being able to use only the muscles necessary to run and not other, extraneous muscles.

Singers are often riddled with unconscious tension when they sing. Good voice teachers, like good athletic coaches, deal with students who lock their hips and legs; raise their shoulders; freeze their ribs and diaphragm; tighten their neck muscles; raise their eyebrows; lock their jaws in place; hold their arms and hands in frozen, rigid postures; and tense their lips. Many singers in training seem to feel (often unconsciously) that assuming such postures will aid them in controlling their vocalism. Nothing could be further from the truth. Tension distorts the voice, causing difficulties such as excessive tremolo or unwanted "straight tone." Tension pushes singers off pitch and impairs rhythmic ability. It also limits singers' ability to create a good ensemble with other singers and with the orchestra. Tension is the enemy of acting as well. One cannot give a convincing, visually realistic performance when the body is rigid and the facial muscles are drawn and tight.

The paradox of performing is that *one gains control by giving up control.* For this reason, the cardinal rule of acting is: "Don't act!" Similarly, the best rule for good singing is: "Don't sing!" An artist must acquire performance skills, learn how to prepare well, become secure, relax, and finally *let* (rather than *make*) the performance happen.

We know how easy it is to say, "Just relax," and how hard it is to do it at will. Some people seem born with the ability to sing with no tension whatsoever—but these are the exception. Most performers must learn how to control their tensions. Many things seem to work. Yoga is widely practiced by professional opera performers. Deep-breathing exercises are thought to be beneficial. Wesley Balk advocates a technique for balancing the physical and spiritual energies of the body called the Radiance® technique. Imaging exercises, such as those advocated by Eloise Ristad, Barry Green, and W. Timothy Gallwey in the books mentioned above have likewise been helpful for many. Alexander technique instructors advise repeating the basic principles of Alexander instruction before performing as a way of releasing tension. The Feldenkrais method for relaxation and reduction of body tension is also widely practiced.[7]

Some people advocate medication—especially the use of tranquilizers to control tension, or so-called beta blockers as a way to control the excess adrenalin that the body manufactures as a response to stress. Our opinion is that singers should avoid any regular use of drugs and medications to perform. It will be far more rewarding (not to mention more healthful) for singers to find ways to train the body and mind to always be at peak condition for performance rather than to let chemicals do the job.

Singers might try the following routine as a means of relaxing and centering the body. We have found that it works well for many:

1. Stand up and let your arms hang down from your shoulders. Spend some time consciously letting them hang. Take regular deep breaths. Try to locate any tensions in your body and correct any obvious posture problems, such as hands in front of your legs instead of at your sides, shoulders hunched forward instead of open and back, one shoulder higher than the other, and so forth.

2. Place your feet approximately 12 inches apart, toes turned slightly outward.

3. Sense the muscle that connects your thumb to your wrists. It is in the thickest part of your palms. Without lifting your hands or looking at them, think of the weight of this muscle. Sense its volume, and let it become loose and heavy. Eventually it will seem as if this muscle is getting warmer.

4. Follow the same process for your thumbs. Sense their weight and looseness, and eventually feel them becoming warmer. Make sure that the first set of muscles are still as heavy and warm as before.

5. Begin concentrating on your fingertips in the same manner as above. Don't lift your hands. Maintain your posture as before. Concentrate

on the fingertips. Realize their size and weight. Think of the little bones inside. Think of the small muscles surrounding them. Think of the fingernails and skin, and sense their total volume and weight. Give this process some time, sensing the warmth. Eventually you will feel each fingertip tingling.

6. At this point, refresh your memory with a review of all the processes you have gone through one more time, starting with the palms and thumbs, and returning to your fingertips.

7. Finally, think of your entire hands as heavy and warm and make sure they are still hanging loosely at your sides, and have not crept to the front of your legs.

8. Slowly proceed to extend the heavy, warm, tingling sensation up to your wrists. Sense the massive weight of the wrists, hands, and fingers pulling your arms and eventually your shoulders down further and further. Sense the weight of your forearms, your elbows, and then all the way up to your shoulders.

9. Think of the curve in your back between your shoulders and below your neck. Imagine it becoming more and more elongated. Feel the skin on your neck from your ears to your shoulders pulling down, and realize that all of this is happening because of the weight of your hands.

10. By now, if the exercise has been successful, your hands should be much warmer than before. You should feel relaxed and centered, and ready to use your body for response to the physical demands of performing.

In this book we cannot solve the problem of tension—we can only try to make readers cognizant of its seriousness. In the end, this is a problem each person must recognize and solve for him- or herself. There is no one way to deal with the dilemma of tension. Singers must develop a degree of self-knowledge about the locus and manifestation of their own tensions, and seek the solution that will work best for them.

THE "LOOK"

The ultimate manifestation of an opera performer's mental and physical readiness will be the ability to achieve a "look" appropriate to the character being portrayed, in addition to a "sound" appropriate for the requirements of a given role. The body and spirit of the singer must be ready to do what is necessary to make the character come to life.

One tenor playing the title role in Alberto Ginastera and Manuel Mujica Lainez's opera *Bomarzo* was required by the role to be physically deformed. He spent the entire rehearsal period with large elastic bands connecting various parts of his body to achieve the feel of the deformation needed to portray the character convincingly. This singer is an example of someone both physically able, and mentally willing, to undertake an arduous exercise for the sake of his art. Similarly, a baritone playing Porgy in *Porgy and Bess* once prepared himself for six weeks by walking about his home on his knees in order to become comfortable with Porgy's crippled condition.

Of course, these examples may sound extreme, but they are not at all strange for the spoken stage. Actors undergo all sorts of rigors in order to make their characters come to life. The fact that very few opera performers are willing to do the same is one reason why the public has in the past found opera so artificial and devoid of dramatic interest.

In closing this chapter, we want to emphasize once more that the requirements of the opera stage are both demanding and comprehensive. Vocal production is of great importance, but if singers restrict preparation to vocalism, it will be extremely difficult for them to become total performers. The mental and physical preparation we recommend here is a starting point for them in finding a personal route to comfort in stage artistry. It is a large factor in the process whereby singers come to know themselves and their abilities as performers. It is also the first step in writing the third line. Flexibility, ease, and a capable mind and body, in conjunction with vocal abilities, will always be the most reliable formula for success.

NOTES

1. Wesley Balk, *The Complete Singer-Actor* (Minneapolis: University of Minnesota Press, 1977). Second ed. 1985.

2. Idem, *Performing Power* (Minneapolis: University of Minnesota Press, 1985).

3. Idem, *The Radiant Performer* (Minneapolis: University of Minnesota Press, 1991).

4. Eloise Ristad, *A Soprano on Her Head* (Moab, Utah: Real People Press, 1982).

5. Barry Green and W. Timothy Gallwey, *The Inner Game of Music* (New York: Anchor Books, 1986).

6. Rudolf Kloiber, *Handbuch der Oper*. (Kassel and Munich: Baerenreiter and Deutscher Taschenbuch Verlag, 1985).

7. See the appendix to this book for resources on many of these techniques and methods.

CHAPTER 3

❦

Third Line Skills I: The Opera Performer as Actor

The ultimate goal of performing opera is to make the music and text visual. Since opera is a visual art, opera performers are actors. Thus, in order to write and perform the third line, they must be singer-actors.

There is no way around this fundamental truth. There is no place to hide onstage. A singer cannot hide behind costumes or scenery, unless performing a very specific repertory of offstage roles like the Celestial Voice in Verdi's *Don Carlos* (and even here some directors call for the part to be sung onstage). Somehow the concept of being an actor has to get under the skin of every singer before he or she thinks of working professionally. In short, all performers in opera must think of themselves as singer-actors, not as singers who need to know a little bit of acting.

Everything we spoke of in the first two chapters of this book—having a flexible body and a flexible mind—serves the craft of acting. A singer must perform with the body (not just the throat), with the face, and with the mind. Finally, skills as a musician must be put into the service of the acting craft. Every singer must project the kind of visual image expected of the best actors. Why should anyone settle for less? If a singer's voice is superb, that is wonderful! However, that beautiful voice should be one asset among many, not a pretext or an easy way of avoiding development of other performing skills.

Opera happens only when the curtain goes up in the theater. It doesn't happen in the vocal studio, in auditions, or in contests. As the curtain rises, the audience sees a theatrical event—an audiovisual art. It is theater happening in a theatrical space, within a theatrical environment. If opera is to be a healthy, thriving art form, the skills needed to be theatrical—including acting—must be present in all performers before they qualify as professionals.

THE SINGER AS STAGE ACTOR

All opera performers will at some time be called upon to do things other than singing arias onstage. At the very least, every singer will be required to deliver recitative, which is neither spoken nor fully sung (so pure singing technique will not suffice). Recitative is used for the narrative and dialogue sections of the opera. It furthers the plot in an efficient manner. If singers try to sing a recitative like an aria, it will no longer be a recitative.

At other times, singers will have to deliver plain spoken dialogue on stage. Many singers are uncomfortable speaking on stage. They may have glorious singing voices that throb with emotion, projecting to the top balcony of a 4,000-seat opera house, but when they are called upon to speak, the emotion drains from their voices and all of their performing skills go flat.

Under the umbrella of opera, we see many music theater forms. Opera with spoken dialogue goes under many names. In German-speaking countries it is called *Singspiel*; in French, *opéra-comique*. In the United States and Great Britain, many modern musical theater works—the outgrowth of "musical comedy"—are fully operatic in scope. Not only does one need to perform recitative in many of these operatic forms, but one also has to speak with no musical accompaniment. Very respectable *Singspiele* and *opéras-comiques* are part of the most popular standard operatic repertoire. Some of the most famous are Mozart's *Die Zauberflöte,* von Weber's *Der Freischütz,* Donizetti's *La fille du Régiment,* and Bizet's *Carmen* (in spite of the recitatives added later by Gireaux). There are even entire roles in opera that have only spoken dialogue, such as Bassa (Pasha) Selim in Mozart's *Die Entführung aus dem Serail,* and Frosch, the comic prison guard in Strauss' *Die Fledermaus.* One may say, "Call a theater actor for these parts." This is possible, and it is sometimes done if there is no singing at all in a role. But what does an opera company do about casting Agathe, Porgy, or Rosalinde—all of whom must both sing and speak?

Most roles involving spoken dialogue must be played by a true speech-trained singer-actor. A director must cast a fine singer as Papageno in *Die Zauberflöte,* but that performer must also be able to deliver many spoken lines in the course of the opera. The same is true for the duchess in *La fille du Régiment,* not to mention Carmen, Don José, Escamillo, Zúñiga, and Morales in *Carmen.* Even Verdi and Puccini include speech in their operas. Violetta must read Germont's letter aloud before she dies, and Tosca's most dramatic line ("Questo è il bacio di Tosca!") must be spoken with the greatest dramatic skill for her murder of Scarpia to be effective theatrically.

Someone will always say, "Well I won't do those roles, so I don't need to perfect my speaking or acting skills." This attitude is completely invalid. In opera, where singing/acting stops, recitative/acting or speech/acting begins, and more singing/acting follows. Singers can never escape the need to be an actor. Of course we can go on and on with other examples of nonsinging, verbal performance skills needed for the opera stage, including forms such as *Sprechgesang* repertoire. The point is that singing is just one ability needed to be an effective performer.

THE NEGATIVE VALUATION OF ACTING SKILLS

Singers often fail to see acting ability as having a value equal to that of vocal ability. If a singer's acting is praised without equal mention of his or her singing ability, many singers consider this to be a negative comment—a backhanded way of denigrating their singing skills. Since singers feel they have been primarily trained to sing, it is as if they had somehow failed in their primary function on stage.

This is an unproductive attitude. Being known as an excellent actor can only enhance—never damage—a career as an opera performer.

In the opera profession, performers are onstage for approximately three hours in every performance. Singers had better be visually interesting during that time (unless they are among the sacred few who draw audiences despite lack of acting ability). Most singers venerate the solo aria, but, during the three hours of an opera, a singer in a leading role will sing only one or two arias—three at best. This may consist of ten to twenty minutes of singing. For most of the remaining three hours, he or she will be busy all over the stage doing recitatives, scenes with other characters, or setting up other performers for their own arias.

Still, singers often weigh vocal ability against acting ability in an entirely inappropriate way. A common thought goes something like this: "If I have a drop-dead fantastic voice and I can't act, a director still might give me a role. If I'm a fantastic actor and have a mediocre voice, then I might lose the opportunity to perform."

To this we must answer: no fundamental skill takes precedence over another. If a bad actor has a beautiful face or a well-developed body, he or she can still make a career in certain movies with no other talent. But no serious actors believe that developing a great body is a substitute for perfecting overall acting skills. Again, it is important to ask oneself: whom am I pleasing?

But let us be a little more realistic. It is true that one can get away with being less than a complete performing singer and still get jobs singing in opera. But everyone reading this book should also be aware that the less complete one is as a performer, the less fulfilling one's interpretations will be. Opportunities will be limited to certain tastes, to certain opera houses, and to certain managers. The market for those who bring only a voice and nothing else to opera is thinning. The traditional conservative approach to opera in this country is finally disappearing because we have a fast-changing world in the visual forms of entertainment. As of this writing, virtually all the impresarios now running opera houses grew up in an environment where television and the movies did not provide so much competition. Today, however, both television and the movies are important media for the presentation of every form of entertainment, including opera. These media are reaching millions more people than the live stage is. The media-aware public expects to be entertained by fine singing and acting of at least the same quality they see in these other forms of entertainment. Besides, opera was never intended by its creators to be a lesser child in the family of stage arts.

Quite aside from questions of taste, performing in opera is a high calling. Singers must always ask themselves whether they are fulfilling its *raison d'être* and giving it all it deserves, or creating a half-witted hybrid art instead.

The current generation of opera management is leaving and a new one is coming on the scene. The new trend toward performers who act as they sing has already been established. Of course some people—both audience members and old guard management—complain about this, just as they did in the past when *bel canto* gave way to romanticism, and romanticism to *verismo* styles.[1] For most of the twentieth century, opera was dominated by conductors. This created, in part, an emphasis on music over drama. The present era, like it or not, is one of greater sharing between conductors and stage directors. More and more, people identify great opera with its producers. They talk about Ponnelle's, Kupfer's, or Sellars' productions instead of Placido Domingo's or Claudio Abbado's productions.

It is not surprising that young singers become confused on the question of acting versus singing in developing their careers. There is a tremendous tension in the field of opera performance because people have very few ways of monitoring the development of their own skills. Singers may have enough self-esteem to be able to know in their hearts that they are fine performers, that they are developing their skills, and that whatever other people think doesn't matter. But few people are so strong that they can go forward without some kind of external feedback that reinforces their views of themselves.

Because of this insecurity and need for success, students place heavy emphasis on evaluation that comes early in career training. It is true that these first trials often seem to depend on vocalism: passing juries, winning contests, and succeeding in auditions of various kinds (some of which are for admission to further training, based on promise rather than polished skills). It is the later career successes that depend more on a combination of skills, including acting: obtaining contracts to perform, appearing in increasingly important houses, and receiving good critical notices.

We can assure all readers that success in contests and auditions does not always translate into a successful career. Artists may be successful in a five-minute audition and be engaged once by an opera company. But they may not be invited back if they cannot work well onstage. There is no substitute for complete artistic preparation. There is likewise no substitute for personal fulfillment through a well-rounded product. Maybe this lack of total capability as opposed to mere singing capability is one of the reasons for many singers' emotional fragility, erratic temper, and poor health. In other words, knowingly or not, they are less than total performers, and this brings a tremendous feeling of insecurity.

PREPARING FOR SINGING/ACTING

Many singers will not have devoted a great deal of time to acting preparation. A typical question is: "If I have four hours in the day to work on my craft, can I afford to spend two hours perfecting acting skills, rather than spending all four hours working on my vocal skills?"

In preparing for any profession, one has to divide preparation and practice time among the skills needed to carry out successful work. Singing/acting is different both from singing and from acting. It is a special skill, and it must be practiced using special exercises. When most singers practice arias and scenes, they usually repeat the same arias again and again in much the same way striving for some unattainable perfection of delivery. Mindless repetition in the practice room is extraordinarily unproductive. With exercise and diligence, however, a singer may be able to make delivery of an operatic aria interesting, engaging, exciting, and powerful through practicing singing/acting skills.

Instead of repeating arias a thousand times in order to fix vocal problems, singers should try treating aria delivery as a singing/acting problem. One method is to see how many varied facial expressions can be used in the aria. Experimentation with gesture and movement is also extremely useful. Singing the aria seated, on one's back, or while walking around the room creates a different set of perspectives. Adding different shades of dynamics or vocal color aids in vocal flexibility. In short, discovering how many different ways the aria can be sung effectively can help tremendously in perfecting performance. Moreover, most vocal problems disappear when treated this way, because the singer stops treating them as problems of the voice and starts treating them as problems of performance. One should never forget that the performer's primary task is to deliver a text, a character, and a set of meanings onstage, not just raw sound. Sound alone may find its place in vocalizing or in practicing scales, but it can never be effective in expressing a poet's text or a composer's melody.

Many singers also consider enrolling in acting classes designed for the speaking stage. If singers keep in mind that the skills taught in these classes are somewhat different from those used on the opera stage, they can derive considerable benefit from this kind of study. Acting classes can assist a singer in tapping personal knowledge about emotions and human behavior to create more effective characterization on stage. They can show one how to become comfortable handling the body onstage, and can definitely help in delivering spoken dialogue—often, as we have pointed out above, a difficulty for singer-actors.

Yet one must remember that the task of the singer-actor is different from the task of the actor. The operatic score offers one line of text (as theater does) and one line of music. Singers must be ready to deal with both of these and provide a third line (as we will detail in Chapter 6) that is the artist's own interpretation.

STAGE DIRECTORS VERSUS
MUSIC DIRECTORS

In an opera production, usually both the stage director and the music director have clear artistic goals they wish to achieve. For the most part, both will be professionals used to working cooperatively. Sometimes, however, their artistic visions differ. Who prevails if there is a disagreement?

We believe that, when there is an unresolved disagreement, nothing prevails—nobody wins. The show is not as successful as it could have been. If there is a disagreement between music and stage director and either of the two "prevails," the show is 50 percent less successful than it would have been if both minds had been working together. This is also true if a singer disagrees with a conductor or a stage director. All elements must work together to make the performance successful. There is no such thing as a performance that is successful because the conducting was magnificent in spite of lousy directing, or because one singer was magnificent in spite of the sets, the costumes, and the orchestra. Triumph and success are a combination of all these elements. Otherwise, why not just do concerts and dispense with any staging?

There is no reason to celebrate if it is said of a production that, in spite of everything else, only one singer did a good job. Such an appraisal may feed that singer's ego for a while, but it doesn't do anything for the art of opera. If a singer wants to do something where he or she alone will be praised to the exclusion of everyone else, then he or she should be performing in recitals. However, to do a recital in the guise of opera—to have a chorus dressed up behind a performer as backup singers—is an egocentric exercise that is much too costly. It can only be managed financially if the person in front of the chorus is one of the industry's sacred cows. Otherwise there is no way to sell enough tickets.

A singer who is not flexible as an actor, and cannot follow stage direction, gains a negative reputation. Indeed, anything singers do in this business, good or bad, will follow them. The opera world is very small; people are in contact all the time by telephone, mail, or gossip. It is therefore possible that all a singer's qualifications, limitations, or specific actions in a given production will come to be widely known. There is no place to hide. A poor actor's most recent impresario, director, colleague, or town gossip will tell his or her colleagues, "Listen, she has a gorgeous voice, so she can do stand-and-sing roles, but never ask her to act, perform, or be believable onstage." Singers might even manage to market themselves in this way and make a career out of static roles. For those who choose to do this, more power to them, but they must also know that this limits their repertory and career significantly. A singer can do the Celestial Voice in *Don Carlos,* the stationary Emperor Altoun in Turandot, or the stand-and-sing version of Ramfis in *Aïda* only so many times![2]

The audience is implacable: they pay for a ticket and they want to get their money's worth. There may be one or two singers who can satisfy an audience no matter how unsuited they are for a role because of their rock-star-like status in the profession, but even these performers know that they cannot be continually miscast without damaging their careers.

In ancient Greek theater, the actors were hidden behind masks. It didn't matter how expressive their faces were. It didn't matter if they had warts on their noses—they had those masks covering every blemish. That was a form of theater where nothing was required of actors' facial capabilities. This approach to opera performances is still practiced to some extent in a number of prominent companies in the world. It allows singers to use their voices as a kind of mask. But how often can a singer wear a magnificent voice as a mask? Generally, this can only work at an old guard opera house, and even there it can only work when the singer has sufficient star power to get away with giving a performance of limited artistic dimensions.

DESPAIRING THE PASSING OF THE GOLDEN AGE

Some people complain about the current vocal situation, saying: "Where are the great voices? The great voices are disappearing. All we have now are mediocre singers who look good onstage." Some competitions have refused to award prizes—sometimes for several years in a row—because there "weren't any singers of any quality to award the prize to."

It is a mistake to compare today with some imaginary Golden Age of the past, and absurd to say that there are no more great voices. Such judgments are definitely a matter of perspective: what was a great voice in the past might not be judged a great voice today. Both vocal technique and public expectations have grown tremendously. Recordings of singers in the past are notoriously misleading, as is the human memory concerning live performances. Moreover, most of the operas in current repertoire were premiered in small houses in central Europe where having a monstrous voice was not necessarily important. Singers in those theaters didn't have to carry over enormous orchestras to an audience of 4,000.

To put the matter of the "golden" ages of singing in a more rational light, one must be aware, first, that opera comes in many styles. In the *bel canto* period, singing skill ranked above any other performance element in opera. In that repertoire singers will still be required to excel primarily in vocal technique. Even so, if a Norma (in Bellini's opera of the same name) has a fabulous voice and great acting skills, the pleasure of the performance is doubled. However, *Lucia di Lammermoor* really fails unless the production has a Lucia who is a strong actor! For later musical periods, acting skills are intensely important to the success of the performance, just as they are for periods before the *bel canto* era.

Second, in the past, theater builders in the United States erected huge theaters for economic reasons. Performers who can act and at the same time sing with big enough voices to fill these 3,000-seat theaters are not as easily found as are performers able to do well in the smaller houses. Therefore, there is an increasingly reduced group of people who can project from these enormous stages. It is fortunate that the trend is changing rapidly. There are no longer only three big opera houses in the United States. Hundreds and hundreds of new companies are sprouting all over the country in smaller theaters. Many companies realize that these houses offer them much more flexibility in creating imaginative performances, and also allow them creative selection in casting.

The skills required for smaller theaters are much different. In these venues, opera is not the same kind of theater as it is in a huge house; it is much more intimate. The singers onstage really have to communicate with facial expression and gesture. At the Met, the people next to the orchestra pit are able to see some subtleties onstage since they can see the faces of the performers, but from the last balcony it's really very hard to see anything in any detail. Indeed, one doesn't need to go as far as the last balcony. An audience member in the fifteenth row is already quite a distance from the proscenium. Opera in these two spaces might even be considered a different art form. At the very least, if it is the same art form, the performance requirements are quite different.

Third, more and more opera is being seen on television and in movie theaters. Having a large voice is unimportant for these media. Television sound reproduction is not very good, and the vocal lines in movies will be dubbed from recording studio sessions or be filtered or enhanced electronically. Who gets chosen for a televised production? A smart producer will hire a performer who can act as well as sing. It is unfortunate that the very first personalities to appear on televised opera have been the sacred monsters, the stand-and-sing stars who are the least effective in that medium. National audiences have seen an art form that has not been very engaging, even if people have enjoyed seeing the superstars up close. Opera is now a household word, and most people are as familiar with the names of some opera singers as they are with those of rock stars. But this does not mean that audiences are enjoying what they see for three hours, beyond the shallow pleasure derived from seeing a famous person on TV. (It is of course true that there have been important opera productions with fine acting on television, but they have been the exception.) Moreover, the visual language that most televised opera brings into the home was meant for the stage and not for the small screen.

In order to preserve these audiences for the enjoyment of opera, it must become theatrically competitive, using the visual effects found in other programming in television and the movies. In this way the national entertainment industry and the audience have a chance to see opera as it should be, and not as boring, ridiculous, or unconvincing.

BACKSTAGE SAVVY

One more thing needs to be said about the theater. As part of career preparation, a singer needs to have knowledge of what the theater space is. Singers often feel as if they are an isolated floating island descending to the stage, as if everything is going to be taken care of around them. Real life in the theatre is very different. A professional performer needs to comprehend the mechanics of the theater.

An opera performer should know enough to be able to go through a technical rehearsal without complaining about not having enough light; to be called on the intercom instead of being paged in person; to understand the services provided by members of the costume shop and prop crew without viewing them as faceless, lesser servants; to understand what takes place during a change of scenery without jeopardizing personal safety. In straight spoken theater, performers are trained in all aspects of the stage arts. This creates a working atmosphere that is much more fluid than in opera.

In the theater *everyone* is producing the performance, not just the singer. Therefore understanding the mechanics and the infrastructure of the performance is vital. A properly prepared singer-actor knows what a fresnel is, and what a teaser is. He or she knows that the director cannot always move the light for the singer, because it is often easier for the singer to move into the light. We have actually experienced singers who stop singing in an orchestra rehearsal and say, "Where is the light? If there is no light I won't sing." A production staff often can't fix such things on the spot. A rehearsal is run on union time, and every delay costs money. While the singer is onstage rehearsing, the lighting designer is often simultaneously looking for the appropriate lighting. It is not magic: no one pushes a button to summon an angel descending from the heavens with a reflector to focus lights on the singer's head. Often by moving one foot to the right or left the singer can enter the light. Singers who do not understand such simple technical matters create aggravations that no company needs. Such behavior shows ignorance. In short, lack of knowledge of the mechanics of the theater can be detrimental to an opera performer's career.

Every theater training program we know has actors working in every aspect of theater. They run the lighting board for a while, they make sets and costumes, and they manage the business aspects of the house. In some of the smaller opera companies, everyone is asked to pitch in. Some singers assume that they are too "superior" to touch a wire or move a chair. Other singers may be quite willing to work, but they stand around looking like lost sheep. They really don't know what to do.

Any singer will be much better off professionally if he or she makes an effort to understand what other production personnel are doing and why. The process of contributing to creating the total production becomes truly enjoyable when the work that everyone is doing onstage is understood. Moreover, it is much easier for performers to move around on a stage set if they understand how the set was built, and easier to enjoy the best lighting for their performance if they are not fighting with the lighting concept.

MAKING VISUAL MUSIC: THE COMPOSER AS DRAMATIST

Every performer in opera must learn to read an opera score as a dramatic text. The process of opera is that of making "visual music"—that is, music with action on a stage to be viewed by an audience. Ultimately, the artist has to communicate the music by interpreting it visually and dramatically using the capable body by means of the capable mind mentioned in the last chapter. Opera achieves this visual dramatic interpretation of music in a way analogous to the way in which ballet interprets music through movement.

Boris Goldovsky, as both director and coach, used to insist that there had to be something happening visually not only for every measure of music, but for every note, and for every rest as well. Goldovsky's principle should be a place to start for all artists in determining their own interpretation. The score is the source for interpretation in stage movement and expression in opera. Even if a singer decides not to use movement in interpreting a moment in the score, this lack of movement has to come through a concrete decision not to move and not through paralysis from not knowing what to do or how to do it.

Regarding the analogy with dance, it is impossible for a dancer not to know what kind of movement is required for every bar of music. Opera singers are not dancers, but stage action in opera is choreographed because it has to respond to the music. A dancer doesn't say, "My variation in the pas de deux is done, therefore I'm just going to stand here." No, even when standing, the dancer has to be onstage and be actively involved with what is going on.

Music, through its dynamics and its colors, is continually telling the performer what he or she should do in terms of interpretation. An artist who does not use the music, and the interpretive clues it gives us, is fighting an uphill battle. Every time the singer fights the music, the music wins and the singer loses.

It is important to think of the problem of interpretation in terms of developing acting skills. Simply put, acting skills involve interpreting text and music through motion. A singer uses acting skills to interpret the score.

The score, as a fusion of text and music, is very different from dramatic text alone. An example is a Shakespearean monologue, which is very much like an operatic aria. Just as with the aria, dramatic time is suspended in the monologue to allow a personal emotional expression of great depth. An actor interpreting such a monologue has great freedom in performance with almost every dimension of the speaking voice. He or she can vary the tone, pitch, and volume of the voice; intersperse text with silence at will; and punctuate delivery with sharp breaths, even grunts and moans, if it makes dramatic sense. The singer is much more limited in the freedom that can be taken with the musical score—the composer has "preinterpreted" the libretto. The score designates most of the dimensions of pacing, volume, and articulation, shaping for the singer-interpreter the drama that the composer draws from the text.

In approaching spoken dramatic roles, actors look at their characters in the framework of the whole play. They create "subtexts"—unspoken thoughts or motivations—for the lines their characters speak. They work extensively on the "look" of their characters—how they walk and talk, their typical gestures and body movements. They continually ask themselves, "How would my character inflect this line? What would my character's facial expression be? What hand actions or movement would my character be performing while saying this? Where would the other characters onstage be situated while my character is performing? Who would my character be looking at? What would my character be thinking while saying this?"

Opera performers should be able to look at the score and get answers to these questions as well. The principal difference between the opera score and the text of a drama is that the composer has provided the performer with important hints about interpretation—musical clues which help guide the interpretation. A concrete example of how this works follows.

Count Almaviva's recitative, "Hai già vinta la causa (Have you already won the cause?)" from Mozart's *Le Nozze di Figaro* (Example 3-1) is an excellent example of a good juicy monologue with a superb musical setting which can be interpreted dramatically by a performer with some ease. The "third line" analysis below is typical of what a singer should be able to carry out for any aria he or she is performing. We will show more of this kind of analysis in Chapter 6. In general, we include below: a characterization of the "event" in the score (musical passage, rest, fermata, piece of text, etc.); an interpretation of that "event"; a suggestion of how the interpretation can be realized through movement (or lack of movement), facial expression, or bodily attitude; and finally a dramatic "subtext" which suggests what the singer should be thinking in terms of characterization at that moment. In this example we will emphasize the acting events that follow from the musical text.

A few musical/dramatic principles are assumed in the analysis below which may be helpful to state here. We will repeat these and add more in the following chapter. First, we assume that unaccompanied singing passages, as well as passages where the orchestration is simply a held chord, are the composer's way of telling performers that they have some expressive freedom in the execution of the line (some conductors will agree with this principle, others will not). Second, we assume that dotted rhythms are introduced by the composer for special emphasis, as are held notes—especially when indicated with a fermata. Finally, we assume that melodic contours—rising lines, falling lines, up-and-down

(text continued on p. 40)

Example 3-1. Mozart, *Le Nozze di Figaro,* "Hai già vinta la causa"

Before addressing the aria.
The singer thinks:

> This scene takes place in Seville, Spain, in the seventeenth century.
> The count is a nobleman with a roving eye, concerned about
> his authority. He has also been thwarted by his clever servant

Example 3-1. (continued)

      Figaro earlier in the opera. This aria takes place in the third act of the opera at eveningtime. The count is trying to have a romantic meeting with Susanna, who is to be married to Figaro. The count thinks that he has raised a legal impediment to Susanna's marriage, but he has just heard Figaro and Susanna saying that they will get the better of him, and "have already won the cause." So, when he begins this aria, he is angry and bent on revenge. The count is willful and formal, and intent on asserting his power.

1a. Empty downbeat—no orchestral accompaniment.
    The singer thinks:
    This serves to trigger the thought. I can show the thought with an eye focus shift or a hand/arm gesture on the downbeat.

1b. Inflection (melodic shape).

have you already won the cause?
The singer thinks:
This is a quote from what the count has already heard Susanna and Figaro say. This down-up melodic shape suggests a mocking tone. Perhaps I should experiment with matching the melodic shape with eye focus to reflect a subtext, like, "Is this what has been going on all this time? Well, now I know, and you can't fool me any more!"

2. Dotted musical figures.
    The singer thinks:
    These dotted figures reflect energy that leads to the downbeat. This suggests that the count realizes that people are plotting against him, and is surprised and angry. The dramatic subtext might be: "It is unbelievable!"

3. Text: "Cosa sento! (What [a thing] I am hearing!)" with no accompaniment underneath.
    The singer thinks:
    The lack of accompaniment usually allows me to take as much time as needed to deliver this line. I will take the freedom the score gives me before I verbalize these words.

      Perhaps I should also look again at the melodic design:

(continued)

Example 3-1. (continued)

The rising part of the line might signify growing suspicion, perhaps I could perform an angry grunt on the falling part of the line. A possible subtext might be: "I've been fooled!" or (to follow the design of the line): "My—good—ness!"

4. Another set of energetic dotted figures.
    The singer thinks:
    These dotted figures could be seen as reflecting further realization and anger.

5. The vocal line proceeds above a rest in the orchestra followed by a sustained note.
    The singer thinks:
    Rests and sustained notes are the musical equivalents of dramatic pauses. Perhaps I should take a split second of rhythmic freedom (the orchestra will not come in until after I have started singing) to signal a change in mood with a facial expression, then I can proceed to sing the line: "In qual laccio cadea? (In what noose did I fall?)." A possible subtext might be: "How did I allow this to happen?"

5a. A *forte piano* in the orchestra accompaniment under "laccio."
    The singer thinks:
    Laccio (noose) is an unusual and highly dramatic word. And a *forte-piano* is an unusual orchestral dynamic. The count is angry, so maybe I should try an outburst in the vocal line that becomes immediately restrained to match the orchestra.

5b. The word *cadea* (from *cadere,* to fall) has a sixteenth-note upbeat with a strong downbeat on the accented syllable of the word.
    The singer thinks:
    The music thus suggests falling. I'll convey an accent of pensive frustration through a nod of the head.

6. A fermata over a rest.
    The singer thinks:
    I should discuss the length of the fermata with the conductor or pianist and, during the rest, preannounce with my head shaking or with my pacing of breathing, and attack the coming *presto*. The *presto* should seem to be triggered by my exit from the fermata.

7. The *presto* orchestral section.
    The singer thinks:
    This is a musical release of tension in the orchestra built up by the preceding long rest. I'll match this with some kind of strong release of tension, anger, or both. Possibly I can walk away brusquely or try a noticeable hand gesture. My subtext might be: "What can I do now?"

Example 3-1. (continued)

8. "Perfidi! (perfidious people!)."
   The singer thinks:
   This outcry refers to Figaro and Susanna. The long note in this
   three-note figure is also the highest. I'll accent this word using the
   strength of the consonant "P."

9. Four-note orchestral figure followed by a B on the downbeat.
   The singer thinks:
   This figure serves as a transition between musical thoughts in the
   orchestra. It can be seen as indicating uncertainty. I'll show this
   transition by using a facial gesture to reflect something like, "What
   shall I do next?"

10. "Voglio (I want)" followed by a rest.
    The singer thinks:
    The rest indicates an incomplete sentence. In a play the reading
    would be "Voglio . . ." indicating uncertainty. I should look for a
    gesture or expression of searching.

11a. Repeat of four-note orchestral figure.
    The singer thinks:
    As in 9) above, this is a transition between musical thoughts, again
    signaling uncertainty.

11b. Followed by a D on the downbeat, the highest orchestral note thus
    far.
    The singer thinks:
    This indicates certainty (as opposed to the uncertainty in earlier pas-
    sages). The count has come to a conclusion on this note. I should
    indicate that I have found the words I want.

12. "io voglio di tal modo punirvi."
    Inflection:

    Io voglio di tal modo punirvi
    I want of(in) such a(way) to punish them

    The singer thinks:
    The entire first part of the phrase is done *a cappella*. Thus with no
    orchestral accompaniment I have some freedom to interpret the
    line.

12a. "io voglio."
    The singer thinks:
    The count must be pretty satisfied with himself at this point since
    he now knows what he is going to do to them. I'll try saying this
    with a smirk, showing power and vengeance.

(continued)

Example 3-1. (continued)

    12b. "modo (the way, or the manner)."
        The singer thinks:
        This is the highest and longest note of the phrase. It reflects the idea
          for revenge which Count Almaviva has finally hit upon. I can
          really enjoy it, and let the smirk on "io voglio" grow into a wicked
          smile. Since I am still unaccompanied, I can take a little liberty
          with time. The orchestra will not come in until the next downbeat,
          and I can signal them with the two sixteenth notes that follow this
          note.

    13. "(pu)-nirvi! (punish them!)"—downbeat with fast orchestral figures.
        The singer thinks:
        This musical accent can be interpreted as emphasizing the thought
          of the punishment that awaits the "perfidi." My subtext is: "The
          decision is made! Punish them!"

(text continued from p. 35)

lines—are introduced by the composer for dramatic reasons, not just to make a
pretty tune.

    Let us emphasize that this interpretation is only one of an infinite number
of possible interpretations of this musical passage. It should not be thought of
as a "cookbook" solution for all singers wishing to play Count Almaviva. We
stress in this example the need for the singer to think about the elements of
the score and devise an interpretation that can be realized through acting skills.
As we will indicate below, the annotations here are far more extensive than
any singer will actually write down on the score. They *do* represent a sample
thought process that singers should go through in analyzing the score they will
be singing.

LIBRETTISTS AND COMPOSERS

From Example 3-1, it is clear that dramatic movement and interpretation are
inherent in the operatic score, but it is the composer who has the final word.
Both composers and librettists have these stage factors in mind throughout the
writing and composing process. Indeed, the history of opera writing is replete
with stories of controversies between the two collaborators, so concerned were
they with enforcing their individual view of the dramatic realization of particular
scenes. Verdi's letters to his collaborators show how he struggled to get from
the librettist exactly what he wanted. Verdi knew, as all good composers do,

that he would not have been able to write a particular score if it hadn't been for the libretto—good or bad—but he was virtually always able to improve poor libretti. Although Verdi had some truly terrible librettists, he also had excellent collaborators: the Boito/Verdi works are of particular note.

One of the most illustrious collaborations in opera history was between Lorenzo da Ponte and Wolfgang Amadeus Mozart. Although today Mozart is considered the preeminent contributor to the work, it was not always so. Written on the covers of eighteenth-century scores are the words: "Opera di Lorenzo da Ponte" in big characters, "con musica di Signore Mozart" in small characters. In the case of da Ponte, it is only fair even today to bill *Don Giovanni, Così fan tutte* and *Le Nozze di Figaro* as da Ponte/Mozart operas with characters of equal size. But da Ponte wrote libretti for other composers of operas that never achieved success. Why? Because the ultimate dramatist is the composer. It doesn't matter how good the libretto is, or how bad it is. A very bad libretto can become a decent opera. Likewise, there are excellent libretti that become poor operas.

Thus the value of the work is ultimately determined by the composer. The composer cannot start writing until the librettist supplies the text. The first step is the text; the second, the music. The order of the process tells us what gets done last, and it is this which ultimately shapes the product.

The whole notion of "the third line" as we present it in this book hinges on understanding the concept of the composer as the dramatist who defines the interpretation of an opera text, coupled with the concept of the singer as interpreter of the composer's implied dramatic action. In subsequent chapters, what we are saying to singer-actors and directors is that they must look to the music for the ultimate interpretation of the operatic text. To accept the central message of this book, they must accept the premise that the composer knows what he or she wants dramatically when composing the score and always sees it as a way to shape a text—a literary as well as a musical work.

This process begins from the first downbeat. When composers write a prelude or an overture, they want to put the people in the mood for the work to follow. This is part of the creation of dramatic action. When composers write a ballet sequence, they create action on stage, which also contributes in part to the mood of the piece; this, too, is part of the work of a dramatist.

Peter Kivy's book *Osmin's Rage*[3] explores the philosophy of musical expression in opera. Kivy is a philosopher of music. He bases his discussion on Descartes' little known theory of representation of emotions in art. He maintains that eighteenth- and nineteenth-century composers (Mozart as a prime example) had a very clear notion of coding emotions in music. Key relationships, dynamics, and word settings all play a role in this exercise. The composers were clearly not merely writing pleasant melodies.

Through orchestration, composers are continually painting with sound. They are giving performers colors and textures to match with movement and expression. When Verdi chooses cellos to accompany the duet between King

Philip and the Grand Inquisitor in Don *Carlos,* he is painting the intensity of this drama. If he had used violins, his dramatic statement would not have been so grim and dark. Such instrumentation is definitely a dramatic stroke. The same dialogue with a flute would have been completely different, even with the same melodies. For this reason, as we recommend in the next chapter, singer-actors should learn scores from the standpoint of orchestration, not just from the piano reduction.

There is another interesting example of emotional tone painting in the first act of Puccini's *Tosca.* Cavaradossi is singing, "Recondita armonia (O remote harmony)." It is his opening aria. Puccini brings the sacristan into the scene muttering "Scherza coi fanti e lascia stare i santi . . . (Joke with children and leave the saints alone . . .)" in the background. Although the sacristan is singing a specific text, the words are not distinctly heard throughout. Puccini clearly wants a contrast in the vocal texture. Cavaradossi, the poetic painter, is carried away by creative inspiration. He is transported by his thoughts of art. The sacristan punctures the artist's soaring melodic line with the equivalent of "come on, aw, come on. . . ." This dramatic musical coloring is the work of the composer. The librettists, Giacosa and Illica, may not have told Puccini that he had to superimpose the two melodic lines.

This scene is a grand theatrical stroke which sets up much of the drama of the rest of the opera. The painter gets carried away with himself, and the sacristan disapproves of such conduct in a church. It is the exuberance of art juxtaposed against the disapproval of institutional authority. If the piece is interpreted vocally, it might seem to be a tenor's hit-parade repertoire piece with a bass-baritone spoiling the integrity or spontaneity of a virtuoso aria (as some tenors will say). However, interpreted dramatically (as it should be), it can be seen as Puccini's commentary on a painter's irreverent behavior in church. Cavaradossi's lyricism and romanticism will eventually cost him his life in a city dominated by the authority of the church and the police. It is the sacristan's down-to-earth philosophy that reminds us of this matter-of-fact approach, and why the first act of *Tosca* appears to be a social and political commentary pitting art against church and state. This theme is the vehicle for a whole series of musical events that frame the opera—the "Te Deum" of Scarpia, and eventually the most famous aria of the piece: Tosca's "Vissi d'Arte."

FINDING AN INTERPRETATION: TEXT
VERSUS MUSIC

As a final thought, we wish to reemphasize the concept of the composer as the ultimate dramatist, while restoring somewhat the importance of the libretto. It may be simplistic to say that music is what shapes the ultimate dramatic dimension for the work: the conception of opera at its historical beginning was triggered by the text. There are certainly many excellent sources that deal with the content of opera libretti.[4,5] Indeed, the seed, the origin of the opera *is* the text, which inspires the composer to give a particular shape to the work. This text is a guide for the process the singer has to follow when developing an interpretation for performing a work.

Singers must start with the text, work at understanding it thoroughly, and then ask what is the composer's view of it as reflected in the musical setting. Ideally, in studying a new work, singers should not study the music before becoming familiar with the full text of the libretto—to learn the music before understanding the text is unproductive. Nevertheless, for standard repertoire it often can't be helped. Most singers have had a great deal of exposure to opera before they ever begin serious professional training. A singer who has already heard or even sung the music of *La Traviata* without knowing what the text was all about is certainly not prevented from studying *La Traviata* successfully; however, the process will definitely be harder.

The elements of opera might be thought of as a hand of cards dealt at random. The artist has to reorganize the cards in his or her head despite the order in which they were originally dealt. In opera interpretation, singers have to know how particular text items and particular music elements interact, just as in cards they would understand how cards combine to make different kinds of hands. Any given combination of text and music implies an interpretive action for the performer, just as a particular combination of cards implies specific actions for a bridge or poker player.

In a hand of cards, no one card is more important than any other. All combine to make up the hand. Similarly, in opera interpretation, neither text nor music is more important, although the music, as noted above, is the final determining element. And even if the music establishes the final shape of the implied interpretation for the opera score, the text is not to be secondary in the artist's interpretation.

NOTES

1. Nostalgic remembrance of some imaginary "golden past" in opera, when everything was better, has existed almost since the beginning of the art. Critics of Monteverdi's day complained that his *La Favola d'Orfeo* (1607) was not as good as Peri's *Euridice* from 1600!

2. The opposite comment is just as damaging: "Listen, she has a great stage instinct, but don't ask her to sing!" After all, how many roles are out there that do not require some degree of vocal capability? The overall message is that every singer must have a balance of skills.

3. Peter Kivy, *Osmin's Rage* (New Brunswick, N.J.: Rutgers University Press, 1989).

4. Joseph Kerman, *Opera as Drama* (Berkeley: University of California Press, 1988).

5. Paul Robinson, *Opera and Ideas from Mozart to Strauss* (Ithaca: Cornell University Press, 1986).

CHAPTER 4

— ❧ —

Third Line Skills II:
The Opera Performer as Musician

Performers in opera are musicians. They play an instrument—their voice. In reality, however, a singer's instrument is his or her entire body. The voice can't be "played" in an operatic performance independently of body involvement and facial expression.

We assume in this chapter that all singers aspiring to a professional career in opera understand that they must learn their parts and have them fully memorized before an opera can be successfully staged. This means knowing notes, rhythms, rests, entrances, tempos, and dynamics perfectly. The musical abilities needed for the third line are above and beyond these mechanical skills. They involve learning and understanding not just the scratchings on the score, but also what those scratchings mean in the language of music, and how they interact with the words and the drama.

As we pointed out in the last chapter, singing opera is not just producing sound, it is interpreting a dramatic text set to music. In order to do this, a singer must be able to act, *and* deal with dramatic text through musical expression. To accomplish the latter, the singer must be a skilled musician. Needless to say, the mere fact that an opera performer is capable of producing vocal sound of a particular quality does not mean that he or she is a musician.

Becoming a musician is a long but rewarding process. Besides learning to read any kind of musical literature, a musician should have a thorough grounding in music theory and performance practice for many musical styles. Beyond classroom training, a musician must have experience performing with others, thereby developing a fine sense of ensemble. This is often a difficult skill for singers to acquire because of their isolated studio training.

Some singers come to singing after playing a musical instrument. They were first clarinetists, pianists, or artists with some other instrument. This background is invaluable. Not only will these singers be able to play for themselves, they will have a better understanding of music as a total organized system, beyond mere vocal sound.

Playing in instrumental ensembles is of great value. It sharpens the senses to the interaction of melodies, rhythms, colors, and timbres. It also sensitizes the performer to the intricacies of musical interaction with colleagues onstage, as well as to the dynamics of interplay with the conductor. Because it is necessary at some levels of development to study voice in isolation, working with an instrumental group can help develop a sense of cooperation that is often not emphasized in vocal training.

A singer is indeed one instrument among many. Each instrument in the orchestra has its own timbre and color. The voice adds another sound dimension. Singers who complain about composers who don't treat their vocal lines as central are missing an important point basic to opera performance: the voice *interacts* with the orchestral instruments to produce a total musical effect; the instruments are not there to just accompany the singer. The great opera composers all treat the human voice as an instrument in the orchestral score. To be sure, some are more skillful at addressing the demands of tessitura and the ability of the voice to balance the orchestral sound, but all composers expect singers to work with the orchestra to create a total experience for the audience—even those composers whose orchestration leans more toward accompaniment.

UNDERSTANDING THE SCORE

As musicians, then, all singers must understand the work of the composer—paying particular attention to what the composer wants from performers. Composers want instruments—including vocal instruments—that can interpret, express, and communicate what they had in mind when they were putting notes on paper. To know how they go about the process of melding sounds and ideas, it is necessary to understand both the process of composition and the role of the composer as a dramatist.

Writing music is an intricate process. As an interpreter of music, one must at least relate to, if not fully understand, this intricacy in order to be able to communicate the meaning of a specific work to an audience. To begin with, music in the West is polyphonic. Individual instruments (with notable exceptions, such as the piano) are monophonic—including the voice. Singers sometimes study only their own melodic line without connecting that line with the vertical, polyphonic structure of orchestral texture. Moreover, at times they do not understand the meaning of styles intrinsic to different musical periods. Consequently, they may not always understand how their instrument fits in with the whole musical concept of the work.

It would help most singers to understand how an opera is actually written. Every composer has his or her own way, but all methods will eventually come to grips with the integration of musical and textual lines. There are some composers who may start with melodies. They sketch the tune on a piece of paper with perhaps just a hint of the kind of orchestration they have in mind. With this they start building the overall structure of the opera. They may go to a librettist and tell him or her that they have a concept, and ask them to elaborate on it. They might say something like this: "I think that this tune that I have been hearing in my head tells me a story of silk, beads, wood creatures, and things like that." The librettist, from his or her own imagination or from some previous source will then start developing something on that basis.

The process may also take place the other way around. A composer may discover a text and want the librettist to shape it into operatic form. Occasionally a librettist will have a libretto already prepared. The composer will take the text intact from the source and start writing music for it.

It is important for singers to know as much as possible about the way an opera was composed. The research is almost archaeological in nature, but it is necessary because, the more singers understand, the better able they are to put themselves at the service of the score. The process is much like finding the best way to relate an interesting experience to others. Tourists can visit archaeological ruins in Egypt and enjoy their outward beauty, their massiveness or spaciousness. However, they can enjoy and tell others about what they saw much more effectively if they know as much as possible about why and when these structures were built, who used them, and what the paintings on the walls mean. Similarly, only if singers are good researchers of musical material and the score will they become increasingly capable of telling others about this through their artistry. Of course, anyone can come back from the Egyptian temple and tell their friends, "Oh, it was gorgeous, it was spectacular, it was awesome!" and have that be the end of the conversation. Unfortunately, there are some singers that deliver just that kind of shallow interpretation of the music they are singing.

Naturally, the knowledge needed to provide a rich interpretation of a score doesn't come all at once. One has to work with the material for some time and do some library research. It also takes an experienced eye to see exactly what is going on musically just from looking at the score.

In short, discovering the meaning of a score is an ongoing process. The more singers know, the happier and more comfortable they will be and the more fulfilling the experience of communication on stage. With luck in their professional life, they will be able to sing *Tristan und Isolde,* say, twenty times, *Falstaff* 50 times, and *Les Contes d'Hoffmann* 80 times. Each time the singers approach these works, they will gain increased knowledge of them and will give a richer and more complete performance as a consequence. An intelligent performer will participate fully in the worlds of Nordic myth and legend, Henry the Fifth, Shakespearean wit, and E.T.A. Hoffmann's world of seductive images.

This can only happen if the singers' knowledge base is strong and meaningful. Otherwise they will only scratch the surface of the material and quickly become complacent. That shallowness of preparation will surely communicate itself directly to the audience, or it will manifest itself in self-centeredness, diva fits, or other types of insecurities.

APPROACHING THE SCORE FOR THE FIRST TIME

We'll start with the example of a singer preparing to work on an opera role for the very first time, a work like Debussy's *Pelléas et Mélisande,* which is not done frequently. Often, the best approach to a totally unfamiliar work is not even to open the score at first. One should start by researching historical, literary, and musicological material and begin to ask questions: Where does the story of the opera come from? Who is Mélisande? Why do we need to know about Pelléas?

What about Debussy? What other music of his do we know? What about his composition style? Why and under what circumstances did he write the opera to begin with? Who is the librettist? How much did the librettist alter the original story? What was Debussy thinking in choosing this play for his only opera? Who is Maurice Maeterlinck, the writer of the play on which the opera is based? Why did Debussy write an anti-Wagnerian score that sounds more Wagnerian than the music of any other French composer? Many other questions of this sort need to be addressed. The day the singer finally opens the score, this work—the analysis and discovery of elements from the score—will make the study of the work immensely more meaningful. First, working with the score becomes easier and, second, it becomes enjoyable, since the performer begins to feel like a partner in the artistic operation. The score will already be "talking." This is infinitely preferable to starting in by pounding notes on the piano as an exercise in rote memorization. Instead, the process of learning a role becomes a cultural and an artistic experience that the performer will then be equipped to communicate to others.

Having done this research, the singer is then ready to open the score of *Pelléas et Mélisande* and see it as a musician with the idea of really singing a role. First of all, it is best to use an orchestral score instead of a piano/vocal score. As we have said, composers write horizontally and vertically, not just horizontally. They rarely give singers an unadorned melodic line. Rather they surround the vocal line with a richly textured and colored total musical environment which the singer must be aware of. This environment can hardly be seen in a piano reduction.

Singers must remind themselves all the time, "Wait a second, yes, I am singing this note, but the clarinet is producing a countermelody at the same time. The violins are playing a lush harmony to accompany us both. Moreover, they are emerging from a modulation that took place just two bars before I sing. Why this modulation? What was the mood before the modulation? What is the mood right after? What are the cellos doing at the time I am being accompanied by the violins? Oh, the cellos are playing another character's motif! So while I am singing my own melody, I should probably have this other character in mind, because the cellos are reminding me of it." Occasionally a conductor will sit down with the cast of an opera and really talk seriously about the orchestration and how it works, but this is rare.

We have talked about doing a totally new role. Let's take the opposite case where the role to be performed is quite familiar. Suppose a singer has performed Zerlina in Mozart's *Don Giovanni* a dozen times already, but not in the last two years, and now there is a production for which she is hired to do the role. What does she do now, to refresh herself and improve her performance from the last time she did it?

There are a couple of alternatives. One extreme would be to be bored with the role and just consider it a money-making venture with the attitude: "Oh I have to do Zerlina again. I think I remember it more or less. If I perform the role and I am reasonably good, and my voice is still intact, people are going to like it. I'll get another paycheck and I can pay my bills." Fine. Many people go through life with that kind of attitude, whether they are singers, accountants, or cabinetmakers.

A far more enjoyable (and productive) attitude is to look back, to review the social history of the period, and to look at Mozart's biographical information concerning the composition of the work. The singer can then ask, "What else is there in Zerlina as a character that I didn't see before? Is there anything in Mozart's musical setting of her material that I didn't understand the last time I did the role?" The answer will always be "yes." Every time an artist approaches a previously performed Mozart work there is always something else beyond that which was understood in the previous performance, regardless of how long the singer has been performing the role.

Who is Zerlina? Is she just some cute peasant girl that Giovanni wants to take to bed? She *could* be played that way (and often is!). One of several possible deeper interpretations presents Zerlina as a potential victim of the social class system. One then needs to ask how lower class victims react to exploitation by the gentry. How successful are such people in resisting; who are the good guys and who are the bad ones? What does Zerlina represent in terms of all the complexities of Giovanni's personality?

The answer to these interpretive questions lies in part in the kind of music Zerlina is given. She has nothing of the vengeful swooping lines of Donna Anna, nor the slightly schizophrenic writing assigned to Donna Elvira. Zerlina's music is almost uniformly lyrical and sweet. The tension in her character comes from the disparity between text and melodic line. The text of her arias and recitatives show her to be distinctly piquant, with more worldly knowledge than one might assign to her at first glance. Any portrayal of this character should play up these musical characteristics.

ENJOYING MUSICAL PREPARATION

Singers reading this may be saying at this point, "Oh, come on, do I really have to do all of this preparation before I sing a role?" Well, as with all options in life, one can say, "No, all I need to do is study my own part. I only have a few performances. I will get some money for it and then I will go home." This is almost like saying, "Today I have to type eight hours to bring a paycheck home. Basta."

In the opera profession, directors are not policemen or taskmasters scolding people and saying, "No, No, No—naughty, naughty, you cannot have this kind of attitude!" If singers do not take preparation seriously, it will show in performance. If they choose opera as a profession, they have an unusual task in life: *they must conduct their business in such a way that they will never be bored or seem mechanical. Because if they are bored, their audiences will be bored! If they are mechanical, so is the performance.* If singers know little about Mozart, Don Giovanni, Freud, and machismo, the performance will be shallow, and opera becomes once again the stepchild of the stage professions.

Singers should be concerned with these analytic procedures both for their own pleasure, and for improving their craft. When singers study roles, those roles are going to be in their repertoire. They will make their careers largely through playing those roles. We recommend that all singers learn to enjoy the process of role preparation. That enjoyment comes from knowledge. In developing a friendship, knowledge of one's friends creates enrichment and depth for both parties. People who lack the ability to deepen that personal knowledge have only acquaintances.

It is sad in a way that singing is for many people a very frustrating and unsatisfying profession. The measure of success for many singers is in becoming part of a small elite circle of international stars. These aspiring professionals thus have a tendency to look at the rewards of opera only in terms of glory and shining lights. This should not be so. Singers can have an enriching, fulfilling experience every time they sing, even if they do not end up at La Scala or the Met. This experience should extend throughout singers' preparation for singing. The richer a singer's resources, the more capable he or she will be of offering things to the audience in terms of communication and expression, and a more satisfying personal experience will be the result. Moreover, with this attitude a singer may still reach the top international opera houses, and have enjoyed the process every step of the way.

There are many ways of achieving this, and singers may test one or many of them. Throughout this book we insist on one of these solutions, namely *not* to look at a score as a monumental memorization task, or as a vocal/technical obstacle course to overcome. We suggest that singers consider the two lines of the score, the text and the music, as two treasures which, through study, research, and analysis, will guide them to success in the task of interpreting, communicating, and expressing to an audience. The result of this research and study is the third line.

Many singers, especially at the beginning of their careers, haven't quite gotten it in their heads that there are going to be approximately fifteen to twenty roles that they will do all their lives (with about half that number in their standard repertoire). It behooves them to know as much as they possibly can about those roles. The exercises that we suggest in this book are not just of value for enjoyment of a particular role in a performer's repertoire. They should become examples for a singer's basic professional routine for role preparation. As this work is practiced, it becomes easier and easier to do.

Moreover, even if singers are still in a preprofessional stage in their performance studies, they should consider these exercises as serious professional work. It is much more difficult to develop good work habits if one decides that this preparation now is "pretend" preparation; that it will be done "for real" at some later stage. The habits one builds early in one's career will remain for the rest of one's life. The easy flexibility found in singers at earlier training stages cannot be compared with the rigidity that sets in once they are actively singing professionally. Singers who do not practice from the beginning to approach performance preparation in a more fulfilling, productive fashion may never get around to discovering how to do it.

It is unfortunate that some vocal training programs throughout the nation teach so few skills for interpretation of opera roles. There are vocal programs which, for economic reasons, cannot afford the rehearsal time necessary to train singers properly. The attitude is often: "Let's put something together in a few days." These programs adopt the philosophy that the only way to reward the singers for paying for the training program is to put them on stage to do something, whether they have reached an adequate interpretive standard or not.

For those readers who are currently completing their formal studies, as we have mentioned earlier, they may have to supplement their school training with self-education in many areas. One of these areas is score study. Singers can purchase full scores quite easily in most large music stores. If they find them too expensive, they can always go to a library and spend some hours there. Singers may have friends in Europe (where some materials are easier to find) who can send them scores. Music is a very international business; as they proceed, singers will find that they develop numerous connections abroad that can help them with such materials.

One immediate advantage of studying the entire score of an opera is to break the habit of studying arias in isolation. An entire role is developed by the composer and the librettist in 250 pages or so of a score. That character cannot be adequately portrayed by someone who knows only the three pages of the whole score represented in a piano reduction of one of the character's arias.

Knowing what's in a score and understanding its musical structure will invariably help any singer's interpretation. The orchestral writing signals the performers that they should try to reflect a similar color and texture in their thoughts, reactions, and glances toward each other. Singers who understand this will acquire a completely different atmosphere for role preparation than they will get by just keeping the piano accompaniment in mind.

To take an example, many *bel canto* soprano arias are accompanied with harp and/or flute. The flute will compete with the voice for dominance of the melodic line. It allows no flaws of intonation on the part of the singer. The harp creates a lush, yet precise texture.

At times composers used unusual scorings to create special effects. The famous Mad Scene from Donizetti's *Lucia di Lammermoor* was originally scored for glass harmonica[1] (it is usually accompanied by a flute today). This instrument gives an eerie, haunting sound which Donizetti wanted to use as background to Lucia's insanity. The flute may do almost as well, but the piano can never give you the same feeling in that scene. A singer playing Lucia who does not know this important point of the scoring of the aria will be missing an important clue for interpretation.

Porgy's song, "I got plenty o' nothin,'" from Gershwin's *Porgy and Bess* is another example of colorful scoring. A piano can do its best, but the whole style of singing the piece changes when one realizes that it is scored for banjo, rather than for any of the standard orchestra instruments. This gives the music a folksy element—the crudeness of an instrument that can't be tuned very easily. The implied mood of the piece simply can't be ignored.

UNDERSTANDING MUSICAL STYLE

Style is a controversial term. But, for our purposes, style is all those things that the composer cannot write on the score—things that singers can only know if they know the musical conventions of the period. It could be called "general practice," or "tradition." In understanding style, singers must answer questions such as the following: What happens to the orchestral downbeats in the German repertoire? What happens to portamentos in the Puccini repertoire? What happens to the appoggiaturas in Mozart?

Often the same melody and the same notation on the musical score will be dealt with in a completely different way because of the style. Knowledge of the musical language of each one of the principal musical periods or the conventions of each composer is something every singer must acquire as soon as possible as part of professional training. Application of this knowledge will guarantee that the singer will not read a score in a rough fashion. He or she will rather read it with background information that will demonstrate immediately how to interpret both the written and the unwritten conventions of the score.

For example, in singing a Mozart recitative, the singer will stop and think:

"Wait a second, if the phrase ends in the same two notes after an interval leap it is conventional to insert an appoggiatura. And what kinds of appoggiaturas are there?" Singers must be aware of these options from the outset when first approaching the music. Later it may be too late because by then the notes, as they appear in the score, will already have been memorized.

Having said this, we should point out that there is a healthy variety of opinion concerning interpretation of musical stylistic elements. There are some contemporary recordings of Mozart where singers do not use an appoggiaturas at all, and others where they are inserted wherever possible. In music as in any business, trends and fads come and go, and conductors are entitled to be different. Some of them will insist that they talked to Mozart over the phone and he told them to leave out the appoggiaturas. Performers may have their own opinions about musical interpretation, but it is important to be flexible enough to understand that, once a contract to do work with a particular conductor has been signed, singers must be capable of following what the conductor suggests concerning interpretation, or at least be able to discuss their feelings about the interpretation intelligently. Otherwise the singers will never come to an agreement with the conductor and will probably not have fun doing the part. All singers who wish to challenge the conductor must be on the same level of musical knowledge and skill as he or she is, at least with regard to vocal writing and conventions, so that, regardless of what is said about appoggiaturas or any other stylistic option, the conductor's requests can be handled without extended explanation. Rehearsals are not scholarly seminars, but the scholarly research has to be done at some point—better long before the rehearsals than after (or never).

By all of this we mean to say that there is never a definitive answer to interpretation. There will always be differences of opinion. The job of a performing musician is to be aware of ranges of possibilities and, most important, to have enough skill to be flexible when called upon to do something new. This flexibility can only be achieved through study and practical experience. All individuals in the cast may have their own opinion about this. That is another reason why there are conductors to impose a set of uniform conventions on the musical part of the performance. There are almost always important ways an individual singer can contribute to the process, but an individual opinion on musical matters remains just that: an individual opinion.

Aside from Mozart, most of mainstream opera repertoire comes from the nineteenth and very early twentieth centuries. At the very least, a working opera performer must be conversant in styles from this period, whether *bel canto,* Romantic, Wagnerian, or verismo. Operas from earlier periods may require special study. The stylistic conventions of twentieth-century operas are still in flux. Nevertheless, modern composers have either written enough about their work, or have conducted their own operas, or are still alive to talk about their preferences so that there is some idea of what they have in mind musically.

In the last century, sometimes a composer would emerge who established a new "style." Most people would resist him or her, and a few others would embrace the new aesthetic. Those works that remained in the standard repertoire and those that are forgotten were determined by the popular taste of later times. The twentieth century is a period in which this pattern doesn't function so clearly. Composers in this century have typically searched for new, highly personalized styles. To guarantee uniqueness, everybody began searching in a different direction. This made the twentieth century much richer in terms of possibilities than previous centuries. In the days of Beethoven, there were 50 composers in Central Europe writing in roughly the same idiom as Beethoven, and only Beethoven survived. In our day there are 50 or so leading "Western" composers, but more often than not they are not writing at all like each other; in a way, this is part of the mentality of the twentieth century. Under these circumstances, the best the opera industry can do is to premier all new works possible and serve as a ready base for contemporary composers to express their art. The job of singers is more challenging than ever, because they must be able to read new music and tackle its innovations.

Music culture also implies the conditions under which music is performed. The diversity of music style in the twentieth century is attributable in part to the diversity of the public, and in part to the diversity of media (stage, film, television, radio, recordings, videotapes) which make this available to audiences. Another factor in this century is the enormous cultural difference between "popular" music and "serious" music.

Musical training and practice are also different from period to period. Many baroque operas, for example, are lost because full orchestral scores are required to perform musical stage works today. In the days of Peri and Cavalli, it was assumed that the musicians could improvise from rudimentary sketches—melody lines and figured basses. They knew the style and could fill in their parts. Instrumentalists today who have that particular ability are quite unusual, although we may find some equivalent skills in the world of jazz.

Even with a score, the artistic task of the performer is to interpret music using appropriate stylistic conventions. Moreover, style is not something that becomes fixed and rigid once learned. It is fluid, changing with time and with the current taste.

The task of interpretation of style is also inextricably intermixed with the question of interpretation of action on stage. The tempos, dynamics, and musical performance conventions of composers at various times must not only be observed musically, but must be matched by gesture and expression.

Following are a few examples of stylistic variety from Puccini, Wagner, and Strauss—composers who were roughly contemporaneous. These are not meant to be full analyses of composers' styles, but are only indicative of the kinds of musical structures any singer should be attending to in preparing his or her own interpretation.

Once again, as in the last chapter, we want to emphasize that the singer must develop the skill to be able to interpret musical and textual elements in the opera score dramatically. Each musical element should have a clear dramatic meaning for the performer based on the musical style in which the opera was composed.

Puccini's music cannot be sung or played exactly according to the written musical values. Although Puccini's scores may seem to have been written in standard time signatures, they must be interpreted "conversationally," as if the meter were in constant flux.

In Example 4-1 (pp. 56–57) from *Tosca,* the chief of police, Scarpia, mocks Tosca's attempts to go to the queen to save her lover, Cavaradossi, in a scene that underscores his sarcasm and cruelty. The conducting must be highly flexible to reflect his various changes of mood. Each new thought is punctuated with a new musical theme. Puccini allows a great deal of space for the singer in the form of unaccompanied passages, or sections with only sustained note accompaniments. The direction *col canto* appears frequently in his scores. Accents, use of triplets to help the vocal line approximate speech, and many different tempo markings are highly typical of his style.

On any given page of a Puccini score there will be ten different musical thoughts. In a Wagner opera ten musical thoughts will appear throughout an act. This doesn't make Puccini better than Wagner or vice versa, but it does imply a need for a close knowledge of the two styles. Knowing how quickly "musical thought" shifts are likely to occur when dealing with Puccini and how slowly by comparison such shifts will occur when dealing with Wagner makes singers more flexible, powerful performers. It also helps them prepare for the artistic task before them since their choice of focus and movement will match shifts in the music.

In the passage from *Das Rheingold,* shown in Example 4-2 (p. 58), where Wotan invites Fricka, his wife, to their new home in Valhalla, Wagner uses virtually the same musical vocabulary for many bars at a time. Characters in his operas usually sustain a single thought and a single musical mood for some length of time. Wotan in this passage must be able to portray great strength and nobility for many bars in the music. This means that he will not move or shift focus very much at all.

Richard Strauss uses a great deal of dramatic emphasis in dynamics. The artist must be able to hit a downbeat and grow quickly into a crescendo or diminuendo in many passages.

The trio section from the first act of *Der Rosenkavalier* (Example 4-3, pp. 59–60) requires all three singers, the Marschallin, Baron Ochs, and Octavian, to change dynamics several times in the space of a few bars. They are all reflecting different moods and different attitudes—Octavian expressing his mock fear of Baron Ochs, the Marschallin trying to defend Octavian, and Baron Ochs bragging of his conquests with women. Their actions and facial attitudes should reflect these differences. This is typical of the sound textures Richard Strauss attempts to create in all of his vocal writing.

Shifts in stylistic interpretation can be seen in different readings of much late Baroque music. A pre-1950s interpretation of a work as prosaic as *The Messiah* (often still being used today) may have included productions with 300 singers and monstrous orchestras. These works weren't done that way in the period, but one can never be 100 percent certain exactly how they were done. For this reason it is possible to find a whole range of renditions co-existing at

(text continued on p. 60)

Example 4-1. Puccini, *Tosca*, 2nd act, Scarpia

(Tosca con un grido di gioia fa per escire: Scarpia
con un gesto e ridendo ironicamente la trattiene)

Example 4-1. (continued)

1. "Va pure" with a sudden reduction in temp (*Meno*) and a sudden *pianissimo* series of sustained chords in the orchestra.

   The singer thinks:

   Tosca should express her joy through a facial expression and body attitude any time after I sing the word "Va." An effective place for her to do this would be the chord preceding "Ma è fallace speranza . . ." contrasting with the sudden *pianissmio* in the orchestra. Both the tempo change and the *pianissimo* sustained chord give me a lot of freedom. The music is signaling a clear change in Scarpia's mood, and I could mark this with a shift in eye focus, and a gesture of sarcasm.

2. An eighth rest.

   The singer thinks:

   Scarpia can perform a threatening body gesture on this rest. I should either take a step if I am standing, or rise if I am sitting. This can be the start of my movement toward Tosca which culminates on the downbeat.

3. "Cadavere (corpse)" sung with a strong downbeat on the accented syllable of the word, with no orchestral accompaniment under the syllable "-da."

   The singer thinks:

   This is the climactic word in the phrase. Puccini gives me flexibility by providing no accompaniment for this crucial syllable. I can thus probably take as much time as I wish to create a gruesome effect. The sixteenth note on the syllable "-ve-" will signal the conductor to go on.

Example 4-2.

Example 4-3.

(continued)

Example 4-3. (continued)

(text continued from p. 55)

the same time. In any given year one may hear "period" *Messiahs* with original instruments, pared down choruses, and lots of added ornamentation. On the other side of town, there are others that offer standard twentieth-century or-chestration and a big, lush choral sound, with many options in between.

In operatic examples, this difference is not so drastic. Nevertheless, a pompous modern production of *Die Zauberflöte* in an enormous theater with a big orchestra and elaborate sets differs enormously from the original produc-tion. That first *Zauberflöte* was a popular *Singspiel* which took place in a small, antiestablishment theater on the outskirts of Vienna, without the support of the inner circles of society.[2]

Performers must always have enough knowledge to ascertain how much freedom or how little freedom of interpretation they have with the score. By knowing the limits and the freedom of the style, it is possible for them to deal with their own freedom and limitations.

Some stylistic shifts have directly affected vocal production. A well-known example of this is the vocal interpretation of the upper range of the tenor. In Mozart's day, the tenor's upper range was essentially an enhanced falsetto; after all, there were *castrati* then. If a composer really wanted a powerful sound in the upper octaves, he could assign the part to the *castrato* voice. The tenor wasn't called upon to do it. After the first full-voice high C was sung in the 1840s by Gilbert-Louis Duprez, the entire treatment of tenor vocal technique changed. Now a post-Rossini interpretation style for the tenor's high notes is made and grafted back on to earlier works even though those things were never done that way in their day.[3] Today no one wants to hear tenors singing falsetto high Cs.

Similarly, there was no such thing as the vocal category "baritone" in Mozart's day. All lower male voices were called "basses." Even now, low male voice roles in Mozart operas (except for the very lowest ones such as Osmin or Sarastro) are sung either by basses or baritones, depending on the musical taste of the conductor and the balance needed for a particular production. It was only in the nineteenth century that the baritone became established as a vocal category. Along with this category came expectations about vocal technique and production, and a special baritone vocal style—especially for Verdi works. This style can then be projected backward and applied to Mozart's works or those of earlier composers.

CONCLUSION

In closing, we recommend that all singers acquire both the skills and attitudes needed to be a fully functional musician on the opera stage. Skills can be acquired through instruction or self-study coupled with a good deal of experience. As in all aspects of preparation for opera performing, the best attitudes a singer can acquire are a healthy curiosity, a desire to deepen knowledge of the material to be performed, flexibility, and a cooperative spirit. This, along with a passion for squeezing every expressive possibility from the music, will mark any singer as a real professional.

Armed with these attitudes and skills, singers are able to participate in creating an interpretation instead of just scratching the surface in a production. They can then deliver a role as part of a context aimed at reaching an audience, instead of engaging in a lonely exercise of emoting through sound production coupled with a few multipurpose stock gestures thrown out at random intervals. Learning how to be a complete interpreter in this way will also make performing a joyful and fulfilling experience, not just a job.

NOTES

1. The glass harmonica is a series of glass bowls that are tuned and are arranged on a turning rod. The player wets his or her fingers and touches the bowls on the edge as they rotate.

2. The huge modern production staff needed to produce such an opera was also absent at its first performance. The librettist, Emanuel Schikaneder, was also the producer-director and played Papageno.

3. Indeed, Rossini despised the full-voiced high notes. Reportedly once when Tamberlik came to visit Rossini, the composer told his servant, "I shall be glad to see him—on the condition that he deposits his C outside with the coats. He can take it away with him the moment he leaves" (Ethan Mordden, *Opera Anecdotes* [Oxford: Oxford University Press, 1985], p. 34).

CHAPTER 5

— ❧ —

Third Line Skills III: Movement and Expression

THE OPERA PERFORMER ON STAGE

Both movement and expression are inevitable in opera. There is no way to perform without both. When a performer is in front of an audience, *whatever* he or she does is going to be read as meaning *something*, no matter what else happens. There is no such thing as not communicating and there is no such thing as nonmovement or nonexpression. For this reason all singers who hope to become adequate interpreters of operatic literature must understand what they can do with movement and expression, and eventually write these actions on the third line for every role they do.

Even when singing offstage or behind scenery, this principle is important. Even when doing an audio recording in a studio with no audience, movement and facial expression are still factors. Even if the people making up an "audience" for recorded material cannot *see* what is going on, beyond hearing voices coming closer or going farther away or voices moving from one angle to the next, they definitely "feel" expression.

It happens all the time. We know a student who had to prepare an audio tape for an audition. She was well acquainted with many of the techniques outlined in this book. When she went to the recording studio for a taping, the session did not produce good results even after several hours. She was very unhappy with the results until the accompanist said to her, "Listen, why don't you perform the piece the way you do it in your acting coachings?" She said, "Why? What's the point? Nobody will be able to see anyway!" The accompanist had the good sense to insist. She went in front of the microphone and did all the motions and all the facial expressions that she had worked on in her acting coachings, and that was the tape that finally satisfied her.

This theory makes sense on several levels. Motion and facial expressions have a definite effect on the voice. As a number of master teachers have noted, when performers are singing and concentrating *solely* on vocal sound, they often perform physical contortions to try to produce the "correct" sound. These physical movements usually bear no relation to the text they are trying to convey. Arms move to the front of the body, sometimes touching the chest, trying to reach the elusive diaphragm. This is the characteristic posture known as "holding a dead bird." The eyes bulge from the face, the back of the neck stretches, and the lips try to imitate some unhappy primate. The results are often neither vocally nor visually pleasing. In this way the "singing" often gets in the way of the performing.

The main problem here is the question of layers of approach. Some approaches to singing are based on the theory that when singers are well trained in terms of vocal technique, when the time comes for them to perform, technique goes into automatic mode to allow the *rest* of the expression to somehow magically surface by itself. The trouble with this approach is that there is usually no such magical emergence. When called on to perform, singers trained in this way usually have no resources to tap, and they grope for outward expressions that will complement their musical production, often damaging their vocal technique. We believe the antidote to this is for singers to take seriously such expressive tasks as managing effective movement and facial expression, and to practice them concomitantly with practicing vocal technique. Rehearsing these tasks and making *them* the primary concerns of the actual performance, rather than vocalism, often allows the voice to free up completely.

As far as the "vocal instrument" is concerned, as we have suggested in Chapter 4, an opera performer's instrument is not his or her *throat* or *voice* in isolation. It is the entire body and mind—there is no independent organ inside of the body called the vocal system. The first realization for singer-actors must be that they cannot detach their voice from their body.

Trained singers should be aware of their vocal apparatus as part of a total performance apparatus, but awareness does not end here. The task of the opera performer must be to aim for total expression. This involves every part of the body—arms, legs, trunk, head, and face. This is the most rudimentary truth on the speaking stage, but it still manages to elude many singers. Singers are sometimes first made aware of the connection between the vocal apparatus and the body when they complain to the stage director: "I cannot sing sitting, kneeling, walking, or lying on my side or stomach." Awareness of an inability is, of course, a very unproductive kind of awareness, unless it becomes the starting point for correcting the inability. Rather than look at the body as a limiting factor, all singers should try to train their whole bodies for singing.

MOVEMENT

Every stage action will be read as meaningful movement. The question all singers must ask themselves is: "Am I personally engaged with my own movements?" Every action of the body should be the result of a decision to communicate something to an audience. Even the lack of movement has to be a decision. The all-too-common attitude is: "I am an opera singer, so when I sing I don't move" or "I don't have to move," or "I don't need to move," or "I shouldn't move," or, worst of all, "I *can't* move!" The performer may indeed choose not to move at some point, but that choice should be a theatrical statement, a visual statement, or a characterization statement. The Queen of the Night in *Die Zauberflöte* may not "move" as she sings, but that should be a conscious choice, not a default position taken because she is incapable of movement. If she pauses and stands unmoving for several minutes, she still expresses meaning through her pausing.

There is no way to be in the opera profession without understanding that movement is an integral, carefully considered element in performing. Some singers who are uncomfortable with movement may view a static role with relief, but communication through a static role is not necessarily a blessing. In such roles the singer will still be expected to supply the correct interpretive effects, but he or she must do this with subtle expressions and controlled eye focuses. These are often harder to execute well than more active forms of movement.

In brief, movement must be integral to a well-developed notion of performing. This also means that singers should not conceive of the process of engaging in movement in performance as a layering phenomenon—first getting the vocal mode working and then adding on movement as a kind of icing on the cake. This is actually much more difficult than starting with the concept of movement from the very outset. Every word a singer sings implies a decision about movement, and this should be a part of a singer's conscious preparation from the earliest stages of rehearsal. Otherwise, once the singing mode has "jelled," there is hardly any "space" left to incorporate the rest of the ingredients as an afterthought.

EXPRESSION

Movement is meaningless without facial expression.[1] Expression without movement may be possible onstage, but movement without expression is not, since anything reflected on the face will acquire meaning, as demonstrated in the Queen of the Night example above. It is certainly possible to perform with a deadpan expression, but such a lack of expression should come about through choice and not because the singer is incapable of anything else. The lack of expression can thus be a *form* of expression, just as the lack of movement is a form of movement. Violetta in the last act of *La Traviata,* for example, may choose to read Germont's letter with no facial expression at all. Such an interpretation, in fact, makes an extremely powerful statement given the state of Violetta's health and her emotions. The audience may understand from this characterization that she has read the letter 100 times already, and now she may have become numb—repeating the words mechanically, devoid of expression. Likewise, Bartolo in the first act finale of Rossini's *Il Barbiere di Siviglia* is required to stand stark still with a frozen expression as the military salutes the disguised Count Almaviva, thereby creating a wonderful comic effect.

Audiences have an astounding ability to read facial expression (or lack of it) from great distances. You may test this yourself the next time you are in a large opera house or theater. It is possible to register subtle changes in eye focus or mouth position even from the fourth balcony. This means that nothing done onstage is likely to pass unnoticed. A wooden, deadpan performer cannot assume that no one will be able to see his or her lack of expression.

When do singers need movement on stage? When do they need expression? When does facial expression need accompanying movement and when can it convey meaning by itself? When does movement require a particular expression and when does it convey meaning of its own accord? The answers include all of the above permutations. For example, in King Philip's powerful soliloquy "Ella giammai m'amo" in Verdi's *Don Carlos,* he may be seated at his desk and not move throughout a good part of his aria. Here the lack of movement makes a strong statement, because it *is* a form of movement. It raises important questions. How much expression should be outwardly shown? Is he coming out of a daze, out of a dream, out of this sleepless night? Is he depressed, or tired? He might not be expressive. He might be repeating his lines almost automatically, but the singer should make sure that the lack of expression *is* conscious expression. The performer may actually have to take some care not to allow any uncontrolled facial expressions to cross his face in order to create the desired result.

Most performing on stage should involve a wide range of facial expression. The face is capable of reflecting an enormous palette of emotions. Many singers are afraid to use even a fraction of the power in their faces as they sing. Some believe that using their faces in singing will distort their vocalism. Others look at some professional singers on stage and see little expression, and feel that that is the way to perform professionally.

Neither of these notions is valid. It is true that, when simply told to emote, some singers' vocal technique may be undermined. The act of using unfamiliar muscles while singing will introduce muscular tension which will throw the voice out of kilter. However, singers can be powerful communicators with their facial expression as they sing without interfering with their vocal production. But—and here is the crucial point—they must *practice* using facial expression as they sing. It is only through regular exercise of facial expressive capacities (and body movement—see below) while singing that singers will be able to discover how to use those capacities and not destroy their vocal capabilities through unwanted tension. This is all the more reason for introducing the use of facial expression into their preparation from the very first day they begin to work with material that they will eventually perform. It is often lively facial expression that makes the difference between a lackluster and a truly exciting performance.

FUSING MOVEMENT AND EXPRESSION

Theatrical communication is what distinguishes opera from concerts and recitals. But communication does not take place automatically when a singer moves or uses facial expression. Raising the hand is a simple body movement which may not communicate any particular message. Moving the arm in conjunction with a meaningful facial expression may make the movement meaningful. This added to vocal expression creates a theatrically communicative act.

It is an interesting exercise to stop a scene in the rehearsal process and ask the performers to ask themselves: "What am I trying to say?" The singer will usually answer in a normal conversational mode, "What I am trying to say is this and that." The expression and movement they use in explaining what they are trying to say are often magnificently clear. It is then possible to say, "Well, the movements and expressions you have just used to explain yourself are the movements and expressions you need for your character."

From another perspective: onstage a singer is telling an audience a story or explaining something about his or her character or about the events taking place onstage. He or she is communicating with expression—narrating or representing, in fact. The subjects the singer is communicating are theatrical; they are contained within or implied by the story and setting of the opera. These are the elements that must be dealt with in gauging movement and expression. Actions may be bigger or smaller because of the audience's proximity or the size of the theater, but this is a secondary consideration. Basically, if the elements of movement and expression serve to narrate the story, then the portrayal will likely be successful. If singers are using movement to try to do something else (look the way they think an opera star should look, punctuate high notes, etc.) because they think they *have* to, that's when the use of movement is wrong.

The general public often identifies movement and expression on the opera stage as large and stilted. They still entertain notions of grand stock gestures in opera of the kind mentioned in the first chapter of this book: wrists to the forehead, hands clutched at the breast, arms flung out and up. Unfortunately, there are still singers who believe that this is the proper language of expression and movement for the operatic stage. The general feeling is that if it was good in the past, it must be good today. What these singers do not take into account is that opera, like all art, is continually evolving.

For example, it is indeed true that in opera books of the 1940s, just about any production of *Aïda* has a picture of Radames wearing what seems to be a ridiculous little skirt with pleats. In the 1940s that kind of costume was not ridiculous; it was the accepted concept of what fashion was like in Egypt in the days of Radames. The singer in the picture may also be posed with the back of

his hand on his forehead. So the evolution of fashion in stage costuming par-
allels the evolution of expressiveness, of performance on stage. Audiences would
no longer accept those pleated skirts as a costume for Radames, anymore than
they should have to accept the gestures that accompanied that pleated skirt half
a century ago! This doesn't mean that productions of *Aïda* in those days were
bad, or that singers' notions of expression were wrong. It means that we have a
different language of stage expression today than 50 years ago. The performing
arts have simply evolved along with tastes in food, clothing, architecture, and
every other aspect of human culture.

TRAINING FOR TODAY

Students wishing to become clothing designers today are not going to study
with a teacher whose ideas of style never advanced beyond 1949. Similarly, a
singer pursuing a career is not going to study with a teacher who is stuck in the
1940s. Such teachers are going to teach performing concepts that amount to
museum studies—a kind of artistic taxidermy. This instruction may be fascinating in many ways, but stale and mechanistic for practical purposes in modern
productions.

It is of course interesting to research how opera was produced and performed in earlier periods. For a recent production of Donizetti's *L'Elisir
d'Amore,* the stage director was eager to go and talk to the old masters about
the historical traditions of *opera buffa.* For that production he wanted to recon-
struct some of these old traditions and use them consciously as part of the contemporary work. Such an exercise is certainly valid. But for directors or singers
to slavishly imitate a production or performance style from an earlier period
because they believe that it is the only correct way to perform—or, worse yet,
because they can't imagine any other way of doing it—is certainly wrong. All
past traditions are valid as long as they serve as background for new creative
expression. The attitude "let's do it as they did then because it was better in the
old days" is simply not acceptable.

Some of the famous opera stage tricks from the past are still fun and can
be used to good effect. Many such "bits" can be transmitted to future genera-
tions, but this doesn't mean that future singers are going to adopt a total performing approach that is frozen in time, unless they are making a clear
conceptual choice. Moreover, that choice implies discarding some possibilities
in favor of others. An artist should always know exactly what is being discarded,
and what is being kept and why.

In the theater there are many historic forms, such as vaudeville and burlesque. Performers don't use burlesque *shticks* and slapstick routines any more
unless they are trying to re-create something that really looks like burlesque or
really looks like vaudeville. The movements and expressions associated with
those forms are recognizable. It is the same with melodrama. But singers don't

make melodramatic gestures on the stage unless they are really interested in creating a museum piece, or in referring to that historical form to make a point.

In opera there seems to be a historic divide. After the 1950s, the public began to demand "realistic" acting of opera performers to conform with new aesthetic tastes on the "speaking" stage. The New York Actors' Studio techniques for training actors, based loosely on a version of Konstantin Stanislavski's methods, came to be the stage norm. There are many possible explanations for this development in the theater world. In the 1950s, as the world began to reorganize itself, this postwar attitude in the arts reflected a desire on the part of members of Western societies to find themselves. The cultural and political reshuffling created by the war made it imperative to seek answers to basic questions such as: "Who am I and what do I represent?"

The stage performer always poses this kind of question for the audience. But the *artistic* question is, "What kind of message am I delivering right now?" The fifties was the decade in which opera refocused and reorganized itself along these new aesthetic lines. In Europe it may have started earlier, and in the United States a bit later.

The question of artistic evolution still exists today. Should old performing styles be put on the shelf just because they are old? Or are the old performing styles good enough to support constant revitalization, new angles, new perspectives, and new concepts? We think that the answer lies partly within the individual operatic work. If a given opera is poorly written, it can only be produced in limited ways, and it will die as a piece of living theater. If the opera is good, then it can support a variety of treatments and a continual investigation of its artistic possibilities.

NATURAL LIFE, GESTURE, AND MOVEMENT

The gestures of real, everyday life can serve as a kind of rough guide for singers trying to improve their use of movement and expression, but with some important caveats. If singers are dealing with real-life characters, why should they do anything other than to make them appear like real-life characters onstage? However, there are other kinds of characters than real-life figures in opera. If the work is about the gods and goddesses of Olympus (and there *are* contemporary operas written about such deities, the singers must ask, how do they, as contemporary people, visualize the Olympic deities? They are not going to visualize them in the same way as they visualize "the man on the street." But they are not going to portray them as people conceptualized the Olympian gods 40, 60, or 100 years ago. In choosing appropriate movement and expression, singers have to analyze the entire score: what is the style of the music? What kind of characters are present on stage? What are the contrasts and conflicts of the characters? Are the gods symbols, human prototypes, or much bigger than life entities? The questioning should continue until the singers find specific answers.

Another example is Samuel Barber's *Vanessa,* which takes place right after the turn of the century. The characters in the opera are not going to walk the way people walk today. The length of the women's skirts, their corsets, and the high collars for men imply a different style of movement. Nevertheless, Barber's characters are real people with relatively modern emotions and problems. These are the factors, then, singers must consider before they establish patterns of movement and expression.

Questions of this sort raise important acting problems. How do characters walk? How do they gesture, and how do these movements fit both with the period and with today's standards of performing? This is an elementary problem for the spoken stage, but opera has a special difficulty in that it is especially burdened with its own historical performing styles.

In order to get a start on this problem, a singer must first try to delete all the images of the past. If 40 years ago Bellini's *Norma* was done in a certain fashion, this does not mean that the 40-year-old interpretation is valid today. The way people saw Norma 40 years ago cannot be an accurate portrayal of the way Norma behaved in the days Norma was alive—if there ever was a Norma— or in the days of the Druids. As we have said above, performers in the 1940s had their opinion about that "style" and, if today's singers are true artists, they should have their opinion too. One starts anew every time, even if one accumulates past knowledge.

After erasing all the preconceived imagery, the singer asks: Who was this Norma? Did she walk like a common "person on the street" in those days? One answer might be: No! She walked like a semideity among the trees of the sacred forest. This begins to give the artist some elements for characterization. Did the Druid priests and priestesses walk barefoot? Did they wear something on their feet? What was it? What does that footwear imply in terms of how fast or how slow they walk? Were Norma's thoughts pure? Were her thoughts fickle? The decision here provides clues for determining her physical attitudes. Did she love the people around her, or not? These answers help define a physical and emotional relationship toward the people she confronts on stage. For example, does she look at people over her shoulder or face to face? Answers to these questions provide the kinds of details that help make these characters come to life.

Many of these problems are common to everyone working on the stage, but there is one acting problem of particular importance to opera. The operatic aria presents a special problem for movement and expression. Nevertheless, *the operatic performer should NEVER study arias in isolation from their dramatic context*.

It is a sad fact of life that singers have to study arias because they need arias for auditions. They should, however, study the aria as a conclusion to, and as a result of, studying a role. This doesn't mean that a singer must memorize Carmen's entire role because in two weeks she must sing the Seguidilla for an audition. This means that the singer must have as much information as possible of the whole opera and the background in order to focus this aria within the context. This study will automatically give singers a repertoire of attitudes and movement that will not come from the aria alone—they will be drawing something that is natural for the character within the total role.

An analogy from daily life may be helpful here. Imagine a woman walking into a party. She sees a person talking in a certain fashion, and this person strikes her as somebody interesting. Merely looking at this person does not tell her enough. So she goes to her friends and says: Who is she? How old is she? Where does she come from? What does she do for a living? Where was she born? Finally the woman asks the person herself, but her knowledge of her is not based on just what she tells the woman (party talk can be misleading!), but also on what the woman observed, and what she could find out from other sources. Basically, the woman became interested in the person—this was the only way to get to know her. If the woman is curious, she will try to accumulate as much information as possible to see if she wants to continue seeing this person. Now a singer should imagine that the person at the party is Carmen (or another character that he or she will portray). The singer should replace the party above with the score and replace the friends at the party with information and research from literary and historical sources.

Singers follow exactly this process in preparing an aria. The singer asks him or herself: "Wait a second, do I just take music and words at face value? No. In the same way that I can't find out enough about the person at the party merely by looking at him or her, the aria alone will not tell me enough about the character who is singing it." To arrive at correct gestures and expression, singers must know the character singing the aria intimately. In the case of Carmen, a performer can gain this knowledge from study of gypsies, of Merimée's novel, of the opera's original spoken dialogue, and of the latest productions of the opera by directors of intelligence and knowledge.

HOW MUCH MOVEMENT?

Two of the things with which singers often have difficulty are:

1. determining where movement in singing naturally occurs, and
2. determining how much movement is enough, how much is too much.

The answer to these problems is easier than many singers suspect. In Cherubino's aria "Non so più" from Mozart's *Le Nozze di Figaro* (Example 5-1, pp. 72–73) (we'll assume that the singer has studied both the opera and Cherubino's character thoroughly), there is a lot of vivid expression implied. This doesn't mean that the singer is going to be running madly around the stage. As a general principle, the less a singer does, the stronger he or she appears. Nevertheless,

Example 5-1. Mozart, *Le Nozze di Figaro*, "Non so più"

1. Ostinato figure in orchestral accompaniment with rests on each beat of the measure.
   The singer thinks:
   I can think of the ostinato figure as Cherubino's rushing blood, and the rests as marking the pace of his heartbeat. I should probably think of some movement that will indicate this.

2. There is a rest before this first phrase, and before each similar phrase.
   The singer thinks:
   I must take a good healthy breath for singing, but breathing can also be a gesture. I should make it look hectic—Cherubino is in a sexual frenzy, and the breaths accentuate his passion—they almost seem like panting. In fact, perhaps I shouldn't just breathe because it is physically necessary (audiences are not necessarily interested

Example 5-1. (continued)

>3. in feats of breath control); I should breathe as the character Cherubino would breathe.

3. The overall shape of the line is descending.
   The singer thinks:
   The shape of the line suggests running out of breath (and perhaps of hope as well). I can reflect this (even if I have enough breath) with my facial expression and body.

   3a. & 3b. The longer descending line consists of two shorter descending phrases, the second (3b) rising higher than the first.
   The singer thinks:
   This suggests that I need to finish the thought with strength rather than by fading off.

4. "donna (lady)."
   The singer thinks:
   I should note the special treatment of this word. It is placed on the downbeat, given three notes, and an unusual portamento on the first syllable. Two notes could have done just as well. Mozart is telling me to pay special attention to this word. Cherubino is obsessed with women, so it is appropriate that "donna" should get a special stylistic marking. I could mark this with a gesture as well.

---

there are a few clues for Cherubino's action. First is the sound of Cherubino's heartbeat, implied directly by Mozart in the music of the accompaniment and reinforced by the text. This gives the singer a direct clue: an attitude, a tension in the body, and a nervousness that can be the basis for clear stage action that accords with the music. The "third line" analysis below gives an example of some of the ideas a singer might incorporate into her interpretation. The analysis technique itself will be explained in greater detail in Chapter 6.

In the countess' aria from the same opera, "Dove sono," the music immediately tells the singer what kind of expression is required. The clues coming directly from the score tell the performer that her expression is slow, delicate yet deliberate, and impassioned. Mozart has provided the guide. If a performer tries to do Cherubino standing and doing nothing, it is hardly possible to sing the text. Similarly it is equally impossible for the Countess to move around frenetically during "Dove sono."

In short, if a singer fights the score, the score wins. Which means the singer is the loser.

The score always asks for movement in appropriate places. Movement may be signaled by a musical interlude where there is no singing, or by a sudden shift in tonality, tempo, or rhythm. The score will always win. And this is particularly true regarding most of Mozart, Rossini, Verdi, Wagner, Puccini, Berg, Britten, and other fine opera composers who were deeply involved in producing their own work. There are some scores that need some help from the stage director, but usually in the standard repertoire singers can trust the score to give them the right clues for movement and expression.

TELLING STORIES

Once the singer has established the directions provided by the composer and the score, determining *which* movements and expression is a matter of personal approach and experimentation. But one should never forget that to perform is to tell a story—to relay the text of the opera meaningfully to the audience.

Many singers misplace their gestures, placing them too late, as an afterthought, as if they themselves thought of the gesture after the word triggered the thought. It's helpful to think about how people describe things in a regular conversation. If one person looking at another *first* says, "The sun is setting," and then immediately *after* saying this looks at the horizon, most likely the second person won't find the statement convincing. But if he or she *first* looks at the sun setting and *then* says, "The sun is setting," the second person may be convinced by the statement. The principle is to focus *first,* and then make the statement that relates to the focus.

Of course, the opposite strategy might also be a useful tool if a singer is portraying the role of a deceiver, an intriguer, or someone who is not very convincing. Such a character might well tell a lie, then as an afterthought gesture or focus in an attempt to convince the listener.

In general, then, the order of the elements that the performer must bring to bear in portraying a convincing stage action is:

1. the thought,
2. the focus implied by the thought, and
3. the text that is the outgrowth of the thought and the focus.

Again, the second two elements can be reversed in trying to play somebody who is not to be seen as convincing by the audience. For example, Dr. Dulcamara, the quack medicine showman in Donizetti's *L'Elisir d'Amore,* can only fool the country bumpkins (but presumably not the audience) because he knows his advertising line well. His focus may *follow* his words in order to get a "shifty" reading from the text. Even here, there is a focus and a thought, even if it denotes a subtle search for words. The irony is that Dulcamara delivers his sales pitch by rote recitation (or so it should seem on stage). That is how we sense him as "shifty." But if the singer delivers them in this fashion, unless it is done purposefully, the performance will read as false and hollow.

FOCUS

Eye focus is such a key concept for the stage that it requires a good deal of attention from all performers. There are introverted focuses, extroverted focuses, wandering focuses, lack of focus, but, just as there is no such thing as "nonaction" on the stage, nothing can happen onstage without a focus. The focus is the thought, as well as its direction or its source. The thought is visible through the performer's eyes. Without the eyes focusing, even if the performer tries to show a lack of specific focus, there is no thought. Without the thought, there is no story to deliver—there is no purpose of expression.

An actor can only express thoughts. Even portraying a character's *lack* of thought requires a conscious decision on the part of the performer; hence, another thought. The performance of emotions—anger, violence, happiness, serenity—is nothing but the aftermath of thoughts, some immediate, some buried in memory. One cannot be angry unless there is a thought that leads to the emotional expression of anger. That thought implies a focus. Thus singers should realize that performing is nothing but a constant sequence of focuses—some fast and some slow. The arms, hand, and torso don't express thoughts, they merely accompany them. It doesn't matter how hard performers work with their hands; all that movement won't give them extra expression if the eye focus is not clear. In the end the eyes tell the story and guide the viewer to understanding the thinking process.

Just as humans can detect facial expressions from great distances, so can they detect a focus shift from 600 or 700 feet. Even in an immense opera house, the performer's focus will guide those audience members in the last balcony to understand the thought behind the text being delivered, even though they can hardly see the facial details of a performer.

Signs of ineffective focus are easy to see. Eyes become dull and cloudy, they wander from point to point aimlessly, and the performance becomes mechanized. One gets the feeling that the performer is delivering the text because he or she has memorized it mechanically. The performer then repeats the text but there is no meaning underneath. A performer can be saying the most glorious things or the stupidest ones with the same expression—just going through the motions of repeating the sounds, or searching overtly for conductor's cues with total disregard for continuity in their interpretation.

A singer can't *not* focus. Onstage the performer's eyes are open. They must be directed somewhere. Thus we make a clear distinction between focusing, and focusing *effectively*. Focus is ineffective when the performer is not thinking. The moment there is a thought—presumably the thought underlying the text—there is a focus automatically. Even with the eyes closed, the audience can read a thought in that gesture (however, see below for some of the dangers of closing the eyes onstage).

Effective focusing can be learned and practiced. Most often a performer will want to call up the underlying thought of a section of text before delivering the text, as mentioned above. Sometimes the thought precedes the text by a few bars, sometimes it precedes it by a split second. One way or another, the thought *has* to precede the text, unless we want specifically to either look mechanical or not very believable to suit the requirements of a particular role.

Often singers wish to close their eyes in order to create certain emotional effects. This, however, is very dangerous if used indiscriminately and without planning. Since the eyes are an open window which let the audience see into the character, singers must make sure that they know when they are closing them, why, and how long. They must know clearly the reason behind the eye closure and be aware of the focus that transcends the closed eyelids. Sometimes singers close the eyes to sing about something introverted. This is fine as long as the singer is aware of what he or she is dealing with. How many bars will the eyes be closed? And how is the expression of the rest of the singer's body going to mesh with this? After all, the eyes, along with the few muscles surrounding them, are the only real expressive element of the body. Without their meaning, movement is just that: meaningless motion. If one tried assuming a posture and holding it while changing the expression of the eyes, one would see how the same gesture changed its meaning.

Wesley Balk points out that, when singers first start to develop powers of focus, it can throw their entire performance off. Effective use of focus is very powerful. If they have never experienced that power before, they are disconcerted. We would observe that singers may be thrown off by using focus effectively because they previously had not been thinking about what they were singing.

This underscores the principal insight we must develop about this powerful expressive tool: *Focus is part of the third line.* The moment a singer begins studying the score and producing, making, manufacturing, writing down this third line, he or she should start in planning the focuses. When Mimi sings "Donde lieta . . ." in Puccini's *La Bohème,* what is she looking at? Rodolfo? Fine, but she also could be looking in the direction of the garret the audience saw in act I a few neighborhoods away. There are many possibilities. A singer performing Mimi needs to make a clear decision. It doesn't matter if she changes it later on. To have made one decision means that she may have the flexibility to make another. If she hasn't made any decision at all, she may find herself in an empty space with a blank facial expression. Back to *La Bohème,* if a singer is playing Mimi and singing, "Torna sola Mimi . . ." she is definitely talking about the little room where she lived when she met Rodolfo before. That may be the moment for the singer to focus in the direction of the house where she lived before. Having made this choice, Mimi might therefore focus in the first line on Rodolfo in order not to have a focus (i.e., toward the house) that gets overused.

Example 5-2, concentrates on focus in Mimi's textual line. After all, Puccini is not as careful as other composers in specifying the usage of musical motifs.

Example 5-2. Puccini, *La Boheme,* "Donde lieta"

(continued)

Example 5-2. (continued)

1. "Donde (from where)"
   The singer thinks:
   I could be looking toward the Latin Quarter, but, even if I don't, that should be my focus and thought.

2. "tuo (your)"
   The singer thinks:
   The focus is Rodolfo. Even if my eyes never meet his, I am referring to cry of love.

3. "torna (she returns)"
   The singer thinks:
   I am talking about myself in the third person, perhaps with a focus facing forward, eyes opened, with the realization that I will be alone ("sola"), saying you are going back to the . . .

4. "solitario nido (lonely nest)"
   The singer thinks:
   I am talking about going from *here* (the Barrière d'Enfer) to *there* (the Latin Quarter). My focuses should be very clear to make the audience see this. Even if the variation in focus is very small, going from wide-open eyes facing forward into the void to a slightly lower focus to the side with a small indication of worried concern for the implied loneliness, it will probably communicate well.

Of course these are not the only interpretations the singer might make of Mimi's text, but with these kinds of thoughts in mind, the singer's expression will never be blank and meaningless.

Varying Focus and Refueling

This brings us to another point: focuses do occasionally get tired and overused. When a performer sings an entire line of an aria using one focus exclusively, the focus has strength at the beginning of the line and immediately starts diminishing in power. It takes an enormous amount of energy to create a lasting focus onstage. An example is Azucena's vision of flames in "Stride la vampa" from *Il Trovatore*. The singer for this aria must make the vision live for the audience in a series of powerful staring glances. If her eyes wander, the entire power of the aria is lost.

A focus is like a satellite whose orbit eventually "decays." One way to "refuel" a single fixed focus is to pick an opportune point in the music—a musical interlude or rest—and look away, then return to the original focus. The initial power will then be recaptured. Singers must develop methods for detecting this decline. Sometimes it's a matter of measures. Again, the singer must begin to ask questions: "How many measures? Wait a second, I have this long phrase. How many things am I talking about? If I am talking about two things, shall I use just one focus? No. The composer deliberately gave me the chance to deal with two topics so I don't need to worry about 'refueling' one fixed focus because I am refueling every time I change."

The moment the curtain goes up, the attention of the audience is at 100 percent. As soon as the curtain is open, attention starts declining. It is for this reason that singers need to create visual elements to keep the audience *entertained*. The same thing happens with focus. The moment singers focus on one place, they have 100 percent of their power. Because the power immediately begins to decline, it is the performer's job to keep it strong and vital.

Refueling is an extremely important concept for stage movement, since it allows the performer to recover energy and renew the attention of the audience. Singers should experiment with the toughest, strongest attitude, movement, or expression they can imagine, and establish it through focus and facial expression onstage. If they maintain this for a while, they will see that, regardless of how strong this attitude was when they began, if it is not refueled, it will decay. In other words, if there is not something happening to renew it, it will fade.

A performer can refuel by moving to the next focus, sometimes by adding something to the original focus—an eyebrow lift, a frown, a chin lift, and so forth. This is accomplished by using the elements of the score. If it is another strong focus, or strong attitude, it will last at least as long as the first one, but, if it isn't very good, it will decline much faster.

How does a singer decide if a focus is good or bad? The answer lies in determining how closely the audience is able to match the singer's focus and attitude with the two lines given by the score: the music and the text. The closer the singer can come to the intention of the text and the music in his or her stage actions, the better those two lines are serviced. Presenting a good "third line" through appropriate focus and action will always enable the performer to convey meaning to the audience.

Composers also understand the phenomenon of decline. It is for this reason that they continually come up with different musical themes and variations in the orchestration. This is also why there is a continual text that doesn't repeat itself. If there *is* a repetition, it will happen as a way of underlining or wrapping up the thought of a particular stage sequence. A performer should recognize these elements and use them effectively.

One effective technique for using the music to refuel is to take the focus entirely away from the audience. Here a performer may completely drop his or her eyes, and completely let the body go loose to relieve the tension of the focus before going to another one. This can work well as long as it is justified by a "releasing" chord, a rest, a releasing musical theme, a "releasing" text, or all of the above in the score. A singer cannot release simultaneously with an element in the score that is asking for the opposite. If the score is asking for that release, it is better to follow the score. The next focus by comparison will be much stronger because out of the release singers have infinite room for growth with their next gesture or focus. To continually go from one strong gesture to the next is tiresome, just as continual *forte* singing is tiresome. Some composers will help more than others in this respect.

It is also possible to renew focus from within. Even a steady gaze can have variation. The eyes can widen or narrow. Facial expression can shift subtly. A slow rather than a rapid blinking of the eyes can also be expressive. Singers may find themselves performing an aria that demands a rather fixed focus, such as in a prayer or invocation. Renewing their focus from within will aid in making even such static situations vital.

Many singers, especially in opera, have become so conditioned to facing the audience at all costs, all the time, even when they are not singing, that this has translated into a habit of always keeping their gaze outward, and always keeping their eyes opened. This can be extremely boring. Singers must remember that if there is no contrast in the stage presentation, the interest of the audience will fade.

An example is the closing phrases of Cherubino's aria from *Le Nozze di Figaro,* "Non so più" (Example 5-3). This example deals with a set of long changes rather than word-by-word or phrase-by-phrase changes in the text. This should provide singers with an awareness that inner-melody changes are still

Example 5-3. Mozart, *Le Nozze di Figaro,* "Non so più" (2nd theme)

Example 5-3. (continued)

1. Adagio phrase.
   The singer thinks:
   This indicates an immediate musical release just in the change in tempo. This is a good point to fix my initial focus in the aria—probably on the countess.

1a. Two-note figures.
   The singer thinks:
   These little eighth/quarter figures separated by rests give the chance to reflect some emotion, perhaps a kind of a petulant sob to show self-pity. I might quickly glance away, then back at the countess to see if she sees my state.

2. One-and-one-quarter beats of total silence.
   The singer thinks:
   This is an excellent opportunity to refuel. I will look away and pout, but check the reaction of Susanna and the countess with the corner of my eye.

3. Repetition of two-note phrases.
   The singer thinks:
   I can refuel again with a new focus—perhaps on Susanna this time to see if my game is paying off.

4. Another whole beat of silence.
   The singer thinks:
   Here again I can refuel, refocus, and prepare a mood shift.

5. Tempo I—"parla d'amor con me (speak of love with me)."
   The singer thinks:
   This indicates a complete mood shift. I will shift focus again and try delivering this phrase impishly and pointedly.

6. One-half beat of rest.
   The singer thinks:
   Another good opportunity to interject a pointed sigh and refocus.

7. "con me (with me)" with a fermata on "me."
   The singer thinks:
   This can be very romantic with a long lingering focus on the countess.

8. A second fermata.
   The singer thinks:
   Another chance to refuel, gain increased vigor by refocusing.

9. "parlo d'amor con me (speak of love with me)."
   The singer thinks:
   This can be delivered in an explosion of self-assuredness with a very clear stare at the countess or Susanna or both.

operating under an umbrella of larger patterns that respond to the overall concept of the aria.

There are rapid sixteenth notes all the way through the aria. Suddenly there is a slower part. This gives the performer a signal for dropping or releasing. Cherubino is supercharged in the opening of the aria. The performer relaxes the pace at the slow section to refuel and comes back with a burst and a strong ending—really an explosion at the end. Clever composers like Mozart always present elements of contrast of this sort, so a clever singer should match the elements of musical contrast with her contrasting focuses. It is sad to see this aria in the context of the opera delivered straight out to the audience with no acknowledgment of the dramatic situation or the other performers at all. Unfortunately, it is done this way all too often.

There are many times when a singer must deal with repetitious material, such as strophic songs with much the same music repeated again and again and again. In this case one hopes that the set will be interesting enough so that the performer can execute the first verse while sitting, the second standing, the third resting one foot on a stool, and so on. Those are the cases in which the stage director and the performer have to help the composer a little.

An example is Lindorf's aria in the beginning of *Les Contes d'Hoffmann*. He sings three verses more or less on the same theme: how he seduces and misuses women. If a singer is playing this role, he must find something for the character to do on stage for all three verses. The singer can do a lot in presenting this. Of course, the ultimate shape for the stage movement will be given by the director and the stage designer. (One hopes that the designer is providing what the director wants because otherwise things become difficult for the entire production.) So given a varied stage set, Lindorf's song can be visually different even if the verses have much the same musical setting. The singer can do most of the work in this preparation. He might note that, even though the music is the same, the text is not. Having a different text already gives him different possibilities for different focuses because he is telling different parts of the story. That already enriches the presentation.

Sometimes, however, a singer must repeat the exact same text and the same music. So what does he do in this case? He starts thinking: "How can I bring some contrast to do this?" Here again, the operative word is *contrast*. Maybe the first time through, the music will be sung *forte*; the second, *piano*; and the third, *forte*. This means the first time will be extroverted, the second introverted, and the third will wrap up the dramatic moment with extroversion. For example, the phrase "It's a nice day" can be said many different ways to mean: "I guess it's a nice day," "It is definitely a nice day!" or "Do you think it's a nice day?" The more such situations can be dissected, the greater the performance will benefit.

Returning to Lindorf's song, one can cut verses, but there is a risk of losing the balance and format of the work. Still, when it comes to Offenbach, cuts are common because attention spans today differ from those of audiences in Offenbach's time.

FOCUS AND FACIAL EXPRESSION

We have spoken thus far about body movement, then of the question of the eyes and focus. The third element is facial expression. This is not really a separate topic. Once the concept of focus is clear, facial expression should follow naturally as an outgrowth of that focus.

Using Carmen once again as an example, if a singer has a clear conception of the role of Carmen, she knows how she faces fatality, destiny, predestination, and all the other elements in her life. From this knowledge, the singer may come to the conclusion (perhaps in conjunction with the stage director) that she *knows* what is going to happen to her with absolute certainty. During the well-known "card scene," she might seem to be looking at the cards she is drawing, but her eyes might be positioned on the horizon because she sees the future in front of her; the cards are just secondary. She is in stark contrast with the other girls telling their fortunes in parallel action with her. Those girls are just out to see how much they can amuse themselves with immediate things—what's going to happen tomorrow and how they can have fun "seeing their future" through the cards. Their focus is the realistic focus—the immediate pleasure derived from playing with the cards. For Carmen the event is death, unavoidable death. She sees that no matter what she does, the end result will be death. This establishes the focus for the performer. If Carmen merely looks at the cards, she will become absorbed by the actions of the other two girls, and the trio becomes just that—a musical trio—instead of a monologue with a sharp contrasting element in the words and music of the other two characters. The audience then sees three women having fun rather than the contrast between Carmen's destiny and the two girls' amusement.

Even when singers have a single focus, they can change the meaning of the thought through alternation of facial expression. It is vital to remember that *focuses are thoughts*. They are not mechanical points where singers look, and something happens magically to make that moment meaningful. A singer can be looking at a point on the horizon with a blank expression in terms of focus, as King Philip might choose to do during his aria "Ella giammai m'amo" (Example 5-4, pp. 84–85).

As happened with King Philip, a singer's eyes can be wandering and then suddenly see something: because a new thought or image came to him, the thought worries him, and so on. Therefore, focus is a result of thought or image regardless of where it's directed. Carmen can be looking at a lantern and still be thinking about her death card. The meaning will be a result of the expression growing out of the focus, because otherwise focus is just another mechanical thing that is completely useless. Anything that is mechanical is useless, unless it is mechanical by choice (e.g., the doll Olympia in *Les Contes d'Hoffmann*).

Wesley Balk makes an important distinction between "thought process" focuses where only the eyes move, and "kinesthetic shift" focuses where the head moves as well as the eyes. The thought process shift indicates to the audience that the character is changing his or her thought. It thus indicates a change in

Example 5-4. Verdi, *Don Carlos,* "Ella giammai m'amò"

1. Orchestral introduction.
   The singer thinks:
   I am thinking of desolation and emptiness of my emotional life. A slight nod of the head might precede the first negative phrase that follows. I may stare blankly into space to reflect this thought.

2. "Ella giammai m'amò (She *never* loved me)."
   The singer thinks:
   I may continue staring and repeating the slight nodding gesture

Example 5-4. (continued)

through this phrase, as though it is only the ending verbalization of a long thinking process.

3. "No!" followed by a sixteenth rest.
The singer thinks:
This is a definite conclusion. Here the nodding may disappear. Closed eyes indicate very strong emotion, so I may close my eyes to reflect this.

4. "Quel cor chiuso è a me (that heart closed is to me)."
The singer thinks:
This is a strong emotion. The eyes remain closed.

5. "amor per me non ha (love for me doesn't have)."

5a. C# is the highest note in the phrase, on "amor."
The singer thinks:
The emotional message is even stronger, but since my eyes are already closed, the only thing to do is to intensify the focus. On the C# I can tighten the closed eyes just as pronouncing the "m" of "amor" to show my extreme anguish.

6. Repeat of "amor per me non ha" on a falling musical line.
The singer thinks:
I'll try keeping the eyes closed, but signal that I am coming out of this state by resuming the slight nodding of the head. The remaining energy of the body may drop on the downbeat, on the word "ha."

7. First orchestral transition—cellos.
The singer thinks:
On the downbeat of the orchestral transition, I can finally begin the process of opening my eyes and staring into space once more. I can let my neck release and my head tilt forward on the rising phrase.

8. Orchestral figure led with the highest notes thus far in the piece.
The singer thinks:
As the head comes up, I will let my eyes open slowly, guided by the accents on the F-natural beats of the orchestral figure signifying my pain. My eyes can be wandering here in a search of a thought.

9. The orchestral eighth-note figures become sixteenth-note figures.
The singer thinks:
This transition allows a shift in thought. I can again store into space—perhaps with a slight shift in location and see in front of me the image that I will describe in the next phrase.

10. "Io la revedo ancor (I her see again)."
The singer thinks:
Here I can focus on the image of my young bride hovering in front of me, perhaps with a slight increase of attention indicated by widening the eyes.

the internal state of the character. The kinesthetic shift indicates that something external to the character, such as another character entering the stage or a loud noise, has captured the attention of the character. A roving thought process shift indicates that the character is going through lots of different changes in thinking or emotions. A roving kinesthetic shift indicates that the character is beset by a number of competing forces for his or her attention. Singers should distinguish these important variations in focus and practice them as part of their preparation for any role.

We should mention that there are some people who have developed rather rigid expressions in their singing because of a natural habit of showing little facial emotion, or because of methods in the vocal studio that discourage use of any facial muscles. Singers who recognize themselves in this description would do well to exercise their facial muscles on a regular basis while vocalizing or singing, making sure that the facial muscles are always responsive to their thoughts, never held rigidly in place.

ENTANGLEMENTS

One of Wesley Balk's greatest contributions to the study of singing/acting is the recognition that all of these elements of movement and expression create dissonance in the performer. A performer trying to manage eye focus oftentimes loses intensity in facial expression. While a singer is managing gestures and body movement, eye focus may slip. Assuming a strong facial expression may cause gestures to become weak and inexact.

More important for the singer is the realization that all of these can become "entangled" with vocal production and with breathing. Being faced with the task of performing a complicated stage action causes many singers to lose control of breath and vocal support. This is hardly surprising, since it is simply human to lose control over one physical task when asked to do several others at the same time. In opera the difficulty of managing these diverse physical tasks is a serious matter, however, because this is why many singers never want to move or use facial expression or focus. They realize that they are not prepared to do these things and still maintain vocal quality. It is sad that singers often deal with the situation by remaining static and expressionless onstage—far from being the powerful performers they could become with practice.

Indeed, the solution to the difficulty of entanglements is to practice doing all of these things together. Every performer should make it a habit of singing with shifting focus, shifting facial expression, and different body movements and gestures. The first time these are practiced, they are difficult, but in a very short time it becomes quite easy to reflect several emotions on the face, manage gestures, and shift eye focus while breathing, supporting, and singing. This is what audiences want to see.[2]

LOOK AT PEOPLE!

Some singers may find it difficult to prepare a new role, especially in a situation where they are called upon to do something really quite different from what they would normally do in everyday life. Getting a sense of the thoughts and the focuses of a character is a serious acting problem.

For example, few performers have had the experience of being insane, but still they are able to play Lady Macbeth or Lucia. To solve these problems, singers must learn from careful observation of the world around them. One wonderful acting teacher had excellent advice for his students. He would say, "I can't teach you anything here. The only thing I can tell you is, when you come back tomorrow, instead of driving your car, take the bus. If you drive a car you are concerned about traffic lights, and where to park and all those sorts of things. If you take the bus, you have time to look at people."

Singers must look at people! That is what will teach them how to act roles that fall outside their immediate experience. They should be continually absorbing visual information from people around them, noting how people act and react in different circumstances. Taking the bus is, of course, just a symbolic way of saying that singers should be natural observers. The message is clear: Singers must not waste an opportunity to look at people. If they don't have this within them, performing will be very difficult. Singers will succeed if they develop an interest, a curiosity, and a love for seeing how their fellow human beings act and behave around them under different circumstances. This ranges from saying good morning to someone at the elevator, to visiting a psychiatric ward in a hospital. It means that the years of a singer's life have to be utilized in accumulating these images.

Of course, serious actors who are preparing a difficult role often make field trips. Singers rarely do such a thing. The option should be open. Why shouldn't singer-actors take advantage of seeing southern Italy at Easter, if they are preparing for *Cavalleria Rusticana*? Why couldn't they go South Carolina if they are going to participate in *Porgy and Bess*? But this kind of research for a role should be icing on the cake. Singers should be enriching themselves on a *daily* basis; then, if they have the chance to enrich themselves through fieldwork when they have a project, they might well do it.

One caveat should be mentioned concerning extreme measures in studying a role. It might not make all that much sense to go to South Carolina just to get a sense of the way inhabitants of villages similar to Catfish Row of *Porgy and Bess* walk the streets. Such a trip will be a waste of effort unless singers have been going through the exercise of observing people on a regular basis. The ability to see and absorb behavior patterns from others doesn't happen automatically. Singers must not take the attitude that because they have a new project tomorrow they must begin a whole routine of research and study—it is already too late by then. The project started the day they decided to become performers, and began observing and absorbing the behavior of the people around them. For a new project, singers may then underline certain special aspects by taking a field trip, but the basic homework should already have been done.

Charlie Chaplin was hailed as the "actor of actors," the ultimate clown, and the deepest of performers when it came to the expression of pathos and sensitivity. He referred to the acquisition of his famous gait from watching a group of youngsters laughing at a man who was walking with an obvious handicap. Chaplin wasn't making fun of the physical shortcomings of the man, but he understood how to transform the experience to create an acting gesture that would effectively bring out laughter.

In summary, singers must be in the habit of observing and learning to incorporate the things they see. They mustn't go crazy thinking that every time they step out of the house they are going to undertake a special expedition to observe people. Rather it must become a regular habit stemming from their natural curiosity about the human world around them. This practice is the ultimate source for convincing movement, focus, and stage expression. Through it singers will become open-minded and flexible. They will be able to work easily with a stage director, understanding, accepting, enriching, and developing the production concepts that will lead to the creation of a role. Singers will do this by testing their observations within their own body, their own limbs and expression, with the goal to serve a role, develop a character, and create a communicating experience.

NOTES

1. Wesley Balk maintains that movement has no intrinsic meaning, but is interpreted through the facial expression accompanying it. It is for this reason that his training methods place great emphasis on facial exercises. See his three books: *The Complete Singer-Actor, Performing Power,* and *The Radiant Performer* (Chap. 2, notes 1–3) for exercises that will help any performer develop skills in movement, facial expression, and focus.

2. Again we refer you to Wesley Balk's writings for many suggestions on how to increase this capacity through systematic practice.

CHAPTER 6

— ❦ —

Writing the Third Line

In Chapters 3 and 4 we introduced the concept of the third line in addressing the functions of the performer as actor and as musician, respectively. In Chapter 5 we dealt with the dimensions of movement, facial expression, and focus on the stage as they might be incorporated in the third line. In this chapter we will deal with the task of combining all of these dimensions. We will provide some indication of how dramatic realization of the text and stylistic realization of the music in performance can be combined with expression and stage action in writing the third line into the score.

By way of review: the first two lines of the musical score are the textual line and the musical line. The third line, as we have said, is the line that the *performer* "writes." It is his or her interpretation deriving from the first two lines. Actually writing this third line in the score can aid any singer in countless ways to make a performance convincing. It has the added benefit of providing security for vocalism. Above all it will enable a singer to be flexible and thoroughly prepared for work with a conductor and a director on any role.

We repeat a cautionary note expressed earlier in this book. There is no single canonical method for writing the third line. Therefore, when we provide examples or suggestions for the third line, they are just that—examples and suggestions. The actual writing of the third line for the individual performer will be, first, an analytic process—the result of study, consultation, and experimentation. Second, it will be a continual process—performers will write and rewrite the third line for every role they perform throughout their professional career. Finally, it should be a pleasurable creative process—as much the product of an artist's own imagination, taste, and skill as the writing of the music or the libretto. It is our sincere hope that, through this process, every singer reading this book will be able to create memorable performances that will bear his or her personal stamp.

Before the singer begins "writing" the third line on the score, it is essential to understand the complex interrelationship—the "marriage"—between the first two lines in opera: text and music.

THE MARRIAGE OF TEXT AND MUSIC

We like to call the combination of text and music a marriage because of all that metaphor implies: the joys of marriage, along with the difficulties of marriage. Marriage only functions if both parties work for each other. Human relationships fail when either of the two parties does not know how to sustain communication over time. The other party cannot carry on alone. Marriage is also an apt metaphor because in it caution has to be exercised in bringing the two parties together. Matchmaking is, after all, a delicate art.

Sometimes in opera the match between music and text is not a good one. As we have mentioned previously, there are operas that have poor libretti—even by great composers like Verdi. Likewise, some good libretti may not have very good music. Even with the best works there is usually a predominance of one element over the other. Verdi's music is usually so good, one can tolerate a bad libretto. With good libretti like Menotti's, the audience can tolerate a lesser score.

In marriage, if one of the partners doesn't know how to cook, the other had better know how to. If both partners can cook, that is even better! In other aspects of life as well, they have to complement each other and work together. One partner has to understand the limitations of the other and vice versa.

Singer-actors can do little about the material they are given to perform. They are not called upon to become critics and judge the value of, say, Bellini's setting of the stories of Sir Walter Scott. However, every performer *must* be able to identify and work with the strengths and weaknesses of the operatic material.

Singers generally believe the musical line to be primary in preparation and performance. They are so worried about the notes they are singing that they are not willing or able to balance musical interpretation with textual interpretation. The result is often a bland and colorless realization of the role, even when every high note is spectacular.

One way for singers to start developing flexibility in interpretation is to examine the score using questions about the interrelationship of text and music such as the following: "Why *this* note, and not another for this particular phrase? Why *this* particular word on *this* note? Why *this* melody and not another at this point in the story? Why does *this* sentence have *this* particular musical setting? Why did the composer write *this* particular passage or interlude exactly in *this* place in the story line? Why do I have to sing *this* textual and musical phrase here? and—mostly forgotten, but of fundamental importance—Where does the idea for the entire work and its musical and dramatic realization come from?" The answers to these questions will of course be better and more complete as one becomes more familiar with the musical and cultural background of the opera.

The process of making performance choices that enhance the fusion of text and music becomes clear if singers look at the score systematically this way. By asking questions of the score from the first day it is opened, singers will never have to revert to thinking: "What am I saying? What am I talking about?" Or "Why has the composer set the text in such a way?" The result of their analysis will be the basis for writing the third line: a set of natural and effective directions for interpretation in performance.

The composer, being the final dramatist of a score, always has individual ideas about the ways the work is to be interpreted. Throughout the history of opera, composers have often directed or participated in producing their own works and thus have been able to modify the score to meet dramatic needs. The best librettists, when they are writing, conceive of the text in terms of the structure of action onstage. Many write their texts with musical formats in mind: aria versus recitative, for example. Some librettists were even identified in their day as the primary contributor to the work.[1]

For the performer, the principal task is, once again, not to critique the quality of the music or the text. It is rather to learn to see the two lines, the results of collaboration between composer and librettist, as functioning together, *with* each other not as adjuncts of each other.

THE THIRD LINE

Once a singer understands and is able to visualize two lines, music and text, working in tandem, then he or she has a better chance of understanding the idea of the third line. The third line then becomes an interpretive "answer" to the previous two parallel lines: a result of their combined meaning. This is accomplished through an understanding of how each line affects the other, an interrelationship that can be extremely subtle. All elements of the score: words, commas, rests, melodies, fermatas, time signatures, rhythms, dynamics, and tempos are interrelated. Performers must ask how to serve the elements from both lines—not as independent lines but as *interdependent* lines. A singer's interpretation in performance has to provide a continual answer to this interrelationship. Performers are not serving Mozart, nor are they serving da Ponte. They are serving da Ponte/Mozart.

As we have said, however, there is no single correct third line for every opera passage. The interpretation—the third line—is just that: *interpretation,* not dogma. That is why there are multiple artistic interpretations of these works. There were not two da Pontes writing the libretto for *Così fan tutte.* There were not two Mozarts writing the music for *Così fan tutte*. Nevertheless there are endless numbers of interpretations to the two lines these men wrote. Yet these interpretations are only valid if they respond to the first two lines.

In studying a role, performers must take the responsibility of imagining and creating a third line for themselves. This is separate and apart from the direction they receive in rehearsal for a production. The singer has the duty to dig out of the score as many elements as possible based on the concept of text interacting with music. The greatest benefit to singers from analyzing the score in this way is that they gain flexibility in preparation and performance, something that is otherwise difficult or impossible to achieve. The fewer ideas performers have, the less they know about alternative possibilities for interpretation and action—consequently, the more protective, rigid, and closed-minded they are going to be when working with the conductor, the director, and the ensemble. In all areas of life, of course, increased knowledge fosters increased flexibility, but it is interesting that this basic truth has to be emphasized in opera so much more often than in other artistic areas. Fighting this rigidity is constant because the focus in preparation for opera performance is almost exclusively inclined toward the production of vocal sound. Thus for most singers the rest of their preparation becomes blurred and inexact. Many companies take the path of least resistance and resort to replicating "tradition" for standard works, assuming that what was done before must be good today.

Boris Goldovsky cites a sad but hilarious set of examples of completely illogical "traditions" that arise from the whims of singers or conductors which become perpetuated in future productions.[2] In one case in the first act of *Rigoletto* as performed by a famous company, he noted that Count Ceprano, after furiously pursuing his wife and the duke of Mantua across the stage as they proceeded into the duke's bedroom, stopped at the wings, turned around, and sang with the chorus. This made the duke's subsequent complaint about Ceprano's interference absurd. When Goldovsky asked why he had staged the scene this way, the director said that it was a matter of professional courtesy— the conductor was unhappy with the sound of the chorus and needed an extra bass, so the director obliged by keeping Ceprano on stage.

Years later Goldovsky saw a student production in another part of the country where the same thing happened: Ceprano stopped pursuing his wife and the duke, but merely listened to the chorus rather than singing with them. When asked why, the director said that he had made it his duty to study opera as it was done "professionally" for the benefit of his students. Though Ceprano's actions were admittedly illogical, he felt he had to honor "tradition," since this was the way that the scene was done everywhere now.

One symptom of this, which we have mentioned several times, deals with "voice centered-ness" in the training of students of singing. In the best of all possible worlds, the voice teacher will open singers' eyes to vocal possibilities; singers need to remind themselves that the voice teacher provides vocal technique as only *one* of the many ingredients in opera. Acquiring vocal technique and never learning other performance skills may be fine for becoming a voice teacher but not for going onstage and being entertaining for two or three hours. A singer whose entire conception of opera is limited to the execution of arias, even with flawless vocal technique, is crippled as a performer. These individuals are working with a limited view of the second (musical) line of the score, with only the palest view of the first (textual) line, and with no knowledge at all of the third line.

Score study and the writing of the third line will be a matter of self-education for most singers. A singer working with a fine conductor and a fine stage director on a good production with adequate rehearsal time might be led through the process of interpretation. But there is a danger in such ideal situations as well: singers may get into the habit of going into a production expecting to have essentially the entire interpretive procedure provided for them. They may expect textual nuance, eye focus, facial expression, gesture, and movement to be spoon-fed to them by the stage director, rather than them taking on the full preparational responsibilities of performers. In a production process, performers must be ready to give—for this they have to bring some ideas with them to exchange.

The alternative is for the singer to become a puppet, provided there is time for the puppeteers—the conductor and stage director—to provide training as well as staging. Frankly, this will rarely happen. Professional opera is not a training ground. It is, rather, an encounter of professionals ready to utilize their previously acquired skills and contribute their previously acquired knowledge and insights to the production.

THE PERFORMER AS THIRD CREATIVE PARTNER

In writing the third line, the performer becomes a partner in the creative process with the composer and the librettist—a third party in the act of bringing the opera to life. We believe that performers should make this act of creation concrete by *actually notating the third line on the score using footnotes, arrows, asterisks, and any other means available to make the analysis meaningful.* The third line is a personal set of notes that the performer can always translate into real stage action, so it is important to use consistent writing conventions and legible writing.

Before beginning to write the third line it is assumed that the singer has already developed a clear picture of the whole opera, his or her character's place in the story, and the immediate setting for the material being sung. The material the singer writes should encompass the full range of topics we have covered in the preceding chapters. Although each performer must develop a system of notation that works best for him or her personally, we suggest the following four broad areas for notation be considered in writing the third line:

1. *A notation of the important musical events in the score that have dramatic interpretive significance.* This will include notes on musical interpre-

tation—dynamics, tempos, length of pauses, breath marks, phrasing marks, emphasis, and appoggiaturas. Also important to mark are points of articulation with the orchestral accompaniment and with the parts of other singers, such as when the singer's vocal line is doubled by an orchestral instrument, or by another singer. Of particular importance is noting where the vocal line is accompanied and where it stands alone without orchestral accompaniment. Usually, unaccompanied sections allow for greater freedom for the singer, but, when returning to the accompanied section, the singer must be particularly careful to observe strict rhythmic values, since the conductor will expect the singer to lead the orchestra back in correct tempo.

2. *Notes on textual elements needing special dramatic interpretation.* These are indications of the need for particular emphasis on certain words, or for changes in vocal color to reflect certain textual meaning, along with the translation of unfamiliar words or phrases.

3. *Notes on dramatic intent.* These comprise the subtext of the lines being sung, and the dramatic purpose that the character is expressing in his or her singing.

4. *Notes on expressive interpretation.* Included here are:
    a. facial expression and emotional attitude: smiles, frowns, puzzled expressions,
    b. eye focus and shifts in focus, and
    c. body movement including gestures, and body attitude.

Here is an example of the kind of analysis a singer might make, using Fiesco's aria "Il lacerato spirito" from Verdi's opera *Simon Boccanegra* (Example 6-1). The recitative starts with a series of deep, strident chords. The first lines of text say:

A te l'estremo addio palagio altero,
freddo sepolchro dell'angelo mio!
Né a proteggerlo valsi!
O maledetto! O vile seduttore!

To you, the very last farewell, proud palace.
Cold sepulchre of my angel [Fiesco's daughter]!
I was not able to protect you!
O cursed man! O vile seducer!

The singer might analyze the piece in the following way:

Example 6-1. Verdi, *Simon Boccanegra,* "Il lacerato spirito"

Example 6-1. (continued)

1. A rapid descending orchestral line.
2. Ends on a B-minor chord which is held for two full bars. Nearly a full bar after this chord sounds, there is no orchestral movement.
   The singer thinks:
   a. (music analysis) I have nearly a full bar plus the freedom of a sustained note to fill with a gesture, a focus, or an expression.
   b. (textual analysis) There is no text yet, but my actions must anticipate the text to come to give it dramatic impact.
   c. (dramatic analysis) From my study of the opera, I know that I must be bitter, sad, and angry. My subtext is, "I hate that palace and everything it stands for because the man who owns it destroyed my only happiness, and I couldn't do anything about it."
   d. (expressive analysis) Thus I will allow my head to fall from an upright position during the descending line to signify Fiesco's sorrow. Then on the sustained note 2) I will turn, raising my eyes to the palace. With no orchestral movement, a long fixed, bitter stare at 2) might increase the tension of the moment.

   The singer writes:

   - at 1. "head drops"
   - at 2. "lift head, eye focus fixed on palace in distance—bitter, sad, angry"

3. A sixteenth-note upbeat to the next bar.
   The singer thinks:
   a. (musical analysis) The music here suggests a sharp attack. The orchestra is *pianissimo* with a decrescendo. I can therefore choose any dynamic I like. The later curse "O Maledetto!" might be better framed if I keep this piano and very intense rather than blasting with my loudest note.
   b. (textual analysis) "A te . . . (To *you*)." I am referring to the palace. The "te" comes on the downbeat and so should be given a clear emphasis. I must remember that in Italian in such textual situations the "t" in "te" is sustained, almost as if it were a doubled consonant.
   c. (dramatic analysis) The same feelings are sustained as above. I suddenly decide to attack the palace. Subtext: "I am going to curse this place one last time before I leave."
   d. (expressive analysis) A wandering focus until just before the sixteenth note, then, just before I sing, I raise my eyes sharply to

Example 6-1. (continued)

focus on the palace on the horizon. I might also point sharply just before singing "A te."

The singer writes:

- at 3. an accent mark and an arrow over the sixteenth note pointing to the following dotted quarter note
- over the dotted quarter note on "te," a larger accent
- a circle around the "t" on "te," writing "tt" over it
- over the dotted-eighth rest before "A": "focus on palace; point"
- over "A te": "piano—intense"

4. The first line of text "A te l'estremo addio, palagio altero."
   The singer thinks:
   a. (musical analysis) The musical line is sung over a sustained *pianissimo* orchestral chord. This gives me great freedom of expression. The contour falls, then rises slightly, then falls again with a rest before "palagio altero." This musical line could be mirrored in my body movement.
   b. (textual analysis) I am addressing a farewell to the palace where my daughter was raped and died. This is a fairly straightforward line, but the word "palagio" needs special emphasis, so the audience will know whom I am addressing so bitterly. Verdi gives me a chance to breathe before "palagio." I should take the opportunity to set up the word. My attitude is bitter. Perhaps I should spit the consonants to emphasize this. It will also help maintain the intensity when I am singing softly.
   c. (dramatic analysis) This is the preface to my curse. I am clearly leaving, and giving a final farewell, so this means I have been defeated, and I must be bitter about this as well.
   d. (expressive analysis) My facial expression should continue to be sad and bitter—perhaps deflated with defeat as well. The deflation can match the falling vocal line, revive a little on "palagio" and fall on "altero."

The singer writes:

- over all of 4): "focus on palace, bitter"
- lines under consonants as a reminder for emphasis
- circle around dotted-eighth rest
- over "A te . . . addio": "deflate"

(continued)

Example 6-1. (continued)

- over "palagio": "rally"
- over "altero": "deflate"

5. Eighth rest.
    The singer thinks:
    a. (musical analysis) Sustained chords in the orchestra allow me to be a little free here with this rest. The comma separates a falling musical line from a rising line.
    b. (textual analysis) The rest occurs at a comma, but the comma separates two very distinct phrases. A longer break is warranted here.
    c. (dramatic analysis) The next phrase tells why I am so unhappy, so this comma/rest is quite significant. It is a windup for the curse, and marks a clear change in thought.
    d. (expressive analysis) Just time here for a quick refueling. This is warranted as well because there is a clear change of thought. Perhaps a quick flicker of the eyes away from the palace and back. My expression should grow more hostile.

    The singer writes:

- at 5): "refuel, refocus on palace—hostile"

6. "freddo sepolcro dell'angelo mio! (cold tomb of angel mine!)."
6a. With sustained orchestral chords.
6b. The vocal line is all sharp dotted rhythms.
    The singer thinks:
    a. (musical analysis) The sustained chords 6a) give me some freedom. The sharp rhythms 6b) suggest that I should let the text do the dramatic work. A crescendo to "angelo mio" is already indicated in the score.
    b. (textual analysis) The syllables "pol," "l'an," and "mi" are the vehicles for the release of anger, both dynamically and through restrained outbursts. Some measured intensity on "freddo sepolcro"—perhaps by emphasizing the double "d" in "freddo" with a warmer, pathos-filled tone. The "angelo mio" indicates my daughter, and so I should say it with a warm tone.
    c. (dramatic analysis) This is a primary story-telling line. The audience needs to get these words to understand my character. This line is a kind of cursing of the palace. Subtext: My daughter died here because of the cruelty of the owner.
    d. (expressive analysis) I should retain my focus and my bitter

Example 6-1. (continued)

expression. And a facial expression to match on "angelo mio" will provide a good contrast in the line.

The singer writes:

- over "freddo scpolcro": "intense anger"
- a line under the double "d" in "freddo"
- lines under "-pol-," "an-," and "mi-"
- circles around the dotted eighth-note–sixteenth-note combinations
- a circle around the *crescendo* in the score
- over "angelo mio": "add warm pathos"

7a. Dotted figure in the orchestra on the pickup to the next phrase.

7b. "Né a proteggerlo valsi! (Not to protect her was I able!)."

7c. Vocal line in a dotted rhythm begins on the second beat.
   The singer thinks:
   a. (musical analysis) The dotted figure pickup is echoed in the vocal line on "Nè a proteggerlo valsi." The voice should try to match the orchestra line, so I will be limited in rhythmic freedom here; however, the vocal line is unaccompanied, giving me freedom in dynamics. I could do it softly or loudly. Either would make musical sense. Softly might be better, because I have just come off a loud phrase, and will be at my loudest on "maledetto."
   b. (textual analysis) This line is a line of regret. The emphasized syllables are "Nè," "-teg-" in "protegger," and "val-" in "valsi." I could sob on "val-" to emphasize my sorrow.
   c. (dramatic analysis) The theme changes from cursing the palace, to talking about myself and my inadequacy. I can almost sob this line, because it expresses regret. Subtext: "My daughter died, and I couldn't prevent it because I am too weak or I failed in some other way."
   d. (expressive analysis) The music and text both suggest a change in focus. I will shift my eyes with a turn of my head to look straight ahead with a glassy stare, and change my facial expression from one of anger to one of helplessness at 7a). That is what the orchestra figure at 7a) is there for: to give me time to refocus to these thoughts. My attention also shifts from looking at the palace to examining my internal feeling, so a thought-focus shift would be appropriate. Since it is an internal emotional focus shift, I will move my eyes, but not my head.

(continued)

Example 6-1. (continued)

   The singer writes:

- at 7a) a circle around orchestral figure, an arrow drawn from figure to following vocal line, and "match" over the arrow; writes over 7a): "despair, shift internal focus forward"
- at 7b): "piano"
- over "val-": "sob"

8. Three strong orchestral chords separated by rests with sixteenth-note pickups: 8a), 8b), 8c).
9. "O maledetto! (O cursed man!)."
   The singer thinks:
   a. (muscial analysis) Each of these chords—8a., 8b., 8c.—is like a fanfare for the curse at 9). The curse itself, in octaves, is also like a fanfare. The curse should pick up something of the tone of the orchestra, and at least tells me to do something. The orchestra is marked *piano,* so this gives me several options. I can either deliver the line *piano,* or *fortissimo*—the orchestration leaves all options open. Since I just delivered a *piano* line, I will sing this *fortissimo.*
   b. (textual analysis) This is the high point of the recitative. It is a curse, and of course it should be emphasized and delivered in a forceful way. Each syllable should get some distinct emphasis.
   c. (dramatic analysis) This is the culmination of Fiesco's anger, frustration, and misery. The aria that follows talks of his unhappiness and need for salvation from his daughter, so this is the strongest statement in the whole piece.
   d. (expressive analysis) I can use three different focuses, slightly separated, as I search for a new thought. They indicate another shift in thought. The three chords—8a), 8b), and 8c)—give me the chance to shift my thinking from despair back to anger and vengeance. On the rest before the first figure, 8a), I'll widen my eyes and change my expression to one of anger. On the rest before the second figure, 8b), I will shift my focus to the palace again; on the rest before the third figure, 8c), I'll raise my fist in a curse. That way the audience will be expecting the curse at 9) before it comes.

   The singer writes:

- 8a.: "widen eyes, change expression to anger"
- 8b.: "shift focus to palace"
- 8c.: "raise fist"

As one can see in Example 6-1, for each interpretive choice he makes, the singer writes the direction on the score. The more visual this third line becomes, the clearer the process. It is important to note that nothing in this analysis is in any way exclusive—there are an infinite number of possible responses to the particular combination of music and text found in this aria. For instance, the singer might have chosen to make the three gestures at 8a), 8b), and 8c) coincide with the musical figures rather than with the rests between the figures. Moreover, a stage director may have had completely different ideas. But, having gone through this analysis, the singer will be ready to add facial expression, focus, and gesture at the appropriate points in the score without being disconcerted by anything the director suggests. He will know in advance the likely points in the score for movement and expressive change. He will also be ready and able to add interpretive elements of his own if the stage director turns out to be of the "traffic cop" variety who only provides broad blocking with no detailed interpretive suggestions at all ("OK, Fiesco moves down center and sings his aria, and then . . .").

BALANCE AND TASTE

At this point many singers may be saying, "All right, this book is telling me to go through all the roles that I am learning and to start writing a third line in the score for myself. How can I know that what I am writing will be "correct"? Moreover, how much should I be writing? Surely I don't need to be annotating every note and rest!"

Although at the beginning of the chapter we have provided a broad list of elements to consider writing on the third line, we believe it is wrong for singers to write the third line as a mechanical exercise. Once again, we emphasize that this is a *creative* process. This means that not only is it a matter of individual taste on the part of the singer, but it is tailored to the needs of the particular instance of music and drama at hand. The simplest way to answer the question "What should be on the third line?" is: *A constant answer—a "performance response"—to each one of the elements that has been printed on the score.* Although actually annotating every element of the score would be overkill, the singer should genuinely consider a third line response to every comma, rest, accent, key modulation, time signature change, tempo change, or change in dynamics as a conscious choice.

On a *pianissimo* chord, the singer should be prepared to conceive of an action to match it in intensity or lack of intensity, using an appropriate emotion such as pathos or frivolity. If the next chord is written *sforzando,* the action chosen must be noticeably more accentuated than the one on the *pianissimo* chord. If there is a rest after a vocal line, the singer must answer with some action the silent question: "Why is this rest here?" Similarly, a fermata is not just a place to hold a high note—it is a guide to dramatic intensity, or the lack of it.

For example, a rest might be analyzed using questions such as the following: "Is this rest a way of finishing my previous line, or is this rest for me to start the line that follows, or is this rest a combination of finishing a thought and starting a new one, or is this rest a separate thought from the previous and the next?" The singer should not go on to the next page before deciding what the rest is for.

Having considered these possibilities, the singer can then balance action and nonaction so that the ultimate interpretation is pleasing and in proportion. In this way the things the singer really wants to emphasize show up against a field of steady-state music and action. A singer who puts no emphasis on any word, no accent on any note, adds no rubatos to any line, never gestures or moves and sings using only one facial expression will cause the audience to die of boredom. Likewise, a singer who colors every note differently, punches every syllable, varies tempos incessantly, and gestures and changes facial expression on every word is equally boring because there is so much going on, no one element of expression is meaningful—all is lost in a blur of action. The ideal interpretation lies somewhere between the two extremes. Finding that balance is the artistic element in writing the third line, just as it is in any other area of art.

The palette of choice is infinite. In 7a. under Example 6-1, what is the orchestra suggesting during this rest? There are a multitude of possibilities, of course, but one might be: an echo to the previous thought ("angelo mio") or a foretaste of that which will be verbalized with the following phrase ("Nè a proteggerlo"). The singer has enormous choice for interpretation. He can do nothing, in order to set up a gesture or expression in the next passage. He can intensify the action of the previous passage. He can use a shaking, nodding gesture that discards the anger expressed at 6. in order to start anew with thought at 7b. Or he can begin the expression or gesture of the next passage before it is signaled in the music or the text. The actual range of choice of gesture and expression is limited only by imagination.

Interpretive choices are not limited to musical punctuation marks and gestures or facial expression. They also apply to specific words in the text. In looking at the score, one might ask: "Is this word a word to be said gracefully or aggressively? What does the word mean? How many other words in this particular language could have been used by the librettist or the composer instead of this one, and why did they use this one? Why did they use 'amplesso' instead of 'abbraccio' if they both mean the same thing? They both have three syllables. But 'amplesso' sounds softer and more tender, 'abbraccio' sounds sharper and more energetic." The process is endless. Each word, each note, each rest, and each dynamic marking should be studied under this lens.

Working with such detail is admittedly going to be very challenging because there is not always an answer for everything. Singers who are stuck for an interpretive response should write a question mark in the score. At least then their eyes will be opened to something for which they didn't have an immediate answer, and the question mark a reminder to reconsider this problem, instead of assuming that it doesn't really matter or that circumstances will somehow take care of the issue.

In this chapter we have laid out the basic outlines for writing the third line.

We have suggested: first, that the singer consider at least four levels of analysis—musical, textual, dramatic, and expressive; second, that each of these levels be indicated in writing the third line in the score; third, that the singer consider every element of the score for potential notation; and fourth, that interpretive elements be carefully balanced to produce a performance that is neither so static that it is boring, nor so busy that none of the elements of interpretation can be seen or become meaningful.

Having a good idea of the concept of the third line is not enough. It must be put into practice on a regular basis if it is to be an effective tool for the singer. Once the third line process becomes routine, we believe that many of the most difficult stage situations can be worked out on paper and in the practice room before they ever become a problem on stage.

In the following chapter, we will consider how the performer can analyze and find solutions to some specific problematic interpretive problems. In Chapter 8, we will provide some additional strategies for bringing interpretative material into balance, and provide some thoughts about practicing the third line for performance.

NOTES

1. It is fascinating to see how the value of the composer is the determining factor in the overall evaluation of the opera. We have to remember that da Ponte's name often appeared above Mozart's on playbills in his day, but there are many da Ponte librettos for lesser composers (such as Salieri) that have not remained in the standard repertoire. In other words, the opera was not made better just because the libretto was da Ponte's.

2. See Boris Goldovsky, *Bringing Opera to Life* (New York: Appleton, Century, Crofts, 1968), pp. 5–7.

CHAPTER 7

※

Practicing the Third Line

In this chapter we will present some difficult interpretive problems, and discuss how they might be approached through the third line. These are primarily problems centering on singers' expression of their own musical material, but they also include singers' reactions to other performer's material, and to orchestral interludes and silence.

Most of the interpretive problems in singing one's own material center around the tension between musical expression and text. There are times when composers wish to create specific musical effects which are difficult to realize dramatically.

In analyzing arias, one of the most common dramatic problems singers face is singing a song with a simple text that is repeated many times. This is made more difficult when the singer is out onstage alone with no other performers, and perhaps no props. The problem is compounded when the aria has only one emotional theme, such as: "I'm sad now because I'm all alone," or, "I'm happy because I know my lover loves me." Of course, one solution is simply to stand motionless and sing. This is rarely effective.

One important third line technique which the singer can use is to break the aria into a number of logical sections based on the music, the text, or both. Each section then can have a specific emotion attached to it, and a specific eye focus. The singer can then look for transition points in the form of orchestral interludes, rests or other pauses in the singing when the singer can refuel and shift to a new attitude and new focus. An example is Pamina's aria "Ach, ich fühl's" from Mozart's *Die Zauberflöte* (Example 7-1).

Example 7-1. Mozart, *Die Zauberflöte,* "Ach ich fühl's"

Example 7-1. (continued)

(continued)

Example 7-1. (continued)

Example 7-1. (continued)

PAMINA

Ach, ich fühl's, es ist verschwunden,
ewig hin der Liebe Glück,
ewig hin der Liebe Glück,
Nimmer kommt ihr, Wonnestunden
meinem Herzen mehr zurück,
meinem Herzen
meinem Herzen mehr zurück.
Sieh, Tamino, diese Tränen fliessen,
Trauter, dir allein,
dir allein,
fühlst du nicht der Liebe Sehnen,
der Liebe Sehnen,
so wird Ruhe,
so wird Ruh im Tode sein,
fühlst du nicht der Liebe Sehnen,
fühlst du nicht der Liebe Sehnen,
so wird Ruhe,
so wird Ruh im Tode sein,
so wird Ruh im Tode sein,
im Tode sein, im Tode sein.

O, I feel it, it has disappeared,
forever gone is love's fortune,
forever gone is love's fortune.
Never will you, hour of happiness
to my heart, again return,
to my heart, my heart again return.
See, Tamino, these tears flow,
my beloved for you alone,
you alone,
do you feel not love's longing,
love's longing?

(continued)

Example 7-1. (continued)

So will peace,
so will peace be in death,
do you feel not love's longing,
do you feel not love's longing,
So will peace,
so will peace be in death,
so will peace be in death,
be in death,
be in death.

One way to start is simply to lay the text out in logical fashion. The analysis we provide below is based on a pattern of rests in the text. (Other possible schemes might involve taking note of high or low notes in the melodic line, of rhyme schemes in the text, or any other structural feature that yields some logical divisions.) We emphasize once again that this analysis is in no way definitive. Singers should develop an analysis that makes logical sense to them.

The aria is written in 6/8 time. In this analysis each new line is created where Mozart has placed an eighth rest in the score. Each large division is marked by a pause of greater than an eighth rest. Accordingly, subdivisions in section 4 are created where rests of intermediate length occur (two eighth rests, and two eighth rests plus a sixteenth rest, respectively). When the analysis is carried out this way, a larger structure for the aria is revealed, and this can serve as a guide for the singer's interpretation.

1
Ach, ich fühl's,
es ist verschwunden,
ewig hin
der Liebe Glück,
ewig hin
der Liebe Glück,
2
Nimmer kommt ihr,
Wonnestunden,
meinem Herzen mehr zurück,
meinem Herzen, meinem Herzen mehr zurück.
3
Sieh, Tamino,
4a
diese Tränen fliessen,
Trauter, dir allein,

4b
dir allein,
fühlst du nicht der Liebe Sehnen,
4c
der Liebe Sehnen,
so wird Ruhe, so wird Ruh im Tode sein,
fühlst du nicht der Liebe Sehnen,
fühlst du nicht der Liebe Sehnen,
so wird Ruhe,
so wird Ruh im Tode sein,
so wird Ruh im Tode sein,
im Tode sein,
im Tode sein

Sections 1 and 2 can now be seen to be two verses with nearly the same melody. The principal break in the aria is before and after the line "Sieh, Tamino," with the final section broken up into three subsections. Moreover, the structure revealed by this simple process has an internal logic. In the first section, Pamina tells of her feeling that all is lost. In the second, she further exclaims that happiness will never return to her. Both of these sections are soliloquy. The third section is a call to Tamino. The fourth section is her message for Tamino: "These tears flow for you alone. Don't you feel love's longing? I will find peace in death."

We will assume that the singer has gone through the text and performed musical analysis, textual analysis, dramatic analysis, and expressive analysis for the entire aria. Having done this, a simple interpretative scheme would be for the singer to choose a different general focus for each of the four sections, two focuses that could alternate back and fourth, or three focuses that could each be used twice. The focuses can be further modified by shifting the direction of the eyes without moving the head (what Wesley Balk terms a "thought process" focus) at the end of some of the lines, or by closing the eyes on emotion-laden words. A different emotional attitude can be adopted for each section and intensified or relaxed on each line, or "overlaid" with other emotions. Too many gestures in a piece of this kind will make it seem overly melodramatic, but one or two, placed at a critical juncture, may be effective. The following is a possible preliminary sketch the singer might adapt:

Section 1
  Focus: to the right, following Tamino
  Emotional attitude: sadness
  Gesture: hands at sides
Section 2
  Focus: straight out, above the head of the audience
  Emotional attitude: longing
  Gesture: hands at sides

Section 3
  Focus: slightly off to the right again, addressing Tamino
  Emotional attitude: hopeful
  Gesture: both hands out to right to address Tamino
Section 4a
  Focus: back to center
  Emotional attitude: pleading
  Gesture: hands at sides
Section 4b
  Focus: back to the right
  Emotional attitude: anger
  Gesture: one hand out
Section 4c
  Focus: straight out
  Emotional attitude: resignation
  Gesture: hands at sides

This basic working plan is just a start. It can then be embellished, as suggested above, with eye closure on emotion-laden words, and flickers of other emotions such as anger, defiance, even happiness. Working in this fashion in front of a mirror, and perhaps with a coach, the singer can adopt the most effective interpretive scheme—one that has just enough, but not too much movement and expressive variety. The singer can then write this into the score, and practice it while singing the aria until the whole piece becomes an effective and natural dramatic statement.

REPEATED TEXT

Another related problem comes when the singer is called upon to deal with text that seems to be repeated again and again with no obvious dramatic purpose. For example, in a number of works from the *bel canto* period this is a common feature. Often the repetition is done for musical reasons, but the singer still must find a way to interpret the score effectively.

One good example of this comes at the end of Don Basilio's aria, "La calunnia" from Rossini's *Il Barbiere di Siviglia* (Example 7-2). It is easy to come to the conclusion that there is no dramatic purpose to be served at all by those repeated chord sequences. So what answer can one give for interpreting them? The singer may have to dig for ideas and be genuinely creative. Has Basilio gone mad? Maybe. Is he trying to make a point? What about letting him become weaker through repetition? What about making him increasingly stronger by delivering each phrase with different emphasis? If any of those solutions works for the singer, fine—the interpretive problem is solved. Whatever the singer does, however, he cannot avoid the analysis. He mustn't assume the problem will simply take care of itself. The curtain will open and he will be there onstage

(text continued on p. 118)

Example 7-2. Rossini, *Il Barbiere di Siviglia*, "La calunnia"

(continued)

Example 7-2. (continued)

1. "sotto il pubblico flagello per gran sorte va a crepar." Vocal line proceeds with eighth notes separated by rests with only sustained notes in orchestra.

   The singer thinks:

   a. (musical analysis) There are only sustained notes in the orchestra—this may be my last chance to take advantage of the freedom in the orchestration by trying a retard and stepping pompously on each note.

   b. (textual analysis) This line is the denouement of the aria. Its literal translation is, "Under the public scourge by great chance goes to die." It could be translated: "Disapproved by the public, he usually goes off and dies." Basilio is savoring the destruction of the defamed person. I can pronounce the words of this line as if each one were a delicious treat. The text has some prominent doubled consonants and rolled "r's": "so*tt*o il pu*bb*lico flage*ll*o per *gr*an *sor*te va a *cr*epar." I can exaggerate these for comic effect. I will accent each note just as Rossini has written.

   c. (dramatic analysis) Basilio can be played a number of different ways. One way is to assume that he is getting more and more wrapped up in his plot to defame Almaviva, and is getting more and more manic. Subtext: "I'll really get this guy and see that he is ground to dust."

Example 7-2. (continued)

d. (expressive analysis) I'll try an increasing leer on this line to indicate enjoyment of the prospect of destroying Almaviva.

The singer writes: (within phrase 1)

- over whole line: "retard"
- circles around accents on each note
- lines under or circles around doubled consonants and rolled "r's"
- over whole line: "leer"

2. First repeat of "sotto il pubblico . . ."
   The singer thinks:
   a. (musical analysis) The orchestra has a fast *forte* ostinato accompaniment, with rapid vocal line and no rests. By this point I had
   better be with the conductor, or I will be derailed. The pickup
   notes on "cre-" should lead the orchestra in strict tempo. This is
   something I need to work out with the conductor. The orchestration is loud, but if I start the line *forte*, I have nowhere to go on
   the subsequent repetitions. I'll try the line *piano*.
   b. (textual analysis) I can sing this *piano* but, to cut through the
   orchestra, I should make my production very forward, almost
   spoken, with careful patter articulation using emphasis on the
   first and third beats. This is a repeated phrase, but the orchestration and tempo are different from the earlier statement of the material, so variety is provided by the musical setting.
   c. (dramatic analysis) I should find some new reading for this line,
   at the very least: enhanced excitement.
   d. (expressive analysis) I'll reflect enhanced excitement in my facial
   expression. Focus on audience will help the line come across.

The singer writes: (within phrase 2)

- circles around pickup notes, accent on "-par"
- "piano," "articulation," "focus on audience"
- accents over "pub-," "-gel-," and "sor-"

3. Second repeat of same line.
   The singer thinks:
   a. (musical analysis) The orchestration is exactly the same as the previous repetition, so I must provide the musical or dramatic variety. I'll try adding the variety in the expressive interpretation

(continued)

Example 7-2. (continued)

> rather than the musical realization. Therefore I will keep it *mezzo piano*.
>
> b. (textual analysis) The text is the same. Since I have decided to add variety in the expression, I will keep the same forward articulation.
>
> c. (dramatic analysis) Here I can be creative. I can add a pantomime. For example, I can act as if I am literally holding Count Almaviva in the palm of my hand during 2), then drop him through my fingers to the floor and step on him as if on a cigarette butt.
>
> d. (expressive analysis) I will add various focus shifts for contrast. While doing this pantomime, I will change focus from the audience to Don Bartolo, or maybe better from the audience stage right, to the audience stage left, while carrying out my pantomime of stepping on him.

The singer writes: (within phrase 3)

- over "sotto": "focus right"
- over "-gel-": "focus left"
- over "sorte": "open hand, focus on floor"
- over "-par": "step on cigarette butt"
- accents as before over "pub-," "-gel-," "sor-," and "-par"

4. First final cadence.
   The singer thinks:
   a. (musical analysis) These repeated cadences should be varied in volume for variety. I'll sing the first *mezzo forte*.
   b. (textual analysis) Another repeated phrase—I'll keep the strong articulation.
   c. (dramatic analysis) This can be an appeal back to Bartolo for approval.
   d. (expressive analysis) I'll focus back on Bartolo, look for approval.

The singer writes: (within phrase 4)

- "to Bartolo"
- "mezzo forte"

5. Second repeat of cadence.
   The singer thinks:
   a. (musical analysis) To add some variety, it could be either louder

Example 7-2. (continued)

> or softer than the first repetition. Since I've been singing fairly softly, I'll sing this one louder.
>
> b. (textual analysis) Repeated phrase—I'll use the same articulation.
>
> c. (dramatic analysis) I'll assume that Bartolo didn't hear the first phrase.
>
> d. (expressive analysis) I'll therefore sing the next repetition *forte* into Bartolo's ear and look annoyed as if I noticed that he hasn't been listening.

The singer writes: (within phrase 5)

- "in Bartolo's ear"
- "forte"
- "slightly annoyed"

6. Final cadence.
   The singer thinks:
   a. (musical analysis) I know from *bel canto* performance practice there is some flexibility in this final cadence. I could even omit the second repetition at 5). Here there could be a cadenza if the conductor will let me or, at least, since I'm doing this in C and not D, take a high D on "cre-," add a fermata, and make the final "-par" a high C. This should be the loudest repetition.
   b. (textual analysis) For emphasis and variety, perhaps extra attention to the rolled "r's" on "crepar" would make sense.
   c. (dramatic analysis) Basilio is immensely pleased with himself, exited and happy, but also a little frustrated that Bartolo is not paying attention. Therefore I should make this final repetition very assertive.
   d. (expressive analysis) I should probably sing this line directly to the audience with a triumphant smirk.

The singer writes: (within phrase 6)

- "to audience"
- "fortissimo"
- a high D with a fermata on the B at "cre-"
- a high C on "-par"
- "triumph," "smile"

(text continued from p. 112)

alone. A possible set of practical solutions to the end of Don Basilio's aria is given in Example 7-2.

If, however, none of the ideas the singer comes up with really works, he will then place a question mark on the "third line" above the mystery passage. Then, the first thing he must do when called to do the role is to go to the conductor and the stage director and tell them "I have a question here on this series of cadences. What do you want me to do?" The conductor may want to cut some of the cadence repetitions by having him *tacet* while the orchestra plays. The conductor might also totally cut several bars of music. Of the phrases that are left, one might be sung *forte,* another *piano,* or they might crescendo or decrescendo. One might be *legato,* another *staccato.* Here, again, the possibilities are endless.

If, for instance, the conductor doesn't want to cut any of the cadence repetitions, the singer's next stop is the stage director, to whom he says: "Listen, there are not going to be any cuts. Do you have any thoughts about how I should do this onstage?" The director may say, "Oh, by then you will be off-stage. Don't worry," or "No, no, no, here you are going to be punching your partner in the stomach," or, "You will be collapsing on the ground and twitching on every chord," or, "You will be plucking flowers—one for every chord." The singer may not be able to predict the ultimate stage action that will be required in his own writing of the third line, but at least he will know that he has his mind open and is continually telling himself, "I need an answer for each one of these phrases."

If, however, the director says, "Well, I don't know what to suggest that you do. Just stand there." In that case the singer will have learned something about his working situation. The next time he signs a contract with this director, he will remind himself to study the role with a good acting coach beforehand, and to work through the score writing the third line with extra care. In this way he can at least get some additional professional input. Alternatively, the singer can come up with his own radical solution, if he dares. He might decide: "OK, I'll run offstage. And if the director doesn't want me to, I will insist: 'You tell me what to do—otherwise I'm going to run offstage.'"

We are not advocating that singers beleaguer directors and conductors with questions about minute aspects of the score. In real life a performer who comes with a score full of question marks that the director is not prepared to deal with may be a monumental pain. A conscientious performer may ask his or her stage director, "Gee I don't know—what should I do with this rest? What are the guidelines for dealing with fermatas in terms of stage action? I am not clear about the interpretation of this word." Although these are not bad questions, many fine directors are not interested in working on the score at that level of detail—they consider such things to be performers' problems, not directors' problems. It is very likely that these directors will not have answers—yet *another* reason for singers to do their homework and analyze the score themselves. Directors, like all professionals, come in different flavors: some directors put their emphasis on directing the overall production; some will be "singers' directors";

and a few will manage to direct both the overall concept of the production and the individual artists' work onstage.

INTERPRETING LARGE CONTOURS

We do not wish to give the impression that the third line operates only at a microscopic level with the smallest elements of the score. It is also important to take into consideration larger contours—the shapes of musical lines, the thrust and intention of entire textual sequences, and the context within which the performance will take place. These contoured lines can be difficult to interpret as well.

An example of a text with a musical line is the one da Ponte gave Mozart in the famous duet from *Don Giovanni* starting with the well-known phrase, "Là ci darem la mano" (Example 7-3, pp. 120–121). The first line of text means roughly, "There we will give each other the hand." The melodic line has a particular shape with rising and falling contours. Understanding the design of the melodic line is very important in analyzing the stage action that the composer wants (Example 7-3*a*).

Taking text and music, the singers must ask themselves: What has Mozart done to da Ponte's original text in setting it to music? How do the text and the melodic line blend and work together? Is it (Ex. 7-3*b*)

or is it (Ex. 7-3*c*)

No it is (Ex. 7-3*d*)

We see that da Ponte wrote a phrase with an accent on the first syllable: "Là," and Mozart has set it on the naturally accented downbeat. What does the singer do? There needs to be a body accent movement to match this stress. On the third line, to match the previous two, the singer needs an action movement. Here one question does not fit all occasions. The singer must think: "What are the conditions under which this production is going to be staged? Is it going to be in a big theater? If so, I had better point with my hand. If it's a small theater, I can point with my eyes." Eye focus as an indicator might be sufficient in a 400-seat theater, but the eyes alone might not "read" in a big house. This kind of internal dialogue helps in a determination of the third line.

"Là [and I point] ci darem la mano."

To sing "Là" with no directional intention defeats the meaning of the word. Often this duet is performed without any regard to the place where Don Giovanni wants to take Zerlina. Giovanni stands there looking seductively at Zerlina's bosom saying, "Là ci darem la mano" while the supertitle translates, "There we will hold hands." Without an indication of place, the audience will think: "Ah! Don Giovanni wants to hold hands on Zerlina's bosom!"

Next comes a weaving back and forth of the melodic line. There is lots of insinuation; it's not a melody with equal importance for each note or with equal stress on all words. The metrical stress and the musical accents as indicated by the high notes in the melodic line are on the pronominal part of the verb "dar*em* (give)," and on the word "mano (hand)." There is an intention underneath that

Example 7-3.

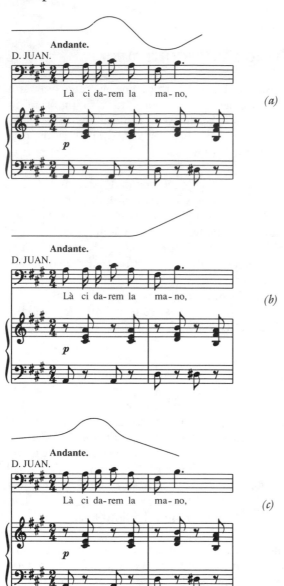

Example 7-3. (continued)

(d)

must be performed—the third line. This is what singers have to notice in order to match the previous two lines that they got at the music store when they bought the score.

Another example of where long contours in the text are very important and are mirrored by the music is the famous "Seguidilla" from Bizet's *Carmen*. Here Carmen is tied up, and the song is a proposition that Carmen is delivering to Don José (Example 7-4, p. 122). But the melodic line runs counter to this. The music does not imply a proposition of anything to anyone. This is not surprising, because Carmen is playing a double game. In effect, she is saying: "I am really propositioning him, but I am technically just singing a song."

Don José stops her and says, "Don't talk to me anymore!" and she replies, "I am just singing to myself" (Example 7-5, p. 123).

Now the singer enters the picture. In analyzing the score, the singer might say: "Wait a second. The text is insinuating. The music seems divorced from the text in character. So I must also adopt a detached manner, but with one eye noting Don José's reaction. I am not *saying* anything in the song that directly propositions him, but if he is listening to the words he cannot miss the implication."

If a singer is preparing to sing the "Seguidilla," then her third line must show a combination of action and expression reflecting two conflicting ends. The internal dialogue might be as follows: "How much do I insinuate with my eyes when I am saying this line—how nonchalant is this? Can I still deliver the message if I show 80 percent nonchalance and 20 percent insinuation, or should I alter the percentages? And how do these percentages change throughout the song—just in case Don José is watching at some point and not watching at some other point? What am I doing? Am I filing my nails to prove a lack of interest? No, wait a second, I have my hands tied behind my back so I can't very well be filing my nails!" All of these elements are typical of those the singer will have to consider. In any case, the singer must be doing *something*—even though she has her hands tied behind her back—tapping the rhythm of the song with

Example 7-4. Bizet, *Carmen,* "Seguidilla"

her heels, lifting one or both shoulders in a naively seductive manner, or even doing nothing as a conscious choice.

Some singers have successfully tried lifting their skirt above the knees with their teeth while seated with their hands tied behind their back. After all it is hot in Seville (Carmen's alibi justifying such an action.) This can be done during empty bars if the singer's figure is svelte enough to allow her to bend over to do this.

The singer will also want to consider motive and background location. How honest is Carmen's invitation—how dishonest is it?. What does Carmen want Don José to understand? What is "près des ramparts"? This is not downtown Seville—this is "près des ramparts"—that is, the outskirts where the gypsy smugglers meet. Next comes: "chez Lilias Pastia." This singer will learn who

Example 7-5. Bizet, *Carmen*, "Seguidilla"

Lilias Pastia is only if she studies the rest of the opera. Otherwise she might as well sing, "La, la, la, la," since Lilias Pastia's place won't mean anything to her. Looking at the whole opera should tell the singer *where* Lilias Pastia's place is, *who* he is, and *that Don José probably already knows about him and what goes on in his place*. All of these intentions will give the singer clues as to what to write on the third line. For a singer playing Don José, this information is equally valuable to gauge his reactions to the song. When singers prepare in this way, they have the possibility of presenting an excellent performance no matter what the production and rehearsal conditions are like. It doesn't matter how much or how little time the director has allotted to stage the scene later on. It doesn't matter if the director has Carmen and Don José sitting on a chair or standing on a table. None of these factors will disturb the well-prepared performer because the intention that the singer has indicated through actions on the third line has already been determined through the analysis of the first and second lines.

INTERPRETING SPARSE TEXT

Sometimes a problem can arise when the singer is given very little to react to by the composer and the librettist because the text and its musical setting are so sparse. Here the singer-actor must do a great deal of the work of interpreting the music, the drama, and the composer's intention to make the scene effective. An example is Desdemona's "Salce, Salce (The Willow Song)" and "Ave Maria" (Example 7-6)—the songs she sings before she is killed by Otello. A singer playing this role may first ask herself: "Why is Desdemona singing these particular songs? They are sweet and simple in contrast to the violence to come. Why a soft little folklike melody and a prayer? Is it because every woman, in those days, before going to bed sang a little song and then said a prayer?" Such a dull reading is probably going to give a very boring interpretation for the scene, and the whole climax of the opera will fall flat.

In writing the third line for the scene, the singer should try to take into consideration something about Desdemona's state of mind. If, for example, the singer assumes that Desdemona is trying to calm herself down, but at the same time remembers a song from her childhood, that may be a clue. Desdemona can have a storm inside her. The song might be something she learned as a girl and always sang when she was sad or afraid. The prayer may give her courage. The text might not be related to the drama directly, although it refers to Desdemona's mother's maid, who had been abandoned by her man. Thus, she can be seen to be fighting an emotional storm with a song. If this is reflected in the singer's face and actions, the song will be heartrending. All of this should be annotated on the third line.

The singer might then note that the "Ave Maria" is a little chant—it is not even a strong melody. The first five bars are actually written on one single note.

One might consider that this constrained prayer shows not devotion, but terror. Desdemona's fears surface with this prayer. The words are borrowed words; the musical accompaniment is likewise minimal. It does not interfere in the least with hearing every word of the prayer. Its entire meaning will rest with the singer's interpretation. There are many choices a singer might make to create a powerful scene: Desdemona is suspicious, resigned to her death, begging for help from God, and so forth. Some choice must be made, however, to determine where and how these choices will be reflected, or the drama will fall flat.

The directions the singer writes for herself in such a situation can be much stronger than in many others because Verdi has given her the chance to supply virtually *all* the drama that this scene implies—drama that is not in the text in the form of direct musical clues. The whole intensity resides in the delivering of a constant, still emotion.

Example 7-6. Verdi, *Otello,* "Ave Maria"

Finally, there are some arias that seem to be "set pieces" because they are "cavatinas" of one sort or another—introductory arias where someone comes onstage and essentially says, "Here I am—this is me—hello!" In these pieces there seems to be no plot action being advanced. The opera in effect stops dead while the character sings. Interpretation is problematic since such a piece can be (and is) performed almost as a separate musical number. The trick for the performer is to acknowledge the showpiece-like intent of the aria, while still finding ways of integrating it into the dramatic action of the opera. Performers who break character to sing such arias, either by suddenly assuming recital stance and expression or by cutting up, mugging, and introducing extraneous *shtick* generally kill the dramatic line and momentum of the whole performance.

Figaro's "Largo al factotum" from Rossini's *Il Barbiere di Siviglia*" is perhaps the most famous example (Example 7-7). There is a lot for the performer to play with in this aria, clearly.

To write the third line for an aria like this, the singer again must first go to the text. "Largo al factotum della città! (Make way for the factotum of the city!)." Taken by themselves, these words could be mock-aggressive or threatening. But is this the way that Rossini shapes the melodic line? No. He sets these lines to a sunny major-key *roulade* figure which he repeats again and again—a very sympathetic melodic realization. Figaro is revealed through the music as a *simpatico* character, not threatening anybody. The problem for the singer is how to reconcile such a strong textual line with the nonthreatening melodic realization and make it *simpatico*? One often-used solution is to assume that Figaro is bragging! This is a wonderful premise to begin with in writing the third line, and it is very much in character with Figaro.

One then comes to endless lines of "la, la, la, la, la." The singer may well wonder: "How do I come up with an interpretation for 'la, la, la'?" Usually there is very little direction given to the singer, leaving him open to show on his face all of his fears about hitting the final G in the vocal line. As a minimal interpretation, he can assume that this is a "vocal release" interposed between the first line of text and the second. The singer thinks: "If it is a release, then I need a body action that will match this release. What do I have in my hand? Maybe the director will give me a guitar so I can just play the guitar. Thank goodness I don't have to think about singing a complicated text in the next line—I can just play the guitar. Maybe the director will have a child run across the stage, and Figaro, to show how *simpatico* he is, will chuck the kid under the chin." So in the third line the singer indicates relief through the music and the "la, la, la" text. Either the director will provide a staged physical response, or the singer will have to manufacture it himself. The singer may reason: "Maybe I will fix my bow tie on the 'la, la, la's.' And with the last 'la' I will finish the bow." There are thousands of possibilities if the singer exercises his imagination. In this way the combination of text and music leaves the singer with a myriad of possible actions and interpretations to indicate on the third line.

One may wonder whose duty it is—the performer's or the director's—to come up with ideas such as the child crossing the stage or Figaro tying up his

Example 7-7. Rossini, *Il Barbiere di Siviglia*, "Largo al factotum"

(continued)

Example 7-7. (continued)

FIGARO.

ran la   la   ran la   le   ra   la.

bow tie or his shoe. A good director will have many ideas for staging the aria. Nevertheless, it *is* the singer's duty to realize that "la, la, la" is a release (even if the melodic line ends on a bravura high note!), that it is not as important as the phrases before and after, and that it must be matched by a physical action of some sort. The performer's annotation on the third line has to match that release one way or another.

Now, for the sake of exercise (and just to make our point), the singer could look at Figaro's entrance the other way around. He could minimize the line, "Largo al factotum della città," singing it *mezzo forte* and somewhat *legato,* then present Figaro's bragging attitude and action through a series of loud "la, la, la, la, la,'s." This should work, too! Yet another solution would be to strike the guitar three times (tra-la-la—tra-la-la—tra-la-la) and finish up the fourth tra-la-la with a bravura stroke of the guitar and an extended arm. All singers should experiment with a number of interpretations and attitudes, eventually finding one or more that represents their own individual reading of the material. No one can say that one interpretation is right and another wrong in this and many other situations in opera—there is no universal truth in the matter of interpretation. Any singer who works extensively with analysis of the third line will have tested this point extensively. Each artist's third line will be rich enough in options and flexibility for him or her to be ready for any task, any production concept, or any stage direction. The singer will then become a team player, and an open-minded creative artist.

USING THE THIRD LINE WHEN OTHERS SING

As a final matter we address one of the least addressed interpretive problems in opera: expression when someone else is singing. It is essential for singers to realize that the third line process is not just for use when they themselves are singing. It must be applied to all music occurring on stage. Nothing is worse to watch on stage than performers who only act and react when they are opening their mouths, and who are otherwise dead. The entire life is drained from the drama. Whenever singers must react to other singers' arias, recitatives or dialogue, the reactions must be keyed to musical events and annotated in the score. The same is true when the only music on stage is orchestral. Indeed, even silence, which occasionally occurs in opera, must embody planned reaction.

This has two virtues. First, coordinated reaction to other singers when they are delivering their music and text enhances the emotional context and impact of their singing. Imagine how destructive it would be for a production of *Lucia di Lammermoor* if the chorus and principals were to stand around looking bored on stage during Lucia's mad scene.

Examples where reaction is essential and must be coordinated with the music of the singer can be brought to mind. In *Le Nozze di Figaro,* Susanna dresses Cherubino up as a maid to disguise him. While doing this she sings the aria *Venite inginocchiatevi.* Cherubino does not sing during this, but he must react. If he does not, Susanna's aria dies. The same is true for Don Jose in *Carmen* during the Seguidilla. He never sings a note, and yet the scene fails completely if he does not react realistically to Carmen's machinations.

Recitative sections are prime examples of musical dialogue. Even when they can deliver their own lines flawlessly, many singers fail at making recitative come to life because their faces go dead and their energy drops on the other performers' lines. Simple planning and writing of the third line for the other performers' music will solve this problem.

CHAPTER 8

━━━━━━━━━━ ❧ ━━━━━━━━━━

Accomplishing the Third Line

In this chapter we wish to consider some important aspects of using the third line to perfect and polish the singer's performance. We begin with a discussion of balance and economy, cautioning that overuse of movement and gesture may be as detrimental to performance as underuse. We then turn to a problem many singers have—performance hang-ups that seem to frustrate even the finest performers. We show how the third line can be used to help singers overcome their fears of troublesome passages. Next we discuss the use of the third line in the formal rehearsal process, showing how it can help in preparing stage roles and in studying arias. Finally we consider the value of the third line as a career investment for all singers, and address the role of the fourth and fifth lines, suggesting how the interpretations of whole teams of directors and artists can enhance the strength of the entire work.

LESS IS MORE: ECONOMY
IN PERFORMANCE

We now want to caution all readers once more about the dangers of excess. Although we consider writing the third line for all the roles a singer plays essential, not every word and every note should be acted out with a gesture, as in children's songs like "The Eentsy Weentsy Spider." In the last chapter we spoke of the importance of balance between action and nonaction. This principle is matched by a principle of economy in characterization. Frequency and intensity of action affect the audience view of a character in very clear qualitative ways. The principle is very simple: *The less singers do, the stronger they appear. The more they do, the weaker they appear.*

There is no value judgment implied here. Appearing strong is only one quality in performance along with many others; it is not always appropriate or desirable. Performers often have to portray weak characters, or portray strong characters who have moments of weakness. For such characters, the performer achieves weakness through extra movement on stage. So the singer may mug, point, or underline words with gestures because he or she wants to show this trait. Antonio, the gardener in Mozart's *Le Nozze di Figaro,* is a weak character. Consequently, a singer might program all sorts of gestures for him. The Count starts out strong, but the singer might need to increase the frequency of his gestures as he gets weaker and more uncertain of his position in some places in the opera. The Count is very powerful when he does very little. At the beginning of the opera his strength is already apparent in the text and the music. So the third line for the Count in the beginning of the opera may consist of just delivering the text and the music with strong inflections and facial expressions, but with least possible movement, since that's where the strength is.

Doing less doesn't mean that the singer works less or that the character is easier to portray or simpler in nature. Usually, doing less takes more concentration. It also requires a longer process of analysis to come up with the minimum set of necessary gestures that create a maximally effective portrayal.

Many stage actors are acutely aware of the process of "indicating" on stage, and avoid pointing or miming their words. Even these kinds of seemingly undesirable actions can be effective for a suitable character, however. When Antonio enters singing, "Dal balcone . . . in giardino," this drunkard with a red nose and dirty shoes can point at the balcony on "Dal balcone," and on "in giardino" at the garden that is beyond the balcony (Example 8-1).

If the singer were to leave Cherubino's broken plants on the floor, engage in hardly any movement at all, and just point with his eyes, he would not be very effective as Antonio. With no movement, he would become a powerful character instead of being a comic figure interrupting where he is not expected. Note by contrast the actions of the Count who asks, "Dal balcone . . . in giardino?" without any gestures at all because he is in control of the scene, while Antonio is only a disruptive force.

It is interesting that the Count and Antonio sing almost exactly the same lines, yet they are very different individuals. The Count says, "Dal balcone," and Antonio repeats it. The Count says, "in giardino," and Antonio repeats this phrase. So, in terms of the third line, is Antonio imitating the Count (probably not)? How then can these lines be different? Character conceptualization is the answer. The Count is strong, Antonio is weak.

In this example, the difference looks simple and obvious, but at other times the contrast between characters can be complex and deceiving. This is why we insist on the study of complete roles with thorough investigation and research. Even in the case of the Count and Antonio, the relationship is not that

Example 8-1. Mozart, *Le Nozze di Figaro,* act II finale

simple. After all, Antonio is Barbarina's father. Barbarina is one of the girls that Cherubino is pursuing, just as Susanna is being pursued by the Count. Susanna is also Barbarina's cousin, meaning that Antonio, the drunkard, the gardener who threatens to spoil the Countess's deception, has a kind of "familiar relationship" to the count.

Here is another example of gestural and vocal indicating that may describe this problem a little better. The Queen of the Night in Mozart' *Die Zauberflöte* sings "Du, du, du, (You, you, you)" in her first aria (Example 8-2, p. 134). If she points at Tamino with individual arm movements every time she says "du," she becomes weaker.

Now, this might be the way the singer wants to portray the Queen of the Night. After all, she is the "villainess" of the opera—or is at the very least pursuing a bad cause which does not accord with her noble attitude.[1] But if she only points once and leaves her hand outstretched, she is stronger. In a small theater, again, this "pointing" might be done with just the eyes. It may be stronger not to use her hands to gesture at all. If the director wants to make her even less powerful, he or she may have the performer walk toward Tamino as she delivers her lines and stand face to face with him on his level.

One might think that if characters simply stand onstage and do nothing, they are not really strong. But to be onstage standing motionless is doing a lot. One has to put lots of energy into standing still. However, when the performer

Example 8-2. Mozart, *Die Zauberflöte,* "Du, du, du"

KÖNIGIN

Du,   du,   du   wirst
You,   you,   you   shall

sie   zu be - frei - en   ge - - ben,
free her from bonds of   slav - - 'ry!

is so tense that nothing can happen, this is a very strong statement itself. In order to work as an interpretation, however, such a statement must be clearly intended and it must accord with the character and situation. Otherwise non-action looks stilted and absurd. A singer delivering a passionate declaration of love standing ramrod stiff with no facial expression looks silly. Inaction such as this is especially inappropriate when it is a consequence of having nothing else planned.

Just to show that all rules have exceptions, we must say that sometimes working against the natural tendency of the musical line can also be effective. If Cherubino is frozen "like a stick" during the first phrases of "Non so più," despite the fervent nature of the music, this could be a strong indication of his emotions at the time.

HANG-UPS AND GESTURES

All singers have hang-ups: physical tension, problems about certain high notes, not knowing how to handle certain aspects of performing. There is a mechanism that performers can use to deal with these, and it never fails. In brief, *discover a sensible action and make it bigger than the hang-up*. The action will then cover up the hang-up onstage. This doesn't have much to do with technique, but tricks are something singers should always have handy, and these need to be indicated on the third line.

Imagine a singer is approaching a high note. The chances are good that it is going to be very beautiful, but it still concerns him or her. If the singer makes a gesture that is more important than the troublesome note, at least a percentage of the audience may be prevented from noticing if it does not come out quite right. One additional benefit is that singers may fool their own hang-ups through this action, and thus guarantee that the note will be executed well. Having a gesture to think about instead of a note may release tension or fear, and singers may thus avoid imposing unneeded stress on themselves.

A famous Wagnerian tenor was doing one of the last performances of his very noble career, singing Herod in Richard Strauss' *Salome*. King Herod sings the concluding line of the opera. The tenor was having a bad evening and his performance was very weak. He came to his last line. He rose, and stood before his throne, even though he was not staged to stand. He had decided to give it his all. The last line he sings is "Man töte dieses Weib! (Someone come and kill this woman!)" (Example 8-3).

He sang the line and put his whole heart and soul into the one note that he knew he could show off—the high B♭ on the syllable "tö-." He held this one note for an eternity, but then there was no sound or breath left for the rest of the line: "-te dieses Weib." Still he made an extraordinarily convincing gesture.

Example 8-3. Strauss, *Salome*, "Man töte dieses Weib!"

His mouth was moving, his arms were moving, he really seemed to be calling the guards with utmost fury to finish Salome off. But no sound came out of his mouth after the long, impressive B♭. Still his acting was so skillful that everyone else got blamed because he couldn't be heard. The director got blamed for putting the throne too far upstage. The conductor got blamed for keeping the orchestra up too loud. Nobody blamed the tenor for not having any voice left for the line. This is a prime example of the gesture being bigger than the hang-up.

There is a very difficult line for the Duenna in the beginning of the second act of Strauss' *Der Rosenkavalier,* where she announces the arrival of Octavian (Example 8-4).

The high B natural seems to be a problem for nearly everyone singing the role. It never emerges purely or cleanly. In a case like this, we advise the singer to do something like the following: If she is looking out the window and describing to Sophie that the Rosenkavalier is arriving and she is relating what is happening, she can move from the window into the room, changing focus as she does it on the syllable "Ro-" (in "Rosenkavalier"). She can express with her eyes and body all the excitement she feels for the arrival of Octavian's carriage. If the sound doesn't emerge cleanly, it doesn't matter because her audience will be looking at the total effect of the scene. Some critics may focus only on the sound she is making at that point, but that is their problem. If their focus is this narrow, they are losing the enjoyment of the opera.

THE THIRD LINE AND THE
REHEARSAL PROCESS

Going through the process of constructing a third line for an opera score amounts to preparing a role completely for stage action before having any benefit of rehearsal. It is a challenging mental exercise to come to the beginning of the rehearsal process with some idea of how to create characterization and work it out onstage. There is some variation in the positioning of the process of writing the third line in the production process. A lot of people prefer to work out their characterization once they get into the rehearsal process and they don't even settle on a final characterization (and this is also true for spoken drama) until the rehearsal process is quite advanced.

But in opera preparation there is usually not enough time for this. Opera professionals often allow six months to study a new role. Writing the third line, like any creative process, requires correct preparation, background reading, organization of thoughts in relationship to what the score provides, and discovering what previous commentators on the score are able to advise.

Once the third line is written, the singer can begin to practice. We advocate working with third line interpretation from the very beginning. Having written the third line for a given passage, the singer can sing through the material, using action and facial expression and actualizing the text with all of the

Example 8-4. Strauss, *Der Rosenkavalier,* act II

indicated verbal emphasis. It may be necessary to work the material a passage at a time in order to make the expressive material smooth and seamless. Just as singers spend a good deal of time getting music "into the voice," so should they think of getting musical expression "into the body."

Once the third line has been written the first time, it should not be thought to be etched in stone. The singer should constantly test and revise the third line material as it is practiced. Technical flaws will usually become quickly apparent. Gestures too close together, vocal emphasis that fights the musical line, long periods of unrelieved repetitive action (or no action), inappropriate combinations of facial expression—all of these problems are easily detectable in private practice sessions. They should be corrected well before formal rehearsal.

They can be further revised once staging directions have been established by the director. Videotaping practice sessions is extremely helpful in this process.

When an effective third line interpretation is finally achieved, the performer can then routinize it through repetition in whole or part. However, in this process, the performer should not repeat actions or singing in isolation from each other. In performance they will be activated together, so it is essential that this process be rehearsed. Working with an acting coach (see Chapter 9) can be essential both in determining the most balanced and economical final form for the third line, and in making sure that the third line is executed fully and effectively in performance.

In general, personal practice should be preceded by analysis of the score, by the creation of a written third line, and by routinization through constant exercise where singing is totally integrated with gesture and expression. Professional help should be sought whenever possible.

THE THIRD LINE AND THE STUDY
OF ARIAS

The third line process is directly opposed to the idea that a career can be developed through learning arias in isolation from their full dramatic context. Singers who study an aria forever are actually at a disadvantage when called upon to do the role associated with the aria. Although, with proper coaching and rehearsal, the singers may come to do an excellent job with the whole role, surprisingly, they may do a poor job with the aria. The reason is that the aria will have been tainted—spoiled by all the routines of vocal preparation, especially when the aria has been used for technical practice or for aria competitions or auditions instead of for interpretation of the role. Because the rest of the opera may have been properly studied within a good rehearsal process, it will contrast sharply with the aria itself, which has become trampled on and stale, embodying numerous old vocal habits from earlier stages of training.

One must not be blind to certain realities in the opera world, however. There are certainly a large number of operagoers who come to the theater to listen only to arias, and who could care less about plot or staging. There are even some "fans" left who are only interested in hearing high pitches—"a few isolated notes in a few consecrated throats," as David J. Baker put it in a recent article in *Opera News*.[2] Many singers and opera companies still cater to those patrons. We believe that opera productions mounted solely with this criterion in mind do little for the art form. It seems to us a total waste of time and energy to spend three hours onstage if all the fans want to hear is one or two arias or a few select notes. For such spectators, one should organize a recital or orchestral concert. In this way, one can give them all the arias they want to hear at once. But, as we have already said several times, opera is not a costumed recital: opera is theater.

THE THIRD LINE AS
CAREER INVESTMENT

The third line process will never be wasted effort. It will remain for future use in every singer's score. This is not to say that every performer must always be the slave of his or her past scribblings, but no performer who has worked through an opera writing the third line will ever have to start from scratch again in preparing the interpretation of a role. In this way, going through the creative process of writing the third line is an investment in the creation of a role.

Every time singers go through a score, they may add different things, elaborate on ideas they have already written, and delete or change notations they have made. The first time a singer does this we suggest using a pencil, the second time a pen, the third time perhaps red ink. By the fourth time, it may be time to buy a new score. But, if performers assume that they will remember their interpretative work from year to year without notating it in their scores, they are wasting their efforts. It *may* be possible to remember some things, depending on memory capability, for a day, for a week, or for a month. But, for opera performers, roles are their most important professional tools. When a singer acquires a role, that role should be with him or her forever. No singer should take the chance that interpretive work will be forgotten. It should always be written down! The third line should continue enriching every singer's interpretation from year to year. It will vary, and grow and change as a result of personal experience: from the work done in learning ever more about the opera and its historical setting; from the surrounding world of human behavior; and from conductors, colleagues, teachers, coaches, and directors met over the years.

As we mentioned in the first chapter, the relationship between performer and role is one of the principal factors making the work of an opera performer so different from other kinds of entertainment. An actor on the speaking stage may play Hamlet once or twice in his (or her) life. However, working actors usually abandon their roles as soon as they are done with them. Indeed, actors on the speaking stage may be afraid of being too closely associated with one role for fear of being typecast.

Opera singers are quite different. Since they are limited to roles appropriate to their specific physical and voice types, they will be known by a specific repertoire throughout their professional life. Because of the way opera is handled in the United States—often assembled from individual fragmented elements rather than produced with a unifying concept—the element of role preparation is even more important. For example, opera companies may hire singers for a production of *Aïda* who have already done many *Aïdas*. If a singer gets sick, doesn't show up, or quits at the last minute, it is expected that someone else who knows the role and can sing and act it with little or no rehearsal can step in at the last minute. A singer's ability to do this will enhance his or her reputation, and may provide an all-important career break. The consequence of this, however, is that in preparation the singer needs to be entirely reliant on his or her own capabilities.[3]

THE FOURTH (AND FIFTH) LINE

So far this book has centered on the responsibilities of the performer in preparing for performance. We do not, however, mean to ignore the director or other production personnel. In an ideal production, everyone understands their responsibilities. The producer hires the best possible stage director and the best possible music director who work carefully with the production staff and with all the performers to extract every last drop of meaning from the score and the text. When this does happen, everyone in the production is participating in a much more enjoyable experience. Moreover, the production has a better chance to excel under these conditions. However, singers must be prepared for the likely possibility that a given production will fall short of this ideal. To save expenses, opera is often produced on a short time schedule with little detailed rehearsal. For this reason, performers must always be prepared to supply their own meaningful interpretation of their roles.

Although we are talking about the third line on the score as the line the performer writes, we must admit that other production personnel are also adding "lines" to the score to reflect their own interpretation. In this situation, the more the better. Just as three lines are better than two (and two are better than one for those who don't even think the text is important), four lines are better than three. The third line is an artist's interpretation, but a fourth line, provided by, say, the director, establishes a dialogue between artists. We can't think of a better way of creating an excellent production than through such a dialogue—enrichment through interchange between colleagues.

This doesn't mean that producing an opera is a democratic exercise—it is not. Ultimately, there must be a unified consensus about a single style and a single concept for the production instead of many "very good ideas." Otherwise the opera will be a messy concoction with no shape or spirit whatsoever. Yet in the development of the production, enriching the process by bringing forth ideas is very important.

In writing the third line, no singers should worry about being too rigidly set in their convictions about interpretation in working with a director. It is the singers who come to a production with blank minds about interpreting their roles who are infinitely harder to deal with. Usually they will not have time to both understand and create a meaningful performance. Singers who approach rehearsal with good strong ideas about interpretation and characterization are always at an advantage. Even if their ideas are completely at odds with what they are going to be asked to do in the rehearsal process, they are already prepared, because they have made the essential connection between music, text, and performance. Yet they must remember that preparation has to include flexibility, open-mindedness, and a sense of partnership. If the windows of interpretation are open, through knowledge, the performer will become accepting of others' knowledge and experience as well.

Good directors are rarely disturbed at working with people who come to a production with ideas about how a role is to be played. If performers have taken the time and effort to work out an intelligent, clear approach to the role, differences in taste and opinion between them and the director are rarely insurmountable. Having a good grasp of the way a role can be approached is not the same as having "fixed ideas." "Fixed ideas" often imply insecurity, and lack of flexibility is usually seen as lack of intelligence. No singers want anyone to apply such a label to them.

Quite aside from considerations involved with working on a particular production, the great operatic works are open to continual interpretation. How can one have a fixed idea about the interpretation of a Verdian or Mozartian character? Perhaps one can have a fixed idea about some lesser work that is so dramatically and musically shallow that it allows only one approach. In general, however, the better the score, the more ideas it yields, the more flexible the possible treatments, the more angles from which to approach it.

Some classic works can bear up even when the singers don't understand the concept of the production well. There was a recent production of *Don Giovanni* where the plot was severely altered. The Commendatore in this production didn't die in the first scene as indicated in the libretto. He remained in the background serving as a kind of *deus ex machina* for the whole opera—making all of Don Giovanni's plans fail. In the end he *pretended* to be a statue, came to dinner, and then fought a duel in which he was killed and Don Giovanni lived. The production was reputedly a success, but it was rumored that the singer playing Don Giovanni didn't have a clue as to what was going on. He didn't really understand what the production was trying to do. Despite this lack of understanding, his performance was successful within the concept set down by the director. This is a case of an opera score and a strong concept pulling a singer through. If the score had been something less sturdy than *Don Giovanni*, the production might not have worked.

There are, unfortunately, many fine professionals at the peak of the opera world who seem to feel that they don't need to study anymore. They have earned their living doing so many standard operas in conventional cookie-cutter productions that they are no longer challenged. We think a general problem in the opera world is that there aren't enough different *Giovannis, Aïdas,* and *Traviatas.* If the audience that saw the Giovanni described above had seen fifteen Giovannis in the last 30 years, all different and innovative, then performers would be better able to continue enriching themselves with the unlimited ways of approaching this wonderful work. Otherwise, again, they are practicing taxidermy instead of art.

The liberty to create on the part of all production members—stage directors, conductors, singers, and designers—must remain alive if opera is to live and grow. Censorship cannot be imposed on stage directors just because they are thought too extreme in their conceptualization. It is not serving Mozart to always do what someone 40 years ago decided Don Giovanni should do. *Don Giovanni* was "given" to us over 200 years ago in a form quite impossible for us to imagine today. Since then, original manuscripts and letters have turned up upon which more research is continually being done. All of this provides ever richer sources for our interpretive imagination.

There is still one more thing of real importance to mention. All opera lovers must be tolerant enough to allow producers, directors, designers, and the whole team, including the singers, to make mistakes. If in opera one always tries to aim for maximum security, never taking artistic risks, then no margin for creativity is left. It is very difficult in this culture to allow for a certain amount of failure in the arts. Opera is, after all, expensive to produce and not well supported financially. Therefore every time a production is done, there is great concern about pleasing everybody so they will be willing to write another check for the next production. The pressure to play it safe with fossilized productions of the most standard operas is very great. Nevertheless, there must be experimentation—some of which will be unsuccessful. Otherwise, opera risks becoming stagnant. Smothering it in this way severely damages the art form, and, when the art form suffers, opera singers will feel the impact first.

NOTES

1. This is not so in the first act, however. Mozart supposedly changed his mind halfway through the opera. The Queen of the Night is thought to have originally been the heroine of the opera and Sarastro the villain.

2. David J. Baker, "High Notes, Pornography and the Death of Opera," *Opera News* 56:7 (21 December 1991):8–11, 51.

3. The exercise of writing the third line well in advance of a production has particular value in the United States because of the unsystematic way in which opera is produced here. This does not mean that the concept of the third line disappears when singers are involved in thorough productions. Good preparation always pays off with a better performance. Some opera companies, however, make it a policy to produce from scratch. Singers then have plenty of time to go through analysis of the score with the production staff before staging takes place. This allows the singer to enrich the third line at a much more meaningful pace.

CHAPTER 9

Help in Writing the Third Line:
Coaches and Other Aids to Learning

In this chapter we talk about vocal coaches and other sources of knowledge and training that can help a singer develop the knowledge to write the third line for any opera score he or she will have to perform.

Coaches can be a singer's greatest source of help in this process. For the vocalist in training, it is essential to understand: the value of the coach, the meaning of coaching, why coaches are needed, what kind of work is done with a coach that is different from other kinds of work done in training for opera performance, and, of course, how this work ultimately enriches the process of writing and performing the third line.

COACHING AS LEARNING

The combination of coaching and voice instruction is one of the most remarkable systems of individually tailored education in the field of learning. Some opera training programs in conservatories and universities barely scratch the surface in supplying personal and professional development for future artists. A serious singer continues to learn and receive instruction throughout life. Practical knowledge in the field of opera is largely transmitted through networks of coaches working one-on-one or in groups with singers. Some singers themselves may eventually become teachers and coaches at some stage in their careers and thus carry on the tradition.

Having teachers and coaches does not relieve a serious singer of the responsibility of learning independently. In opera performance, as with most professions, one must learn to be one's own teacher. The things that will make a performer unique will be the things that only he or she is able to contribute. Opportunities for learning and experimentation are unlimited.

In writing this book, we have suggested continually that singers find the means to write the third line for everything they perform. This, readers can see, requires extensive research and knowledge. We hope that every singer will become as knowledgeable as possible about all aspects of opera, but it is unrealistic at best and pretentious at worst to assume that anyone can acquire total knowledge in any field. While a singer will learn many things throughout training and a performing career, he or she will not necessarily become an expert in the history of art and music, or in musical styles. Whichever area of training a singer lacks, time with a coach can compensate. Even when a singer feels well equipped, it will always pay off to have second and third opinions from experts.

Coaching is first and foremost a learning process. Like all learning, it requires homework. We use the term "homework" in conjunction with coaching because most elements of training are perfected on one's own. There are many kinds of coaches. The vocal coach is the best known, but there are also the style coach, the language/diction coach, the acting coach, and, of course, subdivisions of each. A question about style may be influenced by period, and all the nuances therein.

This doesn't necessarily mean that singers must work with a different individual for each of these skills. If one were lucky enough to find someone who could help in two or more of these areas, so much the better. Perhaps this individual could be a voice teacher as well as a coach. However, in training for a career, it is important for a singer to cover the whole spectrum of needs, even if this requires work with half a dozen instructors.

Sometimes, if singers have the time and are financially able, they will study a particular role with a veteran singer who has done that role before. This is both valid and dangerous. It is valid because, if a veteran singer has done a particular role many times, he or she potentially has a lot to offer. However, any singer pursuing this route of learning would be wise to check other sources as well. Otherwise there is some risk of becoming a clone—someone who, willingly or not, is copying someone else's performance. The best teachers will be flexible enough to say, "This is my opinion, and I can supply other informed opinions as well." Perhaps such a person will refer a student to other sources. One further warning is: just because a person has extensive stage experience does not mean that they have the professional ability to transfer or communicate that knowledge. Merely being in the presence of a famous person might not provide the skills a singer needs. Therefore, regardless of the fame of any potential instructor, all singers should check out the people with whom they want to study. A little investigation will ensure not only that they have the skills or tools the singer is after, but also that they can communicate those abilities on a one-to-one basis.

A review of these individual coaching functions is in order. First, what should one look for in a vocal coach as opposed to a voice teacher? The voice teacher, as such, may be purely a technician who will teach healthy sound production with the vocal instrument. This is a considerable job which we discuss more extensively in the next chapter.

The vocal coach will take instruction one step further, teaching how to use that sound in repertoire. Vocal coaching and voice teaching are often undertaken by the same teacher, but this is not always the case. Moreover, a good voice teacher might be a poor coach and vice versa. The voice teacher works to put the instrument in good working order, and the coach works to help get various pieces a singer is called upon to sing into shape for performance.

Unlike a coach, a pure vocal technician does not necessarily teach recitative or other special vocal performance styles (e.g., dialogue, *Sprechgesang,* and "character voices"). Relying on a technician (or, indeed, *any* individual) to develop all of one's skills is probably unwise—especially when preparing certain specialized stage roles. Even if the voice teacher provides vocal coaching as part of a lesson, he or she may not specialize in opera at all. His or her work may be centered on art songs or oratorio. The opposite is also true. A teacher might do *only* opera; in that case, the singer may need someone to help with oratorio style or French art songs.

A singer may also have a fine teacher of a different vocal type. A bass studying with a female teacher may learn excellent vocal technique but, if she also coaches him, she may lack important information he needs—specifically dealing with bass repertoire and its interpretation—just because she never dealt with it herself. This is not to say that every singer should only study with a teacher or a coach of his or her own voice type. Many skilled teachers are excellent with all voices. Similarly, many skilled singers are not fully effective as teachers even in repertoire they have personally performed.

In getting instruction in general, one has to proceed with eyes wide open, carefully assessing the strengths and weaknesses of teachers and not taking things for granted. Students need not set themselves up as critics or censors but, since they are ultimately responsible for their own training, they must look out for themselves.

FINDING A COACH

Some singers may believe that coaching is only for singers well advanced in their careers. Our belief is that as soon as the singer goes beyond vocalizing and exercises and starts opening scores, that's when coaching must be obtained. The alternative is to risk having to "unlearn" arias later that were butchered for technical training purposes without regard for the artistic care of language, expression, and style.

It may be difficult at times to find a coach. In some of the largest cities, the necessary specialized knowledge is available, but in many places it is extremely difficult to get instruction. As one's needs become more specialized, it may be necessary to travel some distance, or even to move to a place where it is possible to find adequate coaching. But the successful singer will persevere! By shopping around, checking credentials, taking sample lessons, or sitting in on lessons, singers can make sure that a coach has what they need, with coaching that will work for them. After all, it's *their* money now and their artistic future later that are on the line. Above all, singers should make sure that they are there as students and not as followers of the latest fashionable guru.

One more point is worth mentioning. A singer's voice teacher may be teaching in an academic situation. This may mean that he or she is working far away from the actual professional world of singing. In this situation, the singer will want to be especially certain to check with a coach. When it comes to the realities of the repertoire and professional needs in the real-world music marketplace, singers need to be very well prepared. A coach will say, "You need to work on this particular approach to the aria because this is what they are asking for out there." Insights like this can be supplied by an informed coach and may not have anything to do with vocal technique.

It is usually fairly easy to locate people who identify themselves as voice teachers. But the only true vocal *coaches* may be people outside academia who are not identified as voice teachers. Many are associated with opera companies. Singers may have to do some real spade work to find the people they need. It is essential to take the initiative and contact those people who will be of help.

After a student has been studying the basics, a voice teacher may begin suggesting individuals to supply the coaching and the information the singer needs. If a teacher does not do this, the singer should wonder why. Sometimes a voice teacher will say, "Don't go anywhere else until I tell you that you are ready." This attitude must be questioned seriously. If a teacher seems unable or unwilling to help locate coaches, we believe the student should begin to investigate independently. To be useful, this information must be as up-to-date as possible. The business itself is a good place to start such an investigation: an opera company will be aware of coaches in the area. If a singer already knows colleagues who are on their way in their careers, they will be able to recommend coaches. Other singers should be glad to share their experience with their coaches and whether it was positive or negative. Of course, these opinions should not be taken at face value. Singers must go and dig further since they are responsible for their own careers in the end. It would be ludicrous to hear a singer say as the curtain goes up, "I'm sorry, but the first person I asked couldn't give me the names of any good coaches so I didn't get beyond producing vocal sound in these arias, and I haven't really begun to study the whole of this role." It's up to the singer to do a lot of window shopping. In the world of professional opera, a teacher can't be blamed for sheltering a student; nobody will care. Once again, excuses are of no use in the marketplace.

THE ACTING COACH

Many singers never think about working with an acting coach. Nevertheless, they regularly say: "After I study my vocal part, I can't combine it with my movements. And when I'm in the staging process, I forget my music and it interferes with my vocal technique." These sorts of problems arise if acting and staging information are not incorporated when music is being learned. As we said in the previous chapter, the moment a singer opens the score is the time all these questions must come up. In this way the solutions can be found immediately. In other words, the score has to give the singer visual as well as auditory images, physical images as well as vocal images. Singers have to prepare themselves to combine both approaches at the same time.

The same person who is teaching a singer vocal technique may be capable of providing adequate stage training. A vocal coach may also be capable of doing this, although by having both hands tied up on the keyboard during sessions with the singer, the coach may not be able to do this easily. Even a voice teacher or a coach with past stage experience may only be able to teach those things that worked on stage a generation or two ago instead of providing an approach to meet the demands of the art form today and tomorrow.

An acting coach will not necessarily teach acting. He or she will rather provide direction for incorporating expression (sometimes movement) to singing. This will help a singer to begin building a repertoire of stage techniques for future use involving all that we've talked about in the previous chapters: gesture, focus, and facial expression. The acting coach, in other words, will aid the singer in bringing the third line to life.

A singer in training may say, "Well, what do I really need an acting coach for at this stage of my career? After all, I go to auditions, and all they really want to hear is my voice. Whatever acting I need to learn I should be able to get from the stage director in any production I happen to be in." Perhaps a singer can get away with this attitude, but no one can sell a character onstage by delivering only sounds. Not many people want to just hear sounds—this is like hearing *solfeggio*. To stand and sing an aria for an audition is more challenging visually and theatrically than to perform a role with costumes and props. Yet singers *can* sell their talent during a single "stand and sing" audition. Singers with highly developed expressive abilities will stand apart from the other auditionees—this could well be the making of their career.

The acting coach will also help make the transition from the vocal studio to "real life" performing on the stage. This may mean that the coach will directly contradict some directions given by voice teachers. Singers are always making statements like: "I cannot smile," or "I cannot do a character voice because it doesn't match what my voice teacher taught me about correct technique." An acting coach should be able to show a singer how to become flexible enough to meet the demands of the stage. In other words, the opinions of a voice teacher cannot be used as an excuse for not performing. (A singer might think about

changing voice teachers if highly restrictive teaching methods continually lead
to conflict in real performance situations).

The question of vocal technique versus physical flexibility is an ongoing
problem in opera. Singers often justify bad physical habits in terms of vocalism.
Sometimes these have been acquired while practicing scales: raised eyebrows,
tilted head, tense shoulders. This is why singers must consult acting coaches
from the first day they open a score. A particular vocal technique may have been
accompanied by a physical habit for years, through practicing in the same way
all the time while noticing only what the voice was doing. In this way the habit
became ingrained. Once it's ingrained, how can it be deleted? That's where the
acting coach can help, sometimes as an active instructor, sometimes as a "mirror" for the singer's presentation—telling the singer where he or she is using
their body in an awkward or inefficient manner.

Of course, a really good voice teacher will correct many bad physical habits, but in the studio one rarely goes through the motions of playing a role while
singing. And, as we have said before, studying a role stripped of its emotions
and insights is not the best way to go about it. Lauretta's "O mio babbino caro"
was not written as a vocalise, but rather as a dramatic vehicle to depict a young
girl manipulating her father.

Singers may also do many exercises in the voice studio to develop technique which they will never be able to do onstage. The voice teacher may have
a student grab the piano and lean against it while vocalizing; this may be fine
for training, but what will the singer do when he has to portray Méphistophélès
and dance with Siebel while singing? Suddenly he finds he is unconsciously
adopting the same posture and muscle used as when he was grabbing the piano,
because that's what he learned without even noticing. He learned to lean, or tilt
his head in a particular way, or to adopt any number of inhibitory postures. The
acting coach will be the mirror that notices and corrects all this. He or she will
be able to help correct these physical problems or, better, prevent them from
becoming habitual as a part of singing.

VOCAL COLOR AND STYLE

Once the basic technical problems of expression have been addressed, the vocal
coach should help a singer to add interesting color to the voice—all of which
can be indicated as part of the third line. Every voice has many shades of expression, but singers are often petrified at the thought of using them all, because
some may seem less than stunningly beautiful in the mind of the singer. A singer
should be able to "act" with the voice alone when singing. This means adding
forceful attacks, intensified consonant sounds, raspiness, fervor, whispers, and
breathy tones when appropriate for the drama. Indeed, it is hard for some singers to realize that it is important to be able to sing with a range of tones, not
only the single perfect sound they practiced in the studio.

Listening to the recordings of the great Russian bass Feodor Chaliapin is instructive here. Chaliapin did not have the most beautiful vocal instrument, but he used it in all of its capacities. He was able to rivet his audiences with his uses of vocal color—some of it could even be called "unorthodox," but it was nevertheless deeply effective.

While studying the role of Méphistophélès in *Faust,* for example, nothing a bass learns from a vocal technician intent on helping him produce "pear-shaped tones" will teach him all of the vocal colors he needs for this role. In the opening duet between Méphistophélès and Faust (Example 9-1), the devil is quite clear about what will happen at the end of the contract: Faust will go "down below—là bas."

The vocal color for this line should describe the depths of hell—not necessarily through the use of beautiful vocal tones. The "Ha, ha, ha, ha" at the end of the famous second act "Serenade" is a thoroughly ugly rasping cackle (Example 9-2, p. 150). It is unusual for a bass to learn to do this kind of thing in a voice lesson; he must be coached into doing it.

Nasal singing and character voices are another problem. Gianni Schicchi uses a nasal character voice extensively, as do many of the notaries and comic doctors in opera—including Despina in *Così fan tutte.* A singer must develop enough freedom to do all these things in case the character calls for it. The best tenors in the world love to sing Count Almaviva in *Il Barbiere di Siviglia,* except for the third act duet with Bartolo, "Pace e gioia," where Almaviva is in disguise (Example 9-3, p. 151). Why do they object? Because they must use a character voice and "make those ugly sounds." If a tenor came to the first rehearsal of this scene and acted totally surprised when asked to use this vocal color, one could only conclude that he had not done his homework.

There are many situations like this. There are scenes when Sparafucile in *Rigoletto* simply shouts, and there are many occasions where singers must half speak in order to make a particular line work dramatically within a context. The witch in *Hänsel und Gretel* can steal the show with her cackle. Magda Sorel in

Example 9-1. *Faust,* "La bas"

Example 9-2. *Faust,* "Méphistophélès' Serenade"

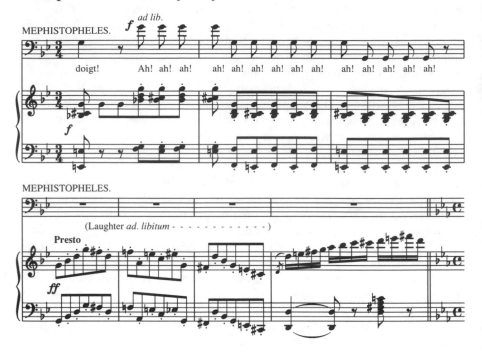

Menotti's *The Consul* must manage a heartrendering cry at the beginning of her great aria: "Papers! Papers!" These are lines where the notes are not as important as the drama.

Some singers are afraid to do these things with their voices—these are singers who have never acquired a correct understanding about the scope of expression in opera. If they believe that singing opera only concerns singing beautiful high notes, they have been deceived, or have been deceiving themselves.

In addition, such singers are cheating themselves of the fun of doing a role if they can't use all the vocal tools at their disposal to make the character come alive. Once a singer is able to flesh out characters and learn how to control the vocal nuances that make them more than cardboard figures, he or she really gets to know them and takes pleasure in making them come to life.

Three potential problems can be precluded by this process of enrichment. First is the question of the singer's sense of security. By knowing what to do at any given point, a singer feels planted on both legs, instead of always thinking, "I hope I can make it through." Second is the issue of competence vis-à-vis one's colleagues. A fully prepared singer will be able to enter into an artistic and intellectual exchange with the other members of the production team: the stage and music directors and the designers. In doing this the singer solves a possible third problem, which we might call "divism" (from diva or divo). This is a

Example 9-3. Rossini, *Il Barbiere di Siviglia,* "Pace e gioia"

lingering attitude permeating the operatic field which deforms the art. Singers who suffer from this condition never feel that they have to serve the opera or the character they are playing—they serve only their own egos, and can often perform only in limited ways. When singers feel flexible and secure, they don't need to engage in this kind of behavior; they serve their role and feel comfortable doing it, employing all of the necessary techniques, colors, and approaches.

THE LANGUAGE COACH

Opera has been written in many different languages, and fewer and fewer translations into English are being done today because of the appearance of supertitles. This means that all singers must become comfortable singing in foreign languages with as perfect diction as possible. The language coach will teach the tricks and twists of each of the languages a singer will need. Some coaches speak all the languages of the repertoire; at the opposite extreme, a singer may need a different coach for each of the languages he or she deals with. In some cases a vocal technique acquired for singing Italian will not be adequate for singing other languages—even English! Indeed, when native English speakers perform in English, they must still have a language coach because the articulation of a spoken language is not the same as when that language is sung. English is, in fact, one of the hardest languages to sing well, *especially* for English speakers—particularly since English seems to be a less favored language in the vocal training studio.

Knowing a language is not just knowing how to pronounce sounds correctly. Nor is it just knowing how to translate or just being able to put vocal technique in gear while singing foreign words. *Truly knowing a language involves understanding the meaning that underlies the literal words*. If you translate *maledizione* as "curse," this is not sufficient, even if that is an academically accurate translation. *Maledizione* is a cultural term of deep significance. In Italy, a *maledizione* was viewed with true horror—it is a promise that the heavens are going to drop on your head. In America, "curse" may raise images of cheap grade-B horror movies. We must always get under the translation, behind the meaning, to understand what the language does, and what the language loses in translation. We must do this because, when we sing in Italian, we have to feel the cultural and emotional overtones of the words.

Another example occurs when the count in *Le Nozze di Figaro* talks about *il dritto feudale* (*droit du seigneur*), the "feudal right." What is he talking about—his rights to the land, his rights vis-à-vis the people? No. He's talking about his right to sleep with young girls working on his estate before they get married. Unless a singer understands this intellectually, culturally, and emotionally, all of the power is drained from the plot of the opera and it becomes a simple bedroom farce.

The straight literal translation of a term will rarely do much, if anything, for a singer. He must go far beyond the dictionary definitions of words. When Figaro sings, "già ognùno lo sa! (already everyone knows it!)" at the end of his third-act aria "Aprite un po' quegli occhi," Mozart conveys the meaning of the line using the orchestra rather than words to make a musical pun (Example 9-4). What is it that Figaro claims everyone already knows? It is that a man is a cuckold, the sign of which is horns on the head. Mozart gives the answer to the question by following Figaro's phrase immediately with French horns in the orchestra in a series of hunting horn calls. In some European productions, Figaro makes the sign of the "horns" with his pinky and index finger at this point.

Once this fact is understood, it will be apparent that there are references to cuckolding everywhere in the opera. When Susanna sings her aria "Deh vieni, non tardar," she knows that Figaro is listening to her (although he doesn't know that she knows). She sings, "Ti vo' la fronte incoronar di rose." This does not mean only, "I want to crown your forehead with roses." It means, "I want to *crown* you (and, by the way) with roses." And the "crowning" is yet another indirect reference to crowning somebody with horns—making them a cuckold. Despite this rather meaningful double entendre, the aria is usually sung in a sweet, melancholic style.

It seems that opera librettos are never annotated to bring out the musical references, innuendos, and asides intended by the composer and the librettist in exactly this way.[1] And this is truly surprising. After all, Shakespeare is annotated—it would be difficult to direct his plays or portray his characters effectively without understanding all of the references. In opera it is up to artists and directors to invest the time and do the necessary scholarship to make the librettos understandable. Cultural annotations of the language of opera are not understood even by literate native speakers, and a great deal of the eighteenth-century Italian, German, and French is already difficult for modern speakers.

For all of these reasons, asking for help with the text of the scores is always appropriate, even for singers who are native speakers of the language to be sung. Furthermore, singers must seek out this kind of expertise for *every* language they sing. A voice teacher might be a good Italian coach but, if he or she does not know French, the singer must find another coach for that language. Maybe a voice teacher is a good Italian *and* French coach—the singer will still have to get a German coach.

Singers should not wait to get language coaching until they have a role they need to do in that language. If, for instance, for the first three years of voice study singers only learn Italian and French arias and only receive coaching in those languages, they will be totally handicapped when they have to sing in German. During the basic vocal learning process, when things were being registered fresh in the brain, German will have been left behind. As a result, that language will always be one in which the singer will be less fluent in relationship to other languages.

Example 9-4. Mozart, *Le Nozze di Figaro,* act III

Some singers will say, "Look, I went to the conservatory. I took two years of diction classes. That really should be enough, right?" Indeed, this may be enough, but it is doubtful. We know some people who have a tremendous facility for languages and others who don't; conservatory diction courses may be sufficient for the talented. No matter how good a singer is as a linguist, however, when working on a particular role, he or she must check with and be heard by people who are knowledgeable in the diction of the particular language of the piece.

Dealing with foreign languages seems difficult for some Americans. Nevertheless, anyone who hopes to have a professional career should not stop short of full preparation in Italian, French, and German (some would add Russian and Slavic languages). Occasionally, one hears singers, Eastern European singers in particular, who never seem to get Italian diction down correctly. This is no excuse, and it's an old story. If one can get away with imperfect diction,

Example 9-4. (continued)

(continued)

fine: a singer may come with an exotic label from Eastern Europe or the Orient and that may be an important marketing tool. Americans, however, may not be able to market themselves as people with a charmingly unorthodox pronunciation. It may also happen that a singer with this weakness is as good as the competition in terms of artistic presentation, voice, presence, suitability for the role, and so on, but if other singers being considered for a given role handle the language of the opera better, that factor will tip the decision in their favor.

We should mention that some of the strongest competition in this area comes from other Americans. Americans have developed a reputation for being good at singing in foreign languages. Thus American singers who present themselves for engagements may be expected to handle the language of the opera well because they are American. This reputation makes it doubly important for American singers to be well prepared in language and diction, since singers

Example 9-4. (continued)

falling short in this area will be seen as deficient not only in the language, but also in comparison with other Americans.

The question of language preparation is actually becoming more complicated. There are now a number of formerly exotic languages such as Czech and Polish which are being used more often in opera productions. Russian has become virtually standard. We don't think that any serious professional company these days would do Tchaikovsky's *Eugene Onegin* in anything but Russian. Supertitles have made it possible for operagoers to hear the original language of the libretto while comprehending the drama taking place on stage.

Of course, the task of preparation could become endless. We don't want to scare anybody. Learning to sing in a number of foreign languages is a professional requirement, but actually learning to comprehend those languages will greatly enhance one's performance. This should become a personal goal for all

Example 9-4. (continued)

singers. Language preparation becomes easier the more one does it; once two languages have been studied, the third is easier, and the fourth easier still. One's flexibility becomes greater in proceeding to the next language. No one will expect a singer to be an expert, but acquiring the ground knowledge will save time and headaches in the end.

Although learning the languages in which to sing is a professional ideal, the vocal, diction, or language coach will have little to do with this process. The learning of diction and the learning of language are confused all the time. Singers will often say, after having sung an opera in Italian, "Next time, I am going to really *study* Italian." This is an excellent thought—a vacation in Italy is a pleasant experience which will help a performer in many ways. Of course, singers must remember that colloquial pronunciation in singing will never be entirely correct for opera. Modern street Italian may not help much in translating

Monteverdi's operas. Languages as used on the stage are different from the colloquial standard languages currently spoken.

With many languages there are special reasons for an opera singer to acquire a speaking knowledge: German is very important for a singer auditioning and then working for German opera companies; Italian is an investment in itself since a large percentage of our standard opera repertoire is in Italian; French, with all its pronunciation intricacies, should be studied from the start; Russian or another Slavic language seems an obvious tool to have at hand in the days of *glasnost,* when the Eastern European opera houses will eventually become another source of work in the profession.

The language coach may go somewhat further and coach the singer musically. The French needed for singing Mélisande is not the French required for Carmen. It's not just the language as an isolated factor that is different, it's the language in relationship to the character. The knowledge of one will come to the aid of the other. But language is also culture, and we know how far away the language of *Porgy and Bess* is from the language of *Vanessa* or the language of *Albert Herring,* even though they are all sung in English.

A subdivision of language coaching is diction coaching. It is one thing to know about languages and another to know about diction and articulation in singing. Some correct techniques of pronunciation for spoken language may actually work against the clear comprehension of those same consonants when sung. In fact, it is not going too far to say that there is no language that is sung exactly as it is spoken. A good example is the guttural "r" of German and Parisian French. Although one must use the guttural pronunciation in literate *speech,* a trilled "r" is usually used when singing.

Vowels pose a particular problem. When spoken, vowel quality in many languages may be highly variable (e.g., note the various pronunciations of the vowel "a" in "cat" in different varieties of English). When sung, all vowels must be carefully examined in order to insure exact control. Vowels may need to be modified slightly in order to work well vocally in certain passages. Here again, the language coach may be a good singing diction coach, but if he or she is not, it's up to the singer to solve the problem through additional study or consultation.

The need for two or more language/diction coaches may be unavoidable. If singers are preparing to do Dvořák's *Rusalka* in Czech, they may have no choice but to go to someone who, while being able to coach them in spoken Czech, will have no idea about vocal technique or singer's diction.

THE STYLE COACH

Once again, singers may find that one of their other coaches has the ability to coach them in the musical and verbal style of the opera they are working on. Styles are many and varied. Musical periods, such as the Baroque, have specific styles. Genres in opera likewise have stylistic conventions. For example, there is a distinct way to sing Russian opera. Certain sounds require nasalization; the voice must often take on a particular metallic quality. There is also a particular inflection for unstressed syllables. All of these matters are difficult to describe in prose. A singer needs someone to show them to him or her directly.

Similarly, one doesn't sing Italian seventeenth-century opera in the same way one sings Verdi. Of course, in a production of an Italian Baroque opera or a Russian opera, the singer can assume that people involved in the production will have some idea about the style. But in the professional world the production staff will not have time to teach this to the singer in detail. If a singer waits until the first rehearsal to prepare, it may be too late. There may be only two weeks to prepare the entire opera. Perhaps a singer can prepare the role and staging and acquire the style in two weeks; if so, this is wonderful—the world of opera loves a fast learner. But most singers need more time; they cannot make excuses if the performance style is wrong when the curtain goes up or when they arrive in the studio to make a recording. Incidentally, a singer may get away with slipshod preparation in a stage performance, but this is inexcusable in the re-cording studio. Unless the recordings are being sold only for a display of a singer's high notes instead of for their accurate rendering of an artistic work, no one will want to preserve for posterity inaccurate pronunciation or mistaken stylistic execution. If a singer decides to wait to tackle the issue of style seriously until the recording contracts start coming in, he or she will have a large prob-lem at that point. A singer at that stage of development will simply not have the time to address the problem of style. Besides, what is not learned properly to start with may become ingrained, making it much more difficult to correct later on.

The issue of style goes even further. It may directly affect the notes of the music to be sung. When working on a Baroque opera, for example, a singer must be acquainted with vocal ornamentation that is not written in the score. Who will provide this information? Singers may do their homework and find books where the principles of ornamentation are explained, or they may go to a coach. It is preferable to do both.

Normally a singer will not see a coach to work with on style as often as he or she sees a voice teacher or a vocal coach. Of course, if a singer is lacking in training and has no knowledge at all of Baroque opera, in the six months before performing a Monteverdi opera, the style coach might be the person to see the most.

Time is never wasted in this kind of study. Clearly, if a singer comes to a conductor or company that's considering a Baroque opera and says, "Look, I've put in a lot of time studying Baroque style," and can then show it in an audition, he or she will be miles ahead of the competition. However, if a soprano has been heard doing Puccini all the time, that company may never even consider her for the Monteverdi opera they are planning because they will have labeled her already. If she had "done her homework," she could then jump in and say, "Wait a second, you've never heard me doing Baroque music. Actually I can sing Poppea much better than I can Musetta." Labels are often the way laziness is justified in the opera profession (and this also applies to the Fach system). Singers shouldn't let this limit their scope. They must be equipped with a variety of options before the label corners them into areas that might not even be what they do best.

The more a singer knows about the style of the work being sung, the freer he or she will feel in accepting conductors' or directors' suggestions. The concept is admittedly elusive. Style cannot be defined exactly; no one owns any definitive interpretation of a particular style. For this reason, opinions about style vary widely. It is certain, however, that the *less* one knows, the less flexible one is going to be. In dealing with informed people, singers may be able to meet them halfway in expressing a difference of opinion, and everyone will win.

A LIFETIME OF LEARNING

To reiterate what we have been saying all along, opera singers have a lifelong task to improve the performance of their roles. It's like any other profession; doctors, lawyers, and engineers continually upgrade their skills. People who don't continue to learn in other professions lose their accreditation. Singers aren't licensed like doctors, but ignorant singers might as well be unlicensed. They are economic burdens for a resident company that has to provide endless extra coachings and rehearsals to prepare them for a production. The word about their inadequacies will get around to people hiring for guest engagements as well.

It is important to remember that any free time, a slack season, or the time between engagements can always be used to learn a new musical style, a new language, or additional repertoire. There will always be people to help. A singer needs a checklist: "What's my weakest point?" When a singer answers this question, he or she can find a coach that will help work on the problem. Sometimes a singer will need to find a coach that can point out the biggest weakness. A lot of this information is never provided in formal learning situations at the university or conservatory—it's something that singers really have to seek out on their own.

Even if a singer is lucky enough to go to a conservatory where some of these things are provided, the instruction in a given topic is usually being provided by *one* individual. That person may be simply imparting his or her personal opinion on a given topic. When it comes to interpreting an opera score, there is no such thing as "the Truth." A singer must eventually form an independent conclusion after accumulating as much information from as many knowledgeable people as possible.

As helpful as coaches are, the learning process will not be limited entirely to working with them. One needs to learn from one's environment. A singer may have traveled a lot or may enjoy going to libraries. He or she may have grown up in a household where cultural and intellectual issues were part of daily conversation, with books on history, music, and philosophy sitting on the bookshelf. The less solid one's background is, the more difficult it is to answer practical questions like: "How did people walk in the streets of Verona in the days of Romeo and Juliet?" or, "What kind of clothing did they wear?"

If singers didn't grow up steeped in such matters, they have to catch up. People who haven't traveled must read books. Of course, going to Verona for two days might provide more information than reading fifteen large volumes, but sometimes the only chance one has to learn about Italian life of that period is by looking at those fifteen volumes. Singers shouldn't have to wait until the first rehearsal of *Roméo and Juliette* to realize that tights will be worn and bosoms will be pushed up. How often is the baritone who will sing Figaro surprised by the fact that his beard *has* to be shaved off? And how many sopranos prepare themselves to sing Susanna by walking about strapped into a corset as they will have to be onstage? Some of this background might be provided by coaches, but the responsibility to come prepared belongs to the singer.

For performing in *Tosca,* a singer needs to know: What was the Napoleonic era in Rome like? Why is Napoleon being mentioned? Who is the chief of police? What happened in Rome in those days? Sometimes, if singers are lucky enough to have traveled, they will already have images to help focus on the place and the period of the opera. Otherwise, extra study must bring that background up to date in relationship to the repertoire.

Of course, there are operas that deal with contemporary times (and many productions that place standard operas in modern settings), but most operas are set in exotic locations or in rather different historical periods than in the present. For this reason a singer should count on doing background work for every production.

Singers also need to know something about the source of the subject for the opera. If it derives from a book or spoken play, they need to know why the book or play was written, who wrote it, what did he or she want to say, what place did he or she fill as a writer? If singers know all these things in addition to the cultural and historical background of the original opera, they might be sufficiently flexible to accept the version of the work in modern clothing. Through background study, singers might understand that the message in the libretto is universal and not necessarily specific to a time period.

Singers with this type of background become flexible performers. They are open to understanding why some director may want to change the clothing of *La Traviata* or *Die Zauberflöte* to something outside its standard setting. This is much better than deciding that the director is someone impossible to deal with (as sometimes happens).

Furthermore, the knowledge of background helps greatly in interpreting the true intent of some operas which had to be altered to avoid censorship. One of the most celebrated examples is *Rigoletto.* When Verdi conceived of the opera, based on a novel by Victor Hugo set in the France of Francis I, the censors disapproved because it cast aspersions on the conduct of a modern sovereign. The implied social critique was too strong. So Verdi in effect said: "Fine, let's put in sixteenth-century Mantua and make the king a duke. The message is universal." If this fact is part of a tenor's background research, he is going to be flexible enough to play the duke of Mantua as a prototype of a certain kind of libertine individual who might conceivably be placed in many different historical periods, and not just as a frozen concept. *Un Ballo in Maschera* was likewise set both in Sweden and in Boston (the latter to escape censorship) without destroying the basic plot.

Once again, this background information may be available from a coach or a sympathetic director, but, once singers start working in more demanding professional circumstances, no one will do this for them. Indeed they may be unfortunate enough to find directors who have not done this work themselves. Suddenly they are there at the mercy of the fates. It's the difference between, "Well, let's see what happens when the curtain goes up," and the security of being able to say, "It doesn't matter. I still have all of my information, and I can perform this role. I can do a believable job of communicating the meaning of my character regardless of what's happening around me."

This underscores an important difference between opera and other forms of theater. Singers in opera are associated primarily with roles and not with productions. The long preparation and rehearsal period that one sees for many professional spoken theater productions is usually not possible for opera. For this reason the opera performer has to internalize much of the information provided in spoken drama by the director or the playwright. Acquiring this expertise is part of the singer's homework. It can be provided by coaches, through personal study, or both. In the end it doesn't matter where the information comes from, but a singer must have it.

Singers may choose to become scholars and accumulate as much information as possible. And why not? It can give them enormous pleasure besides being useful for a career. They may also decide that, because so much is invested in the other aspects of singing, unlimited time can't be devoted to scholarly research. In that case, the solution is to find the individuals that can throw some light on the character, period, or style to be sung. Whatever means is chosen, whether self-study or extensive coaching and consultation, *a singer must not go to the first rehearsal blank*—there will be too little time during the production to assimilate all the information before the premiere. We bring back this image of the curtain going up because, once a singer is onstage and the curtain rises, there can no longer be any excuses. Rigid and exclusive thoughts must be avoided; the scope of *La Traviata* or *Rigoletto* is and will be larger than any one person's convictions or conclusions. Singers must be humble and not only doubt other people's opinions, but their own as well. The singer provides only the third line, the unverifiable one, the interpretive one.

Many great singers end up researching their roles extensively as the years go by, partly in order to keep their interest alive. As they study and research, they always seem to discover more depth in their characters. If it is a good role, the scope for discovery is endless. For example, a mezzo may be set to perform Azucena in *Il Trovatore*. What an interesting character she is! The mezzo begins to realize that this person is not just a woman in rags and messy makeup. Soon she wants to know about gypsies in Europe at that time—how they were treated, what role they played in social life. Her research becomes a whole cultural/historical study.

The mezzo's study also becomes a study in Verdi's work. He uses gypsies and similar figures all the time as a way of introducing a foreign or minority element. Ulrica in *Un Ballo in Maschera* is one figure, and Preziosilla with her whole army of happy-go-lucky shooters in *La Forza del Destino* is another.

Her study may extend to other composers. Carmen is the most famous operatic gypsy; she talks about herself as a Bohemian. That may lead the mezzo to remember: "Wait a second—'Bohemian.' We have an opera called *La Bohème*—what does this have to do with gypsies?" Is Mimi a gypsy? Is Rodolfo? She then discovers that an entire complex of figures and symbolic references derives from the area of Eastern Europe called Bohemia. In Western Europe people thought that this was where most of the gypsies came from because there were important gypsy communities there. So for Carmen to call herself a Bohemian is reasonable—she is a gypsy. On the other hand, why did the French call poor young artists and poets Bohemians? A short answer is that they lived in odd ways and acted in an unorthodox manner. Thus the establishment called them this name—*bohème*—that meant, figuratively, "nonestablishment people," people who don't belong to the mainstream of society. If the mezzo doesn't know this, she may go through seventeen references to "Bohemians," never thinking to relate them back to Azucena.

The most common example we know of singers' lack of preparation is their never wondering, never asking, never inquiring why *La Traviata* is called by that name. The word *traviata* is not in most condensed Italian dictionaries. Thousands of sopranos sing one *Traviata* after the next and if asked, "What does 'La Traviata' mean?" they have at most a very iffy notion. Literally, it means: "the strayed woman" or "the misled one," even "the corrupted woman" from the verb, *traviare*, "to mislead, to corrupt, to lead astray." This should help a singer understand that this woman was not one of those elegant euphemisms: a courtesan or a coquette. She was Violette Valery, a woman led astray, a prostitute, a corrupted woman—a kept woman with whom to go to parties. She was also a woman who sought redemption through true love, but society, in the guise of Giorgio Germont, would not allow her to cross the line back to acceptance. These were the real attitudes of the day. This small example underscores the importance of cultural knowledge and of the accurate knowledge of languages and customs. It should have a strong effect on a soprano's approach to the role.

One other situation needs to be mentioned—working on an entirely new opera. There is a kind of renaissance in new opera production today, and it is likely that sometimes in a singer's career he or she will have the opportunity to sing in a world premiere of a new work. When one does have the luxury of working on an original opera with the composer and the librettist live and present, then there is a very different way of preparing—one must use the people at hand.

It is surprising that singers treat new works as if they were written in the last century. There are so many additional resources available when dealing with a new opera. First of all, the composer and librettist are both alive and available for consultation, yet singers rarely call these people. It is so simple to call and say, "Could we get together? I want to pick your brain." How wonderful it would be to be able to talk to Verdi or Mozart about the interpretation of their operas! Here is the opportunity, and few people take advantage of it. This is something singers can do; it's something they *should* do. It really is their duty as a responsible performer. The composer and librettist may welcome their input as artists. They may have a direct role in shaping the finalized version of the work. Whatever they do, singers must not just memorize like parrots. They should research, question, and help bring meaning and ideas to life. They should work out concepts, ideas, and thoughts, not just sounds pounded on a piano for rote memorization.

From the experience of working with a living composer, singers can have insights into the creators of opera in the past. A firsthand experience of dialogue with a librettist and a composer can help one imagine doing the same with Illica, Giacosa, and Puccini. Singers can imagine themselves providing for these people a third line, giving their input to the creative process.

COACHING AND THE THIRD LINE

All of the learning resources mentioned in this chapter—coaches, self-study, books, and travel—are resources to help singers write the third line to the works they will perform. Pronouncing and understanding language correctly is the most basic tool a performer can have in creating an interpretation for a text in musical theater. Singers haven't the slimmest chance of creating a believable interpretation of a role if they have not solved basic language problems associated with the opera.

Acting and movement skills likewise create a repertoire of skills and possible actions for a performer which he or she can incorporate into an interpretation. Similarly, knowledge of stylistic elements of the music creates a palette of vocal techniques, colors, and embellishments that can be used for total performance effect. These can be written in the third line and used to create a stunning personal style of performance for any given role.

Knowledge of the history, culture, clothing, movement, and bodily carriage of the characters in an opera likewise gives the singer a range of interpretive ideas and action. These help flesh out roles and make them human and three-dimensional, rather than the cardboard figures they so often become on the contemporary opera stage.

To this end, coaches can supply a remarkable range of ideas that a singer, especially one early in his or her training, has never thought about or appreciated. If a singer will use coaches along with the other learning aids suggested in this chapter, writing the third line becomes not only a vital personal activity, it becomes a collaborative activity with many participants.

In this regard, a final word must be said about developing a productive attitude toward learning. Some singers are distressingly passive about their lives and careers. They wait for other people to direct them. They wait for records or video recordings to come out which they can copy. They wait for teachers to utter "the Truth" for them to swallow wholesale. It is as if they have no individualism and no initiative.

No one should have to tell a singer, "Listen, call the composer," or, "Go to this library and find this book." In creating interpretations for the stage, singers should cultivate from the beginning an inclination toward discovery. There are so many resources available—direct experience, books, phone calls to knowledgeable people, proper coaches. The faster the lethargy among artists is reversed and the value of self-activated learning acknowledged, the more everything about opera will improve.

Part of the problem is not always knowing how to get from here to there. Singers, especially those who are just starting to develop a singing career, are told first that they must have a "Voice." The next thing they seem to envision is themselves as stars at the Met. Somehow, bridging the gap between having a voice and being a superstar is a great mystery.

Some career milestones are attributable to good fortune, of course. Nevertheless, developing the personal skills that are needed for a career is something all singers can theoretically do for themselves. We say "theoretically" because no one ever seems to explain exactly how to do it. If a singer is very lucky, a manager from one of the major opera houses will hear him or her at 20 years old and say, "Ah, we're going to take this one in hand." The singer then enters a kind of womb, with unlimited free coaching and immense resources. After a while, the new singer is "reared" into the profession.

This situation is so unusual, it is somewhat like winning the lottery. And even winning the lottery doesn't guarantee that the beneficiary will use the money wisely. For most young singers, whether from New York, Kansas City, Louisville, El Paso, or Anchorage, there is no easy road. Lightning will not strike and make one a star. One of the things that will tip the scales of fortune in the singer's favor is development of a large reservoir of auxiliary skills. Doing this is a lifetime task, and no one rides singers' backs to make sure they do it. They must love the profession enough and believe in themselves enough to keep at it.

Even should someone at the Met tell a singer, "Listen, come here. We are going to make you a star!" this does not mean that there need be no effort on the part of the lucky individual. The only thing available in a prestige training program is a group of people who will try to guide a singer through the necessary steps. If those individuals are not there or the singer fails to learn from them, the singer has no excuse. One still must find a guide, or find a way to guide oneself. Either the third line will be blank, or it will be full and rich. The choice is up to the artist.

NOTES

1. One recent exception is an edition of sections of Richard Strauss' *Der Rosenkavalier* annotated by Evelyn Lear (New York: Schirmer Music Publishers, 1990).

CHAPTER 10

——————— 〜 ———————

Balancing the Third Line: The Singer and the Voice Teacher

This chapter deals with the relationship between student and voice teacher. The relationship with one's voice teacher looms very large in every singer's life. It is demanding of time and energy, and can involve a significant financial commitment over a long period of time. Needless to say, it is a relationship which is also indispensible for the developing of a career. For this reason, choosing a voice teacher and managing vocal instruction is a matter of importance.

This book is primarily about learning to become an interpreter of opera. In this chapter we intend to neither characterize or critique the voice teaching profession. We do feel it necessary, however, to put voice instruction in perspective as part of the total training for performing in opera.

By now it should be obvious that one central theme of this book is self-empowerment. The singer is the author of the interpretation, the creator of the third line. The self-empowerment of the singer applies to voice teaching as much as to any other aspect of career training in opera. Accordingly, we repeat here a central truth, often cited but not always believed, even by experienced performers: *singers must eventually become their own voice managers.*

To this end singers may work all of their careers with others who help to discover and explore their instrument. They may offer help and guidance, but it is the singer alone who will be there selling the product when the curtain goes up. The process of writing and executing the third line, thereby becoming a successful stage interpreter of operatic literature is, as we have presented it, a highly personal process. It requires singers to take primary responsibility for their own education and for their own discovery of the knowledge that will aid them in creating believable performances. This personal responsibility extends to developing intelligent relationships with the people with whom they work in training their basic vocal equipment. Because the concept of the third line is one of balance between all the performative elements in opera, this necessarily means that singers must balance their relationship with their teachers as well, keeping in mind that every element of instruction is part of an *overall* program of training, not an end in itself.

Voice instruction is essential for an opera singer. No singer, no matter how naturally talented, can expect to have a career in opera without competent vocal instruction and advice. After all, singers cannot even "hear" their own sound in the way that others hear it. The standards for voice quality are simply too high and the competition too stiff for a self-taught individual.[1] As we have pointed out earlier, opera singing is an athletic discipline. A singer needs a competent trainer to insure that the basic apparatus is working at peak efficiency— just as Olympic divers or gymnasts need trainers to make sure they are working up to their full potential.

Voice instruction at its best is an extremely exacting job. It is long, hard work performed in excruciating detail. Every singer has a different vocal instrument, a different body and a different temperament. Many students do not have the patience to work on the details of tone placement, development of vocal musculature, vowel production, and self-monitoring skills that are necessary for reliable singing. Other students have conceptions of their performing potential that do not match their basic vocal apparatus or their physical bodies. A good teacher knows how to help students make progress without either discouraging or encouraging them unduly.

Because vocal instruction is so highly personalized, it is easy for a singer to become enveloped in it—even obsessed by it. Our general advice to singers in this book is:

First, never to feel that voice instruction is the only instruction needed for successful performance on the opera stage.

Second, to understand that a voice teacher is not necessarily a licensed psychologist and may not be trained to manage personal emotional development.

Third, to realize that a teacher may help a student make important connections in the artistic world, and may give excellent advice to the singer about his or her capabilities and prospects in the profession, but the primary responsibility for the development of a career in opera lies with the singer.

A high percentage of singers enter the world of opera via the voice teacher's studio. In other words, the teacher serves as the starting point for acquiring information about an opera career. It is regrettable that more singers do not enter the opera profession with parallel information about the spoken stage,

stage craft, music theater, or other entertainment specializations. It is equally regrettable that some students coming into the profession through a voice teacher often do not acquire a wider horizon in these and related areas. This is not a criticism of voice teaching as a profession; it has simply been the standard way of training.

Because they serve as the primary guides for career entry, the responsibility of voice teachers is very great. A superior teacher understands that performing in opera involves much more than just having a beautiful voice, and attempts to help his or her students develop a comprehensive career-training program in which voice instruction is only one aspect.

TECHNICIANS AND GUIDES

Good teachers are good vocal technicians, and they are excellent guides. First and foremost, they know what they are able to accomplish and are honest with their students about it. They warn the student what they can and can't do. A productive attitude in a teacher conforms somewhat to the following scenarios:

> S/he is a vocal technician. S/he works strictly with vocal production. S/he will help a singer gain consistent, tension-free, resonant, and efficient production with the voice on all pitches in the singer's range, on all vowels, at all volume levels, and at all speeds. Unless s/he has good coaching skills, s/he will guide the singer in going to other people for additional training, which s/he can recommend. At all times, this teacher will have in mind the complex elements that need to be blended with technical vocal expertise.

Or the following might apply if the teacher also serves as a coach:

> S/he is a vocal technician who can also coach the singer through romantic and *verismo* styles, but admits to being somewhat weaker when it comes to Mozart and *bel canto* material. S/he will tell the singer how far his/her knowledge goes and when it is time to look for someone else. S/he will remind the singer that success on the stage depends on more skills than the ones s/he can help to master.

The teacher as a guide should convey the knowledge that vocal technique is only good if it enables the singer to become a performer. Technique, regardless of how beautiful the sound that it produces, is useless if it limits the singer's performing capability. There is no way around this. Even if one plans to be a recitalist, one still must perform. A recitalist has to deliver material within a set of stylistic conventions and must engage the audience visually because it is looking as well as listening.

A good voice teacher also understands what his or her students' goals are, and enables them to meet those goals by helping provide a realistic map for training. If a voice teacher says to a student from day one, "Your goal, as I understand it, might be performing in opera. This is a career where you are going to become a total performer. I'm here to help you with the vocal part of that, but you need to know that you're going to have to do many other things, and they're just as important as the vocal part. If, on the other hand, you decide you want to be a recitalist, that requires slightly different training, and I might be able to help you with that, too, if that is your choice."

Good teachers believe in parallel training. They don't start students doing *recitativo secco* before the students know what it is. They don't start students working on foreign language arias before they have the proper diction skills. These teachers might properly say, "First learn some French, and then we'll study a French aria. Until you know French, Italian, and German diction, we are just going to do scales to train your instrument." Similarly, they do not allow their students to approach any musical literature without knowing what's behind the literature. They make their students ask themselves: "What's the style? Who's the librettist? What is the historical period?" Teaching voice in the abstract without regard for these parallel disciplines will only delay the singer, postponing acquisition of the skills that a good third line requires.

Responsible voice teachers also do not teach technique through arias. Most singers are anxious to study the great arias as soon as possible, but there is a primary danger in learning too many arias too soon. A too-eager student may learn them with faulty or incomplete technique and never be able to erase the bad habits. Henri Jacobi, a well known voice teacher, sums it up thus:

> To sing songs and arias, as is frequently demanded of vocal beginners, can become a burden to the unripe organism, causing it to break down all too often. In many cases the effort can also have damaging psychological effects. Songs and arias maneuvered under unripe conditions, by hook or crook, will often turn out to be total losses for a lifetime. Inhibitions, fear and carry-over anxiety will have become so deeply rooted in the mind of a student that he will not be able to free himself from them, even when his voice is finally ready. Though new songs and arias of similar type and range can be handled with ease, the old ones, crippled by old associations, go on limping forever.[3]

Aside from this technical danger, learning arias as material for vocal training can fool singers into thinking that they know how to perform those arias or even the roles associated with the arias. For example, sopranos may claim in their résumé repertoire lists that, because they sing "Mi chiamano Mimì," Mimi's entire role in *La Bohème* is in their repertoire. All professionals know that being able to sing a single aria doesn't mean that they are capable of singing, or of carrying out all the responsibilities of a role. Teaching through arias, without insisting that the student know context or be physically suitable or prepared for the role, is a tremendous disservice to a student.

The teaching/learning situation for opera students is difficult and tricky. Singers must learn arias because that is what must be presented for auditions. For better or worse, this is the system used to cast people in productions. Occasionally certain enlightened companies ask for recitatives or duets with other auditionees. So there is hope out there that companies are starting to be clever and not get stuck with someone who sings a beautiful aria and is inadequate for the rest of the two hours onstage. Presentations of arias should grow out of learning an entire role, from digging under the skin of the character, rather than a facile accumulation of singing material (which is not operatic art but rather a replacement).

The reasonable teacher will thus introduce arias into lessons for this utilitarian purpose, saying, "Listen, we better put a few arias together because you need to have them for auditions." But the teacher recognizes that this is part of the mechanics of the profession, not the goal of the vocal instruction. To make an analogy, a person has to know how to put a résumé together to get work. But being a worker doesn't mean that one specializes in putting résumés together. In the same way, being a singer doesn't mean knowing how to sing a particular aria beautifully—being a singer means presenting a total product.

All of this means that, yes, singers should have arias to audition, and, yes, they should have résumés to introduce themselves, but neither the résumé nor the aria is the goal. They are only things singers have to prepare to get work and they do not define the singer.

THE SANCTITY OF VOCALISM

Singers must also understand that voice teaching is something that works in a generational fashion. Usually the voice teacher is somewhat older, with certain experience, communicating to a younger individual. As in all forms of education, things progress from generation to generation; things progress with time. What is needed today is not what was needed twenty years ago.

In the area of singing, for some reason, the gurus, mother hens, and other controlling types have held back progress in vocal pedagogy and in considering new repertories. Vocal training, like everything else, must progress with the performing art—nothing is static. As we have said in earlier chapters, just because an opera was written 200 years ago, does not mean that singers are performing it as it was 200 years ago. And singers are definitely not singing the same way nor using the same staging as singers of 40 years ago.

The audience is of a different composition now than even five years ago, and it continues to change and develop. It is the nature of art to change. Even if some say that opera is going in the wrong direction, it does not matter. It is going in *some* direction, and that is infinitely better than standing still. Even museums, the repository of static art, are constantly changing. Paintings are rehung in different configurations, exhibits are reworked along different lines, lighting and room decor changes, and explanatory literature is rewritten. Why should people involved in opera do less?

When singers go out onstage as artists, they have to fight for audiences; they have to work hard to interest the public. Funds must be raised and tickets sold. If singers, as the focal point in this process, are incapable of entertaining the audience, the entire enterprise is doomed. This is the bottom line—the rock-hard reality of the business. The simple fact is that the needs of today's entertainment market cannot be met with the product of 40 years ago. And why shouldn't this be the case? It is counterproductive to continue perpetuating the image of opera as the ridiculous art form that nonoperatic audiences claim it to be. Opera shouldn't be the focus of caricature. Most important, opera should not cater to audiences who attend for reasons other than enjoyment of the art.

A singer may have a spectacular voice but, without the other abilities needed to bring a character to life onstage, it does the singer little good, and the art little good. Watching kinescopes of the opera stars of the 1940s is instructive. With a few exceptions, they had no acting skills; many admitted it themselves in their memoirs. It was perhaps not so important: Opera fans could hear them on the radio and think romantically, "What a wonderful voice." To watch many of them in person, however, was like seeing mannequins on parade.

Even today there are some museumlike houses where this kind of style is still preserved, for instance, at the Bolshoi in Moscow. If a teacher has brought a singer to believe strongly in the elevation of vocalism above all other aspects of operatic artistry, that singer's goal might be to reach some of these houses where things are being done in this museum style. But he or she should hurry, because they are rapidly losing ground to the newer, leaner young companies, some 200 of which have sprouted all over the United States in the last few years. Not even Prague, Warsaw, or Dresden produce opera with the Bolshoi mentality today.

It may be useful for a singer to test the attitudes he or she has formed on these questions, by asking, for instance: "Am I more upset if I'm slightly shaky on a high note that was optional to begin with, or am I more upset if I mess up a complete bit of stage business?" From our standpoint, the correct professional attitude is to be equally concerned about both. Today, however, a good many performers will say, "I'm more concerned about vocal shortcomings than I am about shortchanging the audience dramatically." If all we want is pristine sound now and then during an evening, why do we spend so much money and energy staging the opera, making costumes, building scenery, creating wigs, painting props, and hanging dozens of lighting instruments?

In truth, there is no such thing as vocal production separated from action. If singers are taught to understand both at the same time—learning to produce a beautiful sustained high note while executing a corresponding gesture—this separation of the issues will disappear. In the end, it is on the basis of the total execution of skills that audiences will judge singers.

Yes, as we have admitted in earlier chapters, there is a hard core of fans who just want to hear high notes and other vocal fireworks. Singers can do concerts just for them, if they want. But it is important to remember that composers wrote high notes for a specific purpose in a specific place in a specific work. The dramatic moment inspired him or her to place that high note in a specific spot in the score. The only solution to interpretation is to understand the interpretive process in the same way. A singer may say: "Wait a second, this note is not just a high note. It's a high note that has a specific meaning and expression, and I must learn to convey that meaning in my rendition. Otherwise I'm not serving the score, and not serving the art."

A singer may have one of the few voice teachers whose sole concern is sound rather than total performance. This can really cause difficulties with the third line. For example, someone may manufacture flutes that have the best possible sound a flute can deliver, yet the holes of this flute are spaced too widely apart and nobody can perform with it. So what good is the beautiful sound if no one can interpret or communicate to the audience with the instrument? Furthermore, what is a perfect flute good for if it is in the hands of noncommunicative flutists—artless musicians or cold technicians who can play spotless scales, but who have nothing to *say* with their artistry.

The sanctity of vocalism creates some bizarre distortions in singers' own self-images. As we mentioned in Chapter 3, if some singers are told that their acting, or their performance onstage, or their expressiveness was excellent, this is somehow perceived as implying that their vocal skills have been put down. If singers recognize themselves in this scenario, it may be because of a guru or mother hen at some point making them say to themselves, "Oh my God, I did well in my acting, but that doesn't matter—I was *supposed* to do well in my vocalism!" Singers can avoid this all-or-nothing situation if they train themselves to understand how wide the horizon of opera is in terms of all the elements that occur together in a good performance. Then they can take pride in *all* that they do to advance the quality of the production.

Opera in the end requires integrated performance; it is not singing accompanied by some other ingredients for decoration. The third line embodies this philosophy. If a teacher shares this thought, singers should take advantage of it. On the other hand, finding balance in training means not letting personal trips or egomaniacal influences diminish the scope of what will ultimately be the total interpretive rendering of the operatic work.

VOCAL INSTRUCTION AND VOCAL PERFORMANCE EDUCATION

Teachers are human too! The teacher's own economic and career interests may create problems for training. The money the student pays the teacher is an important part of his or her income. It might be tempting to keep students in the vocal studio even when they are not benefiting from voice instruction. We believe that a voice student's budget should not be given over to the technical training of the voice alone. It should be spread out along the whole range of preparations required to become a performer, such as those outlined in Chapter 7. Some teachers may feel that their students' performance is a public demonstration of their own expertise. Some teachers thus take the attitude: "If you go out in public, you will be representing me, so *my* reputation is at stake."

Singers must therefore use their own judgment in determining when to make important career moves. They should listen carefully to their teachers' advice, develop an attitude of trust and respect for their teachers' experience and wisdom, but realize in the end that they have responsibility for their own lives. We know that most teachers work first toward benefiting the pupil, and not themselves, but students must be aware of any attempts to manipulate or control them, consciously or not, and take appropriate steps to improve the situation. Otherwise a whole career may be hampered rather than helped by this relationship.

In extreme cases, stage and music directors may be driven to distraction by conflicting orders to singers from the vocal studio. In a typical conversation with a young singer, the director may finally say, "Listen, how come you did not do all the things we have been working out in staging rehearsals for the past three weeks?" The singer then typically replies, "Well, that's because I was concentrating on singing."

This leads to an impossible situation. The singer is working from the voice teacher's perspective, but the director has the whole production in mind! In the end, all parties must realize that opera is a performing art. Singers are supposed to entertain an audience. Every step taken must be designed to project the motions, the text, the ideas, and the plot of the work to an audience.

Many singers feel that there are certain things asked of them by the stage director or conductor that they really can't do, because it will destroy their vocalism. For instance, as we mentioned in Chapter 2, they can't imagine singing on their knees or their backs, or breathing in a different place from where they are used to. It is curious that many singers will admire those artists that *can* do those things, but can't imagine *themselves* doing it.

If a singer finds the requirements of the stage overwhelming, he or she should rethink the choice of a career in opera. There are many ways other than opera to have a vocal career without having to act or move on stage—or to deal with a conductor's ideas on breathing or phrasing. However, if a singer chooses opera, there are two basic realities he or she must deal with:

First, no opera is produced without a stage director and a conductor.

Second, no opera exists without a story that must be told on stage, theatrically.

Once singers accept that these two elements cannot be avoided, they must ask themselves and their teacher, "How am I going to solve this performance problem? How can I make myself flexible enough to work without running into conflicts between vocal artistry and stage artistry?" *Both* are required, so what does one do? Just as singers practice to develop a vocal technique, they must find an adequate technique for acting while singing. The singers must work to make their body and voice available to sing while kneeling, lying down, walking, or even running if need be.

If a teacher were to tell students that they could only sing in a certain posture and not in another, they would be providing incomplete technical training for their students and an incomplete reality. *Vocal technique is only good if it is serving the total performance, rather than limiting it.*

MANAGING VOCAL INSTRUCTION

Many singers are continually involved in an elusive pursuit of the perfect teacher. We do not believe that there is such a person. Voice instruction is personalized, individual tutelage. There may be a teacher who is good just for one particular student and not for others. It has to do with chemistry, a meshing of personalities, and the combined talents of instructor and pupil for things to click or not to click.

The corollary of this principle is that studying with "famous" teachers will not necessarily guarantee the same results they have had with their most illustrious pupils. Ultimately there are no geniuses or infallible formulas. There are serious and dedicated professionals, and there are those not so well equipped, even if dedicated. Finally, there are those who are neither serious nor dedicated, but who can be very persuasive, magnetic, and smothering. This latter group may reveal themselves when they purport to know the *real* way, the *sure* way, or the *only* way to vocal success.

When singers begin vocal study, many take the luck of the draw. They may not know much about who they are going to be studying with. They may be in a small town with only one or two available teachers. Even in a limited situation, singers should be careful consumers when choosing a voice teacher as they would be with any other major expenditure they make in their life—after all, a singer will be paying several thousand dollars a year to study with this person. It is well worth it for singers to sample several individuals, to "shop around," until they find what they need.

There are lots of ways to do this. A singer can ask fellow vocalists or other respected musicians in the area as a way to check out the reputations of various teachers. Most of all, a singer must think hard, and try to determine what *he* or *she* needs as an individual. If a singer is just beginning, there are excellent teachers for beginning voice students who are not able to help advanced students. Some teachers work best with big voices destined for large opera houses, others with recitalists best suited for performance in more intimate spaces. The search for an appropriate teacher will be much like going to a library to seek out specific books. Each one of those books contains a certain amount of information of a specific type. There's no such thing as one book that contains everything anyone could require.

No reputable teacher will object if a singer asks to take one or two sample lessons and decide later whether to continue. Because the teacher-student relationship is so personal, the quality of instruction alone is not the only factor in making a decision. Personal rapport, convenience of travel and scheduling, and cost are all important. Each of these factors must be weighed to make the best possible decision.

At a university or a conservatory, a different situation arises: teachers are often assigned. No thought may be given to the suitability of a particular teacher for particular students—assignments may only have to do with the teacher's schedule. In this situation, singers ought to resist getting slotted arbitrarily and try as hard as possible from the outset to engineer a choice for themselves. It may be difficult to change teachers later, when hurt feelings, school politics, and all sorts of nonartistic factors come into play.

Aside from this, we maintain that voice teaching in schools with a very limited standard curriculum can fail to produce good results. Unless it's a very special school, students are assigned 30 minutes to an hour a week for a voice lesson. That is probably far too little time. This miniscule amount of instruction seems unlikely to work for anyone no matter how excellent the teacher or how excellent the student. In many schools, even if a student benefits from a teacher and wants to work additional hours privately with him or her, the school will frown on this arrangement because there are all kinds of conflicts of interest at that point (teachers may be accused of exploiting their students if they suggest private lessons at additional fees).

We do not mean to advise singers not to entirely avoid study in a formal school situation. A conservatory or college may be valuable for other reasons. There may be excellent instruction in music theory or music history. Colleagues and friends cultivated in school may become associates for life, creating a valuable network. The school may also provide important performing opportunities, library facilities, and a good place to practice. Singers must simply not be fooled into thinking that all the voice training they need will be obtained in that situation. Often the fault lies not with the institution, but with students who are unaware of how to get the most from the curriculum, the teachers, and the infrastructure of the school.

A singer may say: "I don't have enough money to pay for many hours of lessons per week from a private teacher. My only possibility is to get training through a school." Here we must take what some will maintain is a harsh stand. If a singer is serious about a career in opera, training cannot become an issue of money. If the singer lacks the money personally, he or she must find a sponsor, work out something with a teacher, or borrow the money. At whatever cost, training that will work for the individual singer must be found. Years lost in inadequate training will never be recovered.

Singers' families have been known to make enormous sacrifices to provide the instruction required to reach internationally recognized standards of excellence. Not everyone will reach the top, but those who have the possibility and don't make the effort usually live with regret. If a singer has the basic talent, he or she is aspiring to a career that is as difficult as professional athletics, and just as narrow in its opportunities for success. An aspiring professional tennis player, gymnast, or swimmer will see his or her instructor every day for hours at a time.

The costs are great, but success in these areas cannot be achieved without considerable sacrifice. The same is true in developing a vocal career.

Even when singers have located a teacher and have solved their financial problems, they must maintain a certain skeptical detachment about the training process. Some teachers will accept any student except the most hopeless if they have the time in their schedules, because they have to pay their bills. They are unlikely to say, "Listen, I'm not good for you, go to my colleague next door." If they are employed in a college or university, they're not going to say, "The system of training here is inadequate, so don't work with me." They know, after all, that in a higher education system they have to have a certain number of students in order to maintain the curriculum at a given level. If there are no students, there is no class. If there is no class, the teacher doesn't get paid.

How much should a vocalist study? There is really no set answer. At times study will be very intense, and at other times infrequent. We can tell you from direct experience that in the initial stages of voice study, or when making major changes in voice type (such as going from mezzo-soprano to soprano or baritone to tenor) the best results are obtained by seeing an excellent voice teacher every day. We know that this kind of intensive instruction will be financially or logistically impossible for most people, but we must point out the clear benefits from such frequent teaching. The reason that frequent lessons work so well at initial and transitional stages of voice training is that the voice teacher is effectively re-educating muscles. We know that muscles have a very short memory. They "forget" very quickly, so one has to continue reminding them of what one wants them to do. Just as one must practice yoga or dance or gymnastics every day to make the body conform to new physical demands, so must the muscles of the vocal instrument be trained in a slow but steady manner. The large muscles of the legs, arms, and torso are easier to see and manipulate than the small, hidden muscles of the vocal tract. For this reason expert guidance is needed constantly until the new muscle patterns are established.

Whether with a teacher or not, every singer must engage in daily vocal work. Forty-five minutes or an hour a day may not even be enough time to really establish the vocal apparatus in its most efficient pattern. Forty-five minutes may be adequate to warm up and start to vocalize. However one session of forty-five minutes a week is unlikely to be adequate.

This intensive training will not last forever. As a solid vocal technique is developed, the singer will be able to reduce the frequency of lessons, returning to the teacher for "check-ups" from time to time. Active singers may not be able to see their teachers for months on end. Even so, one must recognize that the need for instruction will vary according to the demands that are being placed on the voice. At some point a singer may need to return to daily lessons. At another point it will suffice to see a teacher every two days, two weeks, or two months.

Many singers believe they should increase the frequency of their voice lessons if they are preparing for something major—a concert, audition, or other important event. However, under such circumstances the voice teacher functioning as vocal technician may not be the person to go to. If a singer is going through a vocal transition, or something technical in the voice is sliding, *that* is when a voice teacher is required. But to prepare something specific for an imminent stage presentation, in concert or audition, our question is: do singers really want to continue to work until the last minute on vocal technique when they are about to render the product that the audience at a performance expects? The dress rehearsal is too late to be working out details of vocal placement. Vocal technique concerns the mechanics of muscles, and muscles are not subject to instant repair. They acquire response only through time. The only thing this kind of study can do at this point is make the singer nervous. A singer with a performance pending might better spend time with a coach. If the teacher also serves as coach, lesson time should probably be spent on coaching rather than vocal technique. At such a time, the singer should be able to trust the mechanics and technique so as to polish the product, fine-tune the artistry, and make sure the third line interpretation is convincing.

FINANCING INSTRUCTION

We hear every voice student reading this crying out at this point: "What do you mean, I should have a voice lesson every day with my voice teacher? Do you know what it costs to have a lesson every day of the week—even for a short period?" We are talking about an ideal situation, and there is ample precedent for doing what we suggest. Some great singers did indeed study every day with their voice teachers. Some people in the business maintain that most of the best teachers will teach a student of significant talent for free or for close to nothing until they begin to earn money. Why should singers not ask? They might be surprised at what a teacher is willing to do (but see our warning below about free instruction). There are solutions to the financial problems, and every singer should find one. A singer may go to a particular teacher as much as possible, perhaps using a tape recorder and replaying lesson tapes to retain more from the instruction. Between lessons, singers can work independently, or find a coach or an accompanist to keep track of their development. Even advanced students in the studio can help each other between lessons. If a singer is determined, solutions will be found. A landscaper who studies voice may say to his teacher, "I'll take care of your property for free if you give me lessons for free."

Some people are fortunate enough to have a relative who is a voice teacher. A number of singers have come far being coached by their parents or their spouses. However, one should recognize that there is always a certain danger in receiving instruction for free. Psychiatrists have a very strong concept of this. They believe that people benefit most when they take personal responsibility for being helped. If singers pay for instruction, they will respect and value it more. We have seen cases of excellent teachers opening their doors to some particular student that they believe in, and saying, "Okay, I am going to give you lessons for free." Their student then fails to take advantage of this opportunity. S/he values the instruction less just because it's free. It does not have to be this way, but it happens often.

Some singers may flatly say, "I will never need daily voice lessons." Fine. Once every few days for initial or transitional vocal training is fine, as long as the singers have made that decision conscientiously, and realize what they must do themselves in order to put their voice in shape. Above all, they should pay attention to their needs and be flexible enough to adjust their instruction to meet conditions as their career changes.

MAKING THE MOST OF LESSONS

Students have to take responsibility for their lessons and make sure that the time is well used. Some teachers are not as sensitive as they might be about using time in lessons efficiently; it is not unreasonable to complain if a teacher is late, takes phone calls during the lesson, or spends ten or fifteen minutes engaging in conversation about other aspects of singing that have little to do with building a voice and training an instrument.[2] A singer must approach teachers and coaches in quite a businesslike manner. If a professional discipline is established during the early years of study, the singer will be more of a professional as he or she grows in the business.

The singer has a responsibility to the teacher as well. The person who asks his or her teacher: "Can I pay you later on?" or "Can you give me a break in the price?" may be a person who can pay without difficulty. Those who may have more difficulties in terms of their budget will often go out of their way to pay without delays. If they value what they are getting, they know that they might have to wait on tables or get an extra job to pay for lessons. It can be extremely difficult, but if one is investing in oneself then the investment must be made with full commitment.

The singer should also be warned about a few additional difficulties inherent in studying voice within a formal conservatory or college situation. One lesson a week per semester is the normal, standard situation, with thirteen weeks in a semester. A teacher is allowed to be unavailable or absent once or twice, and the student may also be indisposed once or twice. Although these lessons are supposed to be made up, the extra sessions may not be easy to schedule. Added to this are school holidays and lateness on the part of the teacher or the student for a variety of reasons. This means that there will probably be ten or eleven lessons in a six-month period. There is no way that a singer will be able to develop his or her instrument with this limited amount of study.

Unfortunately, both singers and teachers are trapped in this system. This is where honesty begins to be a prime factor. An honest school and an honest teacher will warn students about the possible shortcomings of the system and suggest solutions. Teachers should state precisely what they feel they can offer, while stating at the same time what the student will need over and above vocal lessons. First and foremost, teachers should tell their students that by going through the conservatory or college music program alone, they may not get what they need to start a professional career. They will have to go out and supplement their studies.

As we have said, teachers are human. Some tend to become overprotective of their own work. They know how fragile an affair singing is, and how deceptive the entire process can be. A common defensive posture among a few less-secure teachers is to take the attitude: "Nobody touches my student." Teachers of this sort do not want their students to seek instruction of any sort with anyone else. They exercise pressure (knowingly or not) on their students in order to create dependencies that are difficult for students to break. Among this minority of teachers, two of the most pervasive types are the "gurus" and the "mother hens."

GURUS AND MOTHER HENS

Gurus are teachers who, willingly or not, manage to create a mystique around themselves. Gurus are revered, never doubted, and tell their students things such as: "You must listen only to me. You will hear advice from other people, but that advice will only harm you. You cannot see a coach until I finish training you in three (or four or five or however many) years of my special technique. You cannot go to auditions until I allow you to. You cannot consult with anybody else about your singing because that conflicts with what you're doing in our sessions. What I teach is so superb and so different you can only get it from me, and I know because it worked on so-and-so whom I taught (however many) years ago, and look at the career that singer has."

All of this is a mystification of the vocal training process. For a young singer with a limited income, a guru can be very tempting as a teacher. When confronted with such people, singers may think they are receiving extra-special treatment, that they are "saved." Yet singers finding themselves in this situation should be very careful. There is no such thing as a single source for the training of a singer. Singers will have to use many sources, and as we have said, they will have to create their own constellation of trainers.

Mother hens, like gurus, can be male or female. Their chief characteristic is overprotectiveness. Mother hens in essence say: "You come under my wing, and don't breathe unless I give you permission." Even private lives are guarded, guided, and scrutinized: "Nobody can hear my pupils unless it's under my guidance, when I decide, using the repertoire that I want, under the conditions that I establish." For very young singers, this may actually be helpful. Certainly very young vocalists have been ruined by being pushed into repertoire that is too heavy, too soon: 20-year-old Toscas usually burn out at 25. However, when this attitude persists even after singers' voices have matured, it becomes detrimental.

As we have maintained again and again, singers must be responsible for their own careers. If a teacher is helpful, so much the better. But if a teacher holds singers back and prevents them from taking advantage of important opportunities, the training is doing the singers little good. In the opera profession, singers advance most often by being at the right place at the right time. If a student is under a teacher's wing, the chances of being at the right place at the right time are not as great. It is up to the singer to realize when protection has extended to the point where it becomes smothering.

Some mother hens will show up at rehearsals and try in one way or another to interfere with professional or semiprofessional performances. From the standpoint of opera management, this is intolerable. It is also sad for the student, since it implies that they are unable to take responsibility for their own professionalism. Such a scene is a little like a mother or father showing up when their teenager has a date. Parents do their best when they educate their children and then send them off into the real world. At that point there must be trust that they will be able to handle themselves.

Similarly, a reasonable teacher trains a singer to be ready for a performance, but then doesn't undermine the student at rehearsals by showing up to diminish the singer's independence. This only prevents the student from facing professional responsibilities as a member of a performing ensemble. A good teacher realizes that if he or she has not been able to provide students with what they need to get through a performance in the last seven years, seven months, or seven weeks, there is no way in the world to provide them with something to "save" them in the last seven days or seven minutes. The only possible outcome of such a confrontation is the creation of negative energies that actually don't have much to do with what happens in the performance beyond upsetting the performer's composure. Singers have to contend with costumes, makeup, prompters, stage managers, the conductor, the flute being out of tune, and a thousand other details. They can no longer dwell on the possibility that the voice teacher is out in the audience wondering what is going to happen with a particular note. The fact that their shoe is untied may be far more important than the fact that they may be marking on a cadenza during a technical or dress rehearsal.

Mother hens, because of their characteristics, will make it as difficult as possible for a singer to acquire all the other skills that the profession demands. Their position is that all vocal problems must be solved before the student can move on to developing other skills. This is, we believe, entirely incorrect. The development of other career skills should be happening in parallel with voice training rather than in serial order. Singers cannot be limited to singing arias while standing with their arms at their sides if they hope to perform onstage. They will eventually have to be able to sing while handling a sword, running up steps, or dancing. They cannot learn to do that under the mother hen's wing. Singers have to learn these skills under the supervision of someone who can teach fencing, dancing, or acting. In this way they can immediately test whether their singing is going to work with the dancing and vice versa. Our insistence on parallel rather than sequential learning is therefore especially crucial—singers must make all the ingredients work with each other from the beginning. Here again, the mother hen is not likely to allow this blended training to take place.

In the end, the third line is the interpretation singers must write and execute by themselves. Nobody can interpret a performer's own thoughts or artistry but the performer. Teachers and coaches will guide, suggest, and polish, but the training they offer must be inspiring and not smothering for it to feed the performer's skills. A true artist cannot hope to have the third line continually written by a mother hen or guru and have it succeed.

NOTES

1. There are a few notable exceptions, but these individuals are rare. At some point, too, all active professional singers (as we mention in this chapter) must learn to be their own voice teachers. The demands of a career simply do not permit frequent studio sessions. Even the most seasoned performers, however, return to their primary instructors for "checkups" from time to time.

2. *The New York Opera Newsletter* has dealt extensively with this problem. The editor wrote the following advice in the July 1989 issue:

> As soon as the interruption (in your lesson) occurs, meet the other person's eyes, then look at your watch. They will likely catch on and keep it short. If not, then at the end of the lesson, you smilingly say, "We lost 10 minutes of my lesson because of your phone calls. I hope we will have time to make it up next week." Then make a note of it in your calendar. Do this every time it happens.
>
> When the time is 20 minutes or more, you sweetly say, "I have it noted down in my calendar that you owe me 30 minutes from time lost on May 3, May 15 and June 1. Do you have time in your schedule next week to put me down for it or should I just deduct the amount from my check today?" If they give you a hard time or try to embarrass you, you say "I can see your point but I really value my lesson time with you. I look forward to it all week and work hard to earn this money. I'm really upset about losing all this time, which is more important to me than money." Unless they schedule you for extra time, you write out the check for a reduced amount.
>
> If the person is someone you are really close to personally, or you have known a long time then something more informal will take care of it: "We really get along so well and I have a great time chatting with you when I'm here, but I'm afraid if we don't get down to business my voice will start to suffer!" Or even more informally: "All this kidding around is going to catch up with me. If I don't stop goofing off my voice/role/career is going to go down the tubes." By blaming yourself, you take no risk of offending them and at the same time put yourself in the driver's seat. (Pp. 14–15)

3. Henri N. Jacobi, *Building Your Best Voice* (New York: Prentice-Hall, 1982), p. 206.

CHAPTER 11

———————— 🐌 ————————

Using the Third Line: The Audition

The third line process should help all singers in dealing with two important events that are essential for developing careers in opera: auditions and contests. These are two of the most crucial and frustrating events in the profession. Singing in auditions and contests is more difficult for most people than singing in the performance of an opera. Singers can be emotionally destroyed through the process. We cannot lessen the difficulties inherent in audition and contest situations, but we hope in these chapters to reduce the anxiety singers feel by explaining what happens behind the scenes, and explaining how a singer can use the third line to become better prepared for these ordeals. We will deal with auditions in this chapter, and contests in the next, with a short set of observations on recitals and concerts.

Although there is little written on auditioning for opera, there are a number of books written on the audition process in spoken and musical theater, because the audition process is so crucial in these related fields. We urge all singers to consult these as well.[1]

The singer's mental and physical *attitude* going into an audition or contest is perhaps most important factor in performing at peak level. In order to be mentally prepared, singers must first understand what an audition is designed to do, and not to do. The second set of factors affecting audition performance has to do with the material and physical *preparedness* singers bring to the event: what singers present to auditioners and how they present it. Singers who are comfortable in these two areas should be able to overcome most apprehensions about auditioning.

WHAT IS AN AUDITION?

As important as auditions are for a singing career, they are usually not designed to be personal judgments on a singer's abilities. This is one of the great confusions that singers get into when they think about auditions, especially if they've been to a conservatory. An audition is *not* equivalent to a jury in a conservatory or a vocal contest. In an audition, it is rare that auditioners will be judging the total set of abilities of any singer. Even though they may wish to see a range of things a singer can do, they are most often looking for somebody to fill a particular slot—maybe even to fill a particular costume they have hanging in the wardrobe, or to find someone who can be hired for a fee that lies within their budget.

An audition fulfills many purposes for a company beyond casting parts for an upcoming production. First and foremost, an audition is an important publicity tool. Through auditions, an opera company can quickly make a reputation for itself throughout a region, state, or nation. The reaction they wish to elicit is: "Look at this company. They are holding auditions!" The company's name is then on the lips of several hundred people who have to do with the business. It is a wonderful way of promoting word-of-mouth recognition in the profession.

Auditions may also be ego trips for the judges. Willingly or not, auditioners play God. They get to decide who will be engaged and who will not (even if the final casting decision is made on the basis of dress size, hair color, or the probable size of the artist's fee). Being auditioners also puts people in a higher position within the profession. They become kingmakers to whom others will defer. Thus they may be quite happy to go through a long audition process even when there are only a few—or even no—parts to cast because of precasting of the roles.

Some readers may be surprised that we are starting this discussion by mentioning two factors that do not have anything to do with how good or how bad people are as singers. We are doing this because we feel that singers must face reality rather than fantasies if they are to survive the audition process. A singer's fantasy might be something like the following: "I will prepare myself; I'm an excellent singer; I will go to the audition; they will like me, and they will give me a contract (and if they don't it is because they are unfair, they are playing favorites, or they can't recognize talent)." Unfortunately, that scenario doesn't have anything to do with how the company makes publicity for itself, how the judges fulfill their egocentric needs, or how casting is really done. Once singers start understanding how they fit into the wider picture of the audition, there will be fewer problems facing "defeat," or "success." In other words, by understanding the realities of auditioning, singers will not get an inflated head because an audition resulted in a job, nor will they jump off a bridge because they were not cast.

If auditions so often do not result in the hiring of talented singers, why do they exist? The short answer is that they are a necessary evil. There may not be a better, more efficient way for singers to be heard and seen. This is true even though the audition is a deeply flawed process; it doesn't adequately serve any of the purposes for which it is designed. For the singer, it is nerve-wracking. It also costs a great deal of money: singers buy clothes, pay coaches, fly great distances, print résumés, have photos taken, and make tapes—and all perhaps with no direct result.

For the company, auditions don't function well either. Three to five minutes of singing can't tell the auditioners much about how it is to work with the people they hear. It doesn't answer essential questions for the company's management such as: "Can I communicate with these people at an administrative level for the next three weeks if I cast them? Do they need a personal page to be awakened in the morning? Will they require all sorts of pampering? Will they be interesting onstage and capable of carrying a role? Will they be able to work with an orchestra and follow the conductor in performance?"

Most companies thus hedge their bets. It is often the case that a production has been all but cast before auditions begin. Between the artistic director, the conductor, the stage director, and other company personnel, the production staff already knows enough people to fill the available roles. In fact, most intelligent companies will announce their season *only* after they know that they have the people to fill the roles. It is very risky (although some companies do it) to say, "Oh, we feel like doing this or that opera," and then go out searching for some unusual singer to fill a problematic role: a lyric heldentenor for Hoffmann, a dark contralto for Ulrica in *Un Ballo in Maschera,* or a bass with a very wide range for Osmin in *Die Entführung aus dem Serail* (The Abduction from the Seraglio). An imprudent company runs the danger of announcing their season, selling tickets, and not having adequate singers to fill crucial roles. They are left with having to fill in the gap as best they can with a virtual certainty of losing quality in the production.

If singers are aware of these things and take them as part of the rules of the game, then they have a chance of keeping themselves sane. But are singers wasting time and money auditioning, when it seems that they are hitting their heads against the wall? The answer lies in understanding the real reason why singers should continue auditioning even when no roles seem forthcoming. Occasionally lightning will strike, and a singer will be cast in a production for a company where they were previously unknown but, for the most part, auditions are held for the long run. Three years down the road somebody may remember that a singer did a good job in an audition. The director will be considering doing a production and will say, "If she has continued to mature, she would be excellent. I'll call a few of my colleagues who cast her in the last three years, and if their experience was positive, then I will cast her." That's why that audition three years earlier was important.

So, if singers are not cast in a particular audition, this doesn't necessarily mean that the company never wants to hire them. It is likely building a pool for future seasons to which singers who present themselves well in auditions will be added. A good company has to be organized, depending on how solid the infrastructure is, far ahead of time. It cannot plan on someone jumping down in a parachute onstage when it needs a singer. This does not mean, however, that there are never any emergencies—another reason why singers must always be ready.

For all these reasons, singers should go to an audition, *even if the season has been announced, and there is no clear role for them.* If singers are well prepared, the production staff is going to remember them. Moreover, down the line, that same company is going to do other auditions, and the singer will then no longer be a newcomer—an unknown. In addition, one never knows who is listening. The pianist may be involved with another company; if singers deliver a great audition but aren't cast, the pianist might take the word around. Someone who is just passing through on a visit who wants to sit in on the audition might be listening. Even other singers who are auditioning may hear and recommend people to other companies they are working with. In other words, the auditioners are an audience—and a very qualified audience. This is an audience that is involved in the profession, so the word spreads very fast. The downside of this situation is that there is also the possibility of not doing especially well in the audition for one reason or another. That can, of course, be damaging. So singers should not go unless they think that they can do their best.

The bottom line is that *auditioning is an investment for everyone.* It is an investment for the company because it keeps informed of the talent that is available. The production staff puts the names of good singers in its files; when something is needed, they pull out an appropriate folder, make a couple of phone calls to assure themselves that they are not getting a white elephant, and then call the singer.

Of course, two or three years down the road is a long time to wait when singers are trying to get a career started. But there are a lot of talented and deserving people waiting in line. Singers can only invest time and effort, and this investment has the same value as any other form of investment. Nobody will come and knock at the door and say, "Hey, listen, are you good? Would you like to sing for us?" Singers have to go out and knock at all the doors with the best possible spirit. And remember: the judges are not infallible. Their reasons for casting a role are not necessarily the same reasons the singer may perceive; singers cannot change that. A fine soprano may not be cast because the precast tenor is too short. A superb tenor may have a voice that is too big, small, or bright to balance with other members of the cast. If singers are aware that these variables exist, they should not stake their emotional balance on the audition.

PREPARING FOR AN AUDITION

Once singers understand that auditions are practical affairs, not pure judgments of their abilities, they must be mentally, physically, and materially prepared for auditioning. The better prepared the singer is, the better his or her chances of success.

First, all singers should make sure that they have a budget reserved for yearly ventures into auditioning for the local, regional, or national arena. Auditions take place well in advance of a company's season—sometimes a year or more ahead. Every singer should call or write opera companies in their immediate area and ask to be placed on their audition mailing list.[2]

It is wise to develop the mental habit of never taking anything that happens at the audition personally. It is not the fault of the company if the singer flew 3,000 miles and only got to sing five minutes. The company is not conspiring against the singer! They have a budget and have to pay for their pianist, the rental of the hall, and a union electrician to turn on the lights. The pianist charges so much per hour, as do those who rent the hall, and the company only has so many hours budgeted. Alternatively, the company may rent a hall and, at five o'clock, the janitor may come and turn the lights off. If a singer is cut off, it may not have anything to do with how good or how bad he or she is—the staff may not be able to listen to another aria because they will be kicked out if they run over schedule. Singers who think that the company should organize its auditions differently may be right! However, having chosen to audition, the singer should do it with a good spirit and understand the rules (and the breaks) of the process.

It is simply foolish for singers not to provide themselves with the best possible chances for success in auditioning. Some factors that will help include: having a good résumé that is concise and well presented, providing a memorable head shot, and wearing clothes the auditioners are going to remember, not because they are outrageous or because they are out of style, but because they complete the singer's image. A singer interested in Octavian should come in pants instead of a skirt. A singer auditioning for Carmen should wear a dress with a low neckline instead of a tweed skirted suit. If the auditioners want to hear a strikingly different aria later on, a singer can say, "Listen, I would appreciate a couple of minutes to freshen up." Most likely, they will say, "Yes, sure, go ahead." They will hear someone else in between and then the singer can come back with different clothes and a new image. That way it is possible for the singer to show the ability to do more than one thing. If the company calls the singer back to sing on another day, however, he or she may find it advantageous to wear the *same* clothes worn on the first day. After having heard hundreds of singers, many auditioners only remember people by their appearance. A singer who thinks that she made a good impression in a red dress the first time should by all means wear it when she returns.

It is a little harder for men than women to make a strong impression with clothing. Most auditioners will expect men to wear a coat and tie, and that provides little leeway. Nevertheless, there are still things men can do with dress when auditioning to make an impression. A man might want to take his jacket off to do Escamillo, and then he may want to put his jacket back on in order to do Count Almaviva in *Le Nozze di Figaro*.

As we have said earlier, all singers must be realistic about their physique. A 5'5" bass might not want to showcase himself as the Commendatore in *Don Giovanni*. A soprano should not audition for Salome if she weighs 300 pounds. The reverse is also true: a slim, blond baritone with a baby face will have a hard time being convincing as Falstaff.

If a tenor is prematurely bald, in order to audition he might want to get a hairpiece. To be considered for romantic tenor roles, a hairpiece might be just the thing to help create a suitable image for the auditioners. For a character tenor role, the hairpiece should be left at home or in the dressing room. In normal everyday life, if a man feels comfortable being bald, he should stay as he is; if not, he should buy a hairpiece, have implants, hairweaves, or some other treatment. But if he is in the performing business, he owes it to his audience to present a suitable stage image. His audience is, of course, auditioners, general managers, directors, and eventually the public in the theater. Of course, once a singer is in a production, being bald doesn't matter, because there are wigs, makeup, and all sorts of devices to alter stage appearance. In the meantime, to deliver an image in an audition, every performer should choose the proper clothing, makeup, and hairdo.

A singer may want to look *less* attractive or older in an audition. A basso buffo might even welcome the fact that he is balding. Even if he is 25 years old, if he has a bald head, he might pass for someone many years older. Since the entertainment business consists to a great extent of appearance and illusion, singers must create their own image, even if it means "helping" their physical appearance.

This is equally true for women. A woman may say, "I'm thinking about playing Carmen but, you know, I'm just not appropriately endowed." The answer is to wear a padded bra. That's what the production staff is going to give a less endowed singer to wear on stage anyway; it is best to take such matters in good humor. The opposite strategy can be applied for a singer who is going to audition for Cherubino. She should strap herself in if necessary, in order to sell herself as a trouser-role performer and wear clothing that will hide that which needs concealing.

PREPARATION AND THE SOUL OF
THE SINGER

Singers who have made the decision to audition must tell themselves that they are ready to audition. They must do this in a committed way. They must believe in themselves and be willing to sell themselves. They must find a way that will work for them to eliminate self-doubt and develop a strong, positive self-image. One of the ways for them to get over self-doubt is to throw themselves into the audition process, again, as long as all other aspects of preparation are taken care of. Singers should remember that it is their audition. The anticipation of failure will show clearly in the audition performance.

It may be necessary to try several ways to become involved in the audition process. One way, for instance, is for singers to try to concentrate more on the character being portrayed and less on themselves. The third line process will help singers immeasurably here. Having thought through the nature of the character and characterization, singers can then concentrate on a portrayal of the character rather than on their nerves.

All singers have to understand that they are at the service of a character when performing—even in auditions. Some people have trouble convincing themselves to sell themselves as the characters they want to portray. They feel that they are betraying themselves somehow if they do this. One doesn't have to have experience as a prostitute in order to portray Lulu with suitably convincing gestures and expressions. Likewise, a singer will not diminish her self-esteem by lowering her neckline to audition to do Carmen. Tenors need not feel that they are being dishonest in buying a toupee to audition for a glamorous romantic role. After all, opera is theater, not real life. These are decisions singers can make in order to gain some control over the audition process.

This principle also applies to decisions singers make about the course of their own careers. Singers should not feel guilty, for example, going to an audition when their teacher said not to, or failing to go to an audition when a teacher, a mentor, a friend, or a colleague insisted on it. In the end the decision is the singer's, because it is his or her life and future. Teachers may have good reasons for encouraging or discouraging their students from attending an audition, and singers should consider those reasons. But the teacher may also have weak reasons for this opinion, such as ego problems or old grudges. The teacher may say, "Oh, don't bother. Don't go to *that* audition. I know the judges. They're a bunch of schnooks."

"Don't bother." What does that phrase mean? Who knows? As we have said, auditioning is an investment. It doesn't always lead to an immediate role. Singers might want to audition because they need the experience of auditioning. If they are well prepared and know they are going to do a good job, the experience itself can be an important career investment. Perhaps the singer is not going to take any roles that the auditioners offer—because it may be true that the company is not worth the singer's time. But that doesn't matter—the audition may be a good arena to polish performance skills, not too exposed, and a fine place to gain experience.

Being prepared is the key. Singers should know their music, of course, and also make sure they have prepared their audition pieces using third line analysis. Singers should never audition unless they are prepared, even for those auditions that are not of great interest. The audition should also be used as practice for other auditions. Successful singers remember that they are always investing in their careers; by planting seeds, something may grow.

As part of preparation for an audition, it is important for singers to learn as much as possible about the judges that are going to be hearing them. Who are these people? All the judges may be conductors. One of them may hate it when a singer walks around during the audition, because he or she does not believe in "theatrical opera." A singer who knows this in advance should just stand and sing, because that is the way he or she is going to get the role. Better yet, the singer might "express" the part using the face and eyes while standing still.

Singers who know that the stage director is auditioning on a particular day might decide to emphasize stage action in the audition, with the aim of persuading the director that they are capable of acting on stage. If a singer discovers that one of the judges is looking for good female legs for a role that requires wearing tights, she is not going to sell her soul to the devil by wearing shorter skirts in the audition. This is merely an image that is required from her at a particular moment. At some other time, she might have to do a production in a bathing suit, or she might be auditioning to do Salome and will have to shed all seven veils.

Preparing for specific auditioners is always legitimate, even if it is just catering to their known personal preferences. One may well ask, "How do you find out about unknown judges?" First of all, there is the grapevine. The auditioners may be known by reputation. The singer may also start making inquiries. If the audition takes place in an area where the singer has friends, he or she should give them a call and say, "Listen, have you ever heard of this conductor before?" They may start saying, "Oh, s/he's a nightmare," or "S/he's a consummate musician, and a supportive person." Such informants may know about the auditioners' quirks: "Don't try to strike up a conversation with them, because they hate when singers talk to them. Just sing and leave." Or, "Try to engage in conversation—they really want to know you as a person." All these little pieces of information will help the singer relate to individuals instead of to three little dots sitting there in the dark.

It is always good to arrive early to the audition and see how previous singers are treated. One can discover from others the hot spots in terms of lighting onstage, how close or how far away one has to be from the pianist, the acoustic properties of the room, and much additional information that will affect the audition. It is usually possible to listen to people who sing earlier in the audition and try and figure out what happens to them. One should also try to talk to them and benefit from their experience. In some auditions it is possible to sit near the judges while waiting to sing. Watching their reactions can be invaluable.

Some judges or companies may issue checklists for their judges, which will allow them to compare singers later. Figure 11-1 is a typical checklist.

All singers should reflect on how they score in these categories and try to improve their weaker ones. Most of all, it is important for singers to continually compare their own vision of themselves with what the company or the judges are possibly looking for.

Figure 11-1.   Audition Rating Sheet

NAME ———————————————————————————
VOICE TYPE ——————————————————————————
HEIGHT, WEIGHT ————————————————————————
ARIAS PRESENTED —————————————————————————
APPEARANCE ———————————————————————————
FACH ————————————————————————————————
TYPE (HUMOROUS, DRAMATIC) ——————————————————
POSSIBLE ROLES ——————————————————————————
VOICE QUALITY (RATING FROM 1 TO 10) ———————————————
VOICE SIZE —————————————————————————————
MUSICALITY ————————————————————————————
ACTING ————————————————————————————————
OVERALL PERFORMANCE (RATING FROM 1 TO 10) ——————————
MISCELLANEOUS ——————————————————————————

THE ACCOMPANIST

The accompanist is the other person with whom the singer will be working in the audition. The best advice is always to bring one's own accompanist, making sure, of course, that he or she is truly excellent. Occasionally in auditions or contests, singers are prohibited from bringing their own accompanist, or it is not feasible to do this because the auditions are being held in a distant location. Since so many auditions are held in a few big cities, some singers living in other areas try to develop a working relationship with a New York, Chicago, Los Angeles, or San Francisco accompanist who knows their repertoire and is easy to work with.[3]

Occasionally the singer is faced with the worst of all possible situations: there has been no chance to work with the accompanist, and he or she turns out to be very poor or not able to sight-read the audition music well. If that appears to be the scenario and the singer doubts that it will be possible to survive the experience, it is absolutely necessary to be adaptable. Singers should always bring a variety of material to an audition. It is then possible for them to choose some easier pieces, rather than the Stravinsky or Richard Strauss they normally use. Sometimes the accompanist provided for the audition is going to be the pianist for the rehearsals. If this is known to be the case and if the singer finds the situation truly uncomfortable from the outset, it might be best not to audition. We believe that singers shouldn't validate with their presence a company with poor standards. Ultimately, working with poor pianists, conductors, or directors might be something singers are willing to endure to gain experience and enlarge their résumés. Nevertheless, one cannot really shine in performance if the production values are below professional levels.

Singers who decide that they want a career in spite of all these problems, however, should learn how to accommodate themselves to bad accompanists and to bad audition circumstances. Resilience is a great virtue in the entertainment business. Nothing is 100 percent all right all the time.

One of the worst things singers can do is bring their own accompanist and have that person be worse than the accompanist the auditioners provide. This happens all too often. A singer may have a friend who says, "Oh, I'll come with you," or a voice teacher who says, "I want to be there and play for you," or a coach with whom the singer has been working and feels comfortable. However, a world-class accompanist may be playing at the audition. If the singer has chosen to appear with a person who is adequate for repertoire training but not for public performance, this will look bad to the auditioners.

The accompanist is also a co-artist in the audition process. The singer has to make music with him or her. It is important to realize that accompanists may also be nervous, regardless of how experienced they may be; they are performing too. Singers who can sympathize with this, and still realize that they have to make music together with the accompanist, will be in a better position to deal with the problem of working with an unknown partner. This is infinitely preferable to taking the attitude: "Here I am. When are they going to screw me up?" Opera involves teamwork from wherever one looks at it. Egocentrism will undermine a singer *anywhere* he or she applies it. Singers must remember that accompanists can really help if they're good.

Singers should be friendly but businesslike with an accompanist. It is not necessary to become lifelong friends or make the accompanist a musical consultant or confessor during those few moments before or after singing. Some singers go to the accompanist and mumble things after they have sung, about mistakes they made, about mistakes in the accompaniment, or about their feelings concerning the auditioners. This is always a mistake. The accompanist may turn out to be the assistant to the conductor. The first thing he or she is going to say is: "Don't ever deal with that person. She's a troublemaker," or "He's a complainer." The only proper response to the accompanist after the audition is a smile and a "Thank you!"

One of the most common excuses singers give if they are not successful in an audition is, "Oh, the pianist screwed me up." This is never a legitimate excuse. The judges will have heard the same pianist for hours. If he or she is bad, they will already know it. They will appreciate the singers' skill if they can reach the end of the aria and give an artistic presentation in spite of the pianist. Most important of all, singers should *never* criticize the pianist out loud at the audition. That particular pianist was the best the company could do at that time, and no company likes to be criticized for making a poor decision. Worse yet, the pianist may be a member of the production staff—there is no sense making an immediate enemy. It could be that the company went through three pianists who got sick and they were stuck with this one. If the pianist is poor, the judges will be on the singer's side, not on the pianist's side. If the judges don't know the difference, then it may be best not to spend any more time with this particular company.

Learning practical aspects of dealing with professionals in the opera world is another reason why it is so important to work with coaches who will provide the information needed for the singer to become a performer. With this information the singer will be ready to combine artistic efforts with a wide spectrum of individuals. This is far more professional than emerging from a mother hen's nest with the attitude: "Oh, my God, this is the first time I've ever worked with an unknown accompanist!" or, "I'm not accustomed to dealing with opera companies because I never make music with other people." The flexibility that singers will acquire working with vocal coaches, diction coaches, style coaches, repertoire coaches, and so on will make them feel more at ease dealing with whoever serves as accompanist during the audition.

REPERTOIRE AND SELF-CLASSIFICATION

Which repertoire does the singer bring to an audition? We are not talking about competitions, we are talking about auditions, which are very different events. Singers can usually learn through the grapevine what the company holding auditions is doing next season. It is generally no secret; sometimes companies will advertise their season with the roles open at the time of audition. Singers may also learn the type of repertoire the company usually does. Do they do chamber opera, do they do Mozart, do they do twentieth-century works, or do they do Verdi, Wagner, and Puccini? The singer's audition repertoire then will echo the needs of this particular company. The repertoire, as we mentioned before, should also agree with the singer's general physical appearance.

A repertoire should always include contrasting material. Even when auditioning for something specific, the auditioners might want to hear something else. And it should be different from that which was offered initially because they want to see the spectrum of what the singer can offer. If the initial selection was Mozart, can the singer also do Verdi or vice versa? If the singer did Handel, can he or she also do Britten? If the first number was something fast and sparkling, can the singer follow with something slow and *legato*?

This balance needs to be there because auditioners are really interested in seeing the range of the singer's capabilities. They want to take to their files as much information as possible, so when they need to call—three days from now, three months from now, or three years from now—they will have as much information as they need. Also, to determine if the singer can be interesting onstage and be able to entertain an audience for three hours, the auditioners may realize that checking the singer through one aria or one mood may not be good enough.

Singers often wonder about how much acting to do during their audition. Here again, they must ask: "Who is watching and listening out there?" There usually is a conductor/music director and a stage director at auditions. One must not assume that conductors have no theatrical sensibilities, or that stage directors don't care about music. Sometimes it works the other way around. But singers should determine whether they have to please more than one taste. If so, they can do one number without stage actions, but including all of the emotional and expressive aspects from their third line analysis. They can then do a second number that will demand extroversion and a command of space and action using all the third line elements they have written into the score. Usually taking a risk will pay off—at least the auditioners will remember the performance! If the singer doesn't have any clue as to what is expected, it is best to play it safe—middle of the road. Singers can show all the emotion and expression demanded by the music, even if it is necessary to keep physically still. Singers should, under these circumstances, show control but never forget to express. If the auditioners don't like expression, it is because they don't like opera, and singers might be better off not working with them at all.

Another common question concerns standard versus nonstandard repertoire. When auditioning for a regional company that does mostly standard works, the auditioners may feel more comfortable hearing standard repertoire. Those same auditioners may feel a little bit uncomfortable dealing with something they don't know. By offering them something very unusual, singers risk creating a defensive attitude, which establishes a barrier between the performer and the judges. This is all a subconscious process, and it is best to play it safe. If, on the other hand, the company is accustomed to doing twentieth-century works, Baroque or obscure Romantic operas, then selections from these specialized repertoires should by all means be presented. Likewise, a singer shouldn't bring Adele's laughing song to the audition if it is well known that this company does 80 percent contemporary and 20 percent Baroque works every season. Nevertheless, it is always good to have something slightly nontraditional in the five or six arias presented, just in case the auditioners are interested in something beyond the standard repertoire.

There is one other excellent argument for doing standard repertoire. If you do nonstandard repertoire, the auditioners may spend more time listening to the *selection* than listening to the *performance*. Since they want to judge voice and performing ability, this is a disadvantage for the singer. They may come away from the audition with a good impression of the aria, but with little impression of the performer.

Knowing what to present can be a problem for a lot of singers, especially for some of the more unusual voice categories, such as contralto or bass, because a lot of the good repertoire for those voices is not in standard operas. A bass may end up auditioning for roles like Timur in *Turandot*. He doesn't have an aria in the opera but one has to have something to show in audition, and Puccini wrote very few bass arias. Similarly a mezzo-soprano might well wonder whether she should spend the time learning the stepmother's aria from Mussorgsky's *Sorochinsky Fair* when she will probably never in her life perform the role.

It may not matter what singers learn for auditions if they also enjoy performing recitals in which operatic literature is included. Learning nonstandard literature develops the singer's curiosity for other repertoires and enlarges knowledge of styles and composers. It is good training as long as singers learn about the composer, the style, and definitely the whole role, not just the aria being prepared. However, if it is necessary to play it safe in an audition, these nonstandard arias should generally not be used.

Auditioners are generally very pleased when singers choose short selections. Their time is at a premium, and they will usually be able to tell as much about a well-chosen shorter selection than one that lasts ten minutes. With a shorter selection there will also be a chance to sing one or perhaps two additional selections, which may work to the singer's advantage. There is an exception to this principle. When auditioning for a long, tiring role such as in a Wagner opera, the singer must prove to the auditioners that he or she has stamina.

In general singers should do things that they do well under any circumstances, rather than things that are known to be the most difficult in the repertoire (unless they can do them flawlessly). If a singer offers Zerbinetta's aria from *Ariadne auf Naxos,* the auditioners are immediately going to have the attitude: "Well, let's see if she can really do it!" They will scrutinize every note under a microscope. Of course, if singers *can* perform the hardest aria for their voice category perfectly, they are announcing to the auditioners that they can do everything *else* perfectly too. However, coaches who have accompanied numerous auditions feel that doing something simple *well* is preferable to doing something difficult with flaws. Singers win auditions or contests time and time again with a simple aria, just because they are able to sing it with no vocal or interpretive flaws at all, and nobody else among the other singers could do that.

Using the most often performed standard arias can also be a trap, however—particularly if singers are lyric sopranos. If there are 100 singers auditioning on a given day, 70 are going to be lyric sopranos. Out of those 70, half of them will sing all-time favorites, such as: "O mio babbino caro" (*Gianni Schicchi*), "Quando m'en vo" (*La Bohème*) or "Mi chiamano Mimì" (*La Bohème*). This is no longer just standard repertoire—it's potentially boring repertoire. These are not bad arias, but a singer will have to be extraordinarily exciting, unique, and different to be remembered doing them. Even if the singer is able to perform these in a totally fascinating way, how attentive and serious can an auditioner remain when soprano number 59 presents "Mi chiamano Mimì," making it the tenth time they've heard it that morning?

This advice doesn't apply to other vocal categories to the same degree. While the most standard arias might be overdone for a soprano, they might be fine for a bass. If a bass presents "Il lacerato spirito" from Verdi's *Simon Boccanegra* (sometimes described as the bass national anthem)[4] for the second time in an audition section, it doesn't matter because, on average, out of 100 auditioners, only two basses will come to audition, and only one of them, 50 percent, might sing that aria. If 50 percent of the sopranos sing "Mi chiamano Mimì," the sanity of the auditioners is at risk. One exception should be noted: a soprano auditioning for the role of Mimì, must of course sing this aria.[5]

A word of caution is in order here. In general, singers should be careful about offering an aria in audition if they are incapable of performing the entire role associated with that aria. This often happens with tenors who offer "En fermant les yeux" (Des Grieux's Dream) from Massenet's *Manon*. Many tenors can sing this light lyric aria, but the role of Des Grieux demands a second aria: "Ah fuyez, douce image," which is dramatic, *forte,* and high. Many auditioners will not care and will take an aria at face value, but others will see immediately that the singer has no idea what the whole role is about if he obviously cannot perform both arias. This naturally creates a bad impression at the audition.

It is best not to confuse auditioners! A singer with a very wide repertoire and extensive possibilities of expression in temperament and voice should make a choice for that particular audition. No soprano should bring Brünnhilde *(Die Walküre)* and Despina *(Così fan tutte)* to the same audition, even if she is entirely capable of doing both. Auditioners need to classify singers. They need to put a label on the singer's folder. The singer in turn has to make this process easier for the company, even if the system doesn't make sense.

However, singers must be equally careful of defining themselves too narrowly. Some singers have adopted the German Fach system in choosing their repertoire. We discussed the Fach system in Chapter 2, and repeat some of our earlier statements for this chapter. The Fach system is a bureaucratic device for classifying singers into musical and dramatic categories (Fachs). In auditioning for jobs in Germany, singers must determine which of a whole range of Fachs they belong to, from coloratura soprano to serious bass (see Chapter 2, Tables 2-1 and 2-2). Some of the categories are unusual for Americans: young helden-tenor, "romantic" baritone, and so forth.[6]

We consider the Fach system to be a poor, deeply inconsistent system, and believe the Germans have proven to themselves that it is a bad system—largely because it is widely violated by the very people who use it in hiring. Germans talk a great deal about the Fach system. They even publish booklets listing the roles singers must learn if they are in this or that Fach. After they engage their singers, however, they make them sing all the roles for which they have the notes and look the part, whether the role is in their Fach or not. A singer may audition and be hired as a lyric soprano, but if the opera house thinks that the singer can do Tosca or Brünnhilde, she does it; the singer is their employee. They pay a monthly salary, and singers must deliver if they want to keep working.

So, although the Fach system is established as an administrative personnel organizational device, once the season has begun, the administration of the house tries to use singers as much as possible. They can't let a character tenor sit around doing nothing just because there is no role for his specific Fach that month. A very talented singer who has been in the system a while may say, "Wait a second, no. I want it written in my contract specifically that I will not be required to do certain roles." Anyone thinking of working in Germany and specifying this in their contract should make sure that they are in a position to make the demands. These conditions are not found at all times in every German opera house, but singers contemplating a career in Germany should remember to exercise caution when signing contracts.

In the United States, singers should have a general coherence in the arias they present for auditioners—broad enough to show versatility, but not so broad as to confuse the auditioners. Singers should not be as narrow as in the Fach system, although it might be useful to start with the core repertoire of a specific Fach as a guide, adding one or two arias from neighboring Fachs that work well.

It is also important to realize that singers' repertoires will change depending on the size of the house they will be singing in. A singer should find out in advance how big the theater is in which the auditioning company performs, and tailor audition repertoire accordingly. A singer may not have the voice to sing Tosca in a 3,000-seat house, but it might be an appropriate role for a small house. A tenor might be a fine Calaf *(Turandot)* in a small house, and a good Nemorino *(L'Elisir d'Amore)* in a big one. Some singers maintain two repertoire lists: one for auditioning in big houses and one for small houses.

RÉSUMÉS

A résumé is an important document: it presents singers on paper to potential employers. More important, it is the document that allows employers to locate and identify the singers once they have seen them. A singer must always bring résumés and pictures to auditions, even if they have been sent in advance. One never knows who will be at the audition who will not have seen the résumé, and even the most efficient office occasionally misplaces documents.

The résumé must be as concise and short as possible. Nobody has time to read reviews, commentaries, or testimonials. It has to be well presented and easy to read. Nothing should be handwritten. It is a good idea to leave as much space between items of text as possible to increase readability. The auditioners sometimes send forms that singers have to fill out before the audition. These should never be filled out by hand unless it is absolutely unavoidable. Usually the singer will have enough time to fill the forms out at home with a typewriter. Otherwise, if one must fill out the form at the audition site, it makes sense to look for a typewriter in the building. This is, by the way, one good reason for arriving early for the audition. If all else fails and it is necessary to fill out the forms by hand, one should take great care to use careful block lettering. If the auditioners are to know about the singer, they have to be able to read the résumé easily.

It makes good sense to try to present a résumé in an unusual but tasteful way. Marketing strategies people use in presenting their résumés in other professions can be very useful. The résumé should be made memorable through a good typeface or computer-generated font, and a clean, readable layout. *It is essential to be sure to proofread the résumé carefully. Any mistakes made in listing composers, names of operas, conductors, or directors one has worked with will stand out and create a bad impression.*

Singers should list their name at the top of the résumé along with some basic physical characteristics—height and weight (and it is best not to lie—it will show). Usually it is not beneficial to list age, but occasionally it can work to a singer's advantage. A 22-year-old singer with an exceptionally mature voice may stir some additional attention from auditioners. Such prodigies should have no hesitation about listing their age. If a singer's voice and physical characteristics are right for Despina and she is 41, she should not list her age. Here it is best to let image sell, not taking the chance that age will be a hindrance. Although there are age limits on some contests, there are no age limits in professional opera companies.

Some singers may not even want to list weight if they are going to audition in person. A singer who is a little too short or too tall compared with usual artists portraying the role should dress for the audition accordingly. Vertical stripes make a person look taller, and horizontal stripes make one look shorter. Dark colors generally look slimming, and bright colors fill out the figure. Thus the singer should choose accordingly depending on whether he or she is auditioning for a character who will die of tuberculosis, or for Sir John Falstaff.

The singer's address and phone number should come next, followed by the roles he or she has performed.

Some singers list their educational background and their teachers before listing their roles. This is appropriate if one is applying to study in a graduate program or training institute, but not for professional employment. One must be very careful about the content of the résumé. By listing teachers, singers are putting themselves in a nonprofessional situation. If singers are professionals, no one should care who their teachers are. All singers presenting themselves in audition should be finished products ready to work. Singers who announce their teachers are announcing to the auditioners that someone is still holding their hand. Granted, some audition applications may ask about teachers. In that case, singers should list teachers in the application but not in the résumé. As for the prestige of certain teachers, it should be noted that, although some teachers have friends or connections that may be useful, some also have enemies or jealous colleagues.

A singer may have quite a long list of credits. Such a list may be impressive, but it is far better to pare it down to a page or two. It is best to choose those things that represent him or her the best if the résumé is getting too long. A soprano who has done Lauretta in a workshop and Tosca in a regional company should consider discarding Lauretta and listing Tosca. It is important always to tell where the roles have been done. It might look very impressive for a singer to list both Lauretta and Tosca as roles on her résumé, but she is padding her résumé if she has done these roles in a school show consisting only of scenes from the operas without costumes or orchestra. Sometimes, it may be good to list the names of well-known directors or conductors with whom one has worked, because this is also a form of reference.

Although singers sometimes list music directors and stage directors in their résumés, they should make sure that their experience with them was good before listing them. In this business an auditioner will usually pick up the phone and say, "Listen, here so-and-so says that you worked with her. How is she?" It's important to know that person is going to say, "She's excellent." Singers should be certain that other professionals listed in their résumé also know who they are. Very often a person will list master classes with famous teachers and singers, and later it is discovered that they didn't really participate as a singer; they just sat in the last row as an auditor. This kind of thing just makes a singer look bad. If one turns on PBS on television and some star is giving advice to young singers, it does not mean that the person watching participated in a master class. Or if a singer sang briefly for some master teacher who said, "Well, you have to put your hand on the piano instead of grabbing your skirt," it doesn't mean that the singer has participated in a master class. It is surprising what people will claim on résumés. For an auditioner, it is especially disconcerting to be looking over résumés and find that people you have no knowledge of have listed you as their teacher in master classes! Now, if a singer has spent the summer in an institute where a world-class teacher was giving a seminar, this is something different. Under these circumstances, the singer can legitimately list such a class.

Having said all this about résumés, we feel it is important to note that most auditioners rarely have time to read anything. Usually when they are hearing an audition, they will only glance through the résumé. That's why it has to be concise enough so that, if they're really interested in reading, they're not going to stop paying attention to what the singer is singing out there.

In the end, the singers and their presentation are the principal interest for the auditioner. If the voice and the presentation are good, the auditioner will read the résumé more carefully. If the presentation is weak and insecure, it will not matter if the singer sang at La Scala, the résumé may never be opened. So the résumé has to be very carefully put together in the eventuality that the auditioners do open it.

The résumé is also the point of contact between the company and the singer. If one has created a good impression in the audition, it can be a futile effort if the résumé should be lost because the paper was folded the wrong way or presented in the wrong fashion. One of the great tragedies in the entertainment world is having a good audition but a bad résumé that easily gets lost in the shuffle. The auditioners may have liked the singer, but they can never find him or her again. If the résumé is put together in a folder with hard covers and a good photograph that one can see when going through the files, it will perform its function.

Money spent on good photographs is well spent. Photographs should be 8" by 10" and they must be current.[7] Otherwise auditioners will look at the picture three months from now and say, "I don't remember this person." Sometimes it is deceiving when someone comes with short hair and the photograph shows an enormous mane. Men who at some point decide to buy a toupee should have a photograph taken with it; otherwise it doesn't fulfill its function. The photograph should have the singer's name "stripped in" on the front. The auditioners should be able to identify the name with the face, and what better way than to present the two of them together.

MANAGEMENT AND AUDITIONS

Singers often wonder if companies pay more attention to people who come for an audition represented by a professional manager. The short answer is, being introduced by a recognized manager announces that singers are already working at a professional level, and that is good. If the manager is unknown, the singers' association with him or her may hurt them. Some auditioners will ask, "Who is this 'manager'? His/her spouse?" Singers should avoid creating this impression. Many companies use management representation as a guarantee of quality. There are often so many singers presenting themselves for audition that it is impossible to hear them all. Representation by a reputable manager tells them that they will not be likely to be wasting their time hearing the singer. Dealing primarily with managed singers is seen as a kind of insurance policy—a guarantee that the singers will be able to work at a professional level.

Singers who do not have management should not despair, however. Many regional companies will be happy to hear unmanaged singers who are willing to come to their city. Singers who are on vacation or plan to be passing through a city that has an opera company they are interested in should call in advance for an audition appointment. It may work out quite successfully for both the singer and the company.

Some smaller regional companies actually prefer not to deal with managers, because that implies all sorts of administrative difficulties. Usually it means having to negotiate the relationship with the singer at a different level, instead of taking care of things in a more private, direct fashion. A typical reaction for an administrator of a small company is, "My God, now I have to deal with managers! You know how pestering they are, and they're going to ask for more money." Here again, the grapevine will provide information on what is expected from different companies. It may be wise for singers to wait in seeking out a manager until they are so successful that it becomes difficult to sort out conflicting offers. A manager can also serve as an adviser, and not necessarily as a professional representative.

Ultimately the decision to use management largely depends on what level singers are at professionally. It depends on how many jobs the singers have had already, and the quality of the manager. Singers must ask themselves: "Will this person really represent me appropriately, or will he or she just alienate a company because of too many phone calls or too much insistence on getting a higher fee?" Acquiring management is a delicate matter. This person must understand singers' needs and be their representative. Above all, singers should never make the mistake of thinking that management is going to solve all career problems.

Singers are still their own best representatives through their talent and their presentation.

There are some good practical reasons for seeking management. If a singer lives in a remote area where it is uncomfortable to be making continual phone calls, or the singer is traveling a great deal, a manager can solve some of those logistic problems. Singers who don't feel comfortable talking to people and being pushy about themselves may find it helpful to hire someone to do it for them. Some people don't feel comfortable saying, "Hey, listen, do you still remember me?" It's easier for the manager to do it. But singers must be careful, because sometimes people will say, "Who do they think they are? They haven't done anything and they already have a manager."

There is also a basic financial question to consider. How much is this company going to pay? Does it make sense for a manager to get 10 percent of nothing? Singers must ask themselves realistically, "How do I pay the manager if I don't get paying jobs? How many paying jobs did I get last season? If I were a manager, would I be interested in my career at this stage?" It is important for singers to balance things out and keep their career in perspective. Singers are making a statement about themselves as professionals when using management. If that statement is premature, it can turn people off instead of being helpful. Singers must also keep in mind that managers don't just get a percentage of the artist's fee. They will also charge for their expenses on the singer's behalf: phone calls, brochures, advertising, postage, and other office expenses.[8]

DOING THE AUDITION

Last but not least, singers must know how to conduct themselves professionally at the audition itself. The audition is a very special kind of job interview, and it should be treated as such. It involves just as much acting as doing a role on stage. The entire audition sequence should be practiced much as if singers were really doing a role.

The most important factor in an audition is getting the auditioners on the singer's side from the very beginning. Auditioners really want the singer to entertain them and give them a pleasant experience. Thus singers should be well dressed, look pleasant, walk into the audition space (stage, hall, room) at the proper time in a manner that is alive and vibrant and exudes confidence. It is amazing how many singers look afraid, defeated, and depressed before they ever begin to sing.

If the accompanist enters with the singer, the singer should have already given the accompanist his or her music. Otherwise, on entering, the singer gracefully gives the music to the accompanist indicating with one or two soft words the first aria he or she will sing. The other arias the singer plans to offer should be clearly marked so that the accompanist can find them quickly and easily. The music itself should be a bound score with pages that lie flat, or should be in a three-ring notebook or binder. All cuts should be clearly marked. The place the singer is to stand to begin the audition may be quite clearly indicated; if not, the auditioners will usually ask the singer to stand in a particular spot. If this is not clear, the singer should smile and ask where he or she should stand.

If singers are allowed to choose their first selection, the standard opening line for presenting it is: "My name is (name) and I will sing (name of selection) from (name of opera) by (name of composer)." Every singer should practice this simple introduction for every aria they plan to offer. It is essential that the singer's name be pronounced clearly and confidently, and that the aria, name of opera, and composer be pronounced correctly in the language in which they were written. Singers who mispronounce the name of their own aria have two strikes against them even before beginning to sing.

Singers should be careful to use the formula: "I *will* sing (name of aria). . . ." They should not use variations such as, "I would like to sing. . . ." Above all, no singers should ever, under any circumstances, say: "For my first number/selection, I would like to sing (name of aria). . . ." This introduction sounds innocent, but it does not sound at all professional to auditioners.

Singers should begin to use third line preparation even before the accompanist begins to play and present a characterization to the auditioners. It should not be necessary for singers to overtly signal the accompanist. Most professional accompanists know very well when singers are ready to sing.

In executing the aria, singers should aim their eye focuses just above the auditioners heads. It is disconcerting for many auditioners to have the singer stare them in the eyes while singing. Otherwise, all aspects of third line preparation (with some of the caveats about body movement noted earlier in this chapter) should be used in the audition. It is wise to remember that the auditioners are trying to see singers in a role, and it is important that they see that immediately in the audition.

Once the first aria is completed, singers should stand quietly with a pleasant expression and wait for the auditioners to either ask for another selection, dismiss them, or engage them in conversation. Auditioners may ask for a second aria from a list prepared in advance, or ask the singers what else they are prepared to offer. In the latter case, singers can be somewhat more informal, and simply recite the titles of the other arias they have prepared. The full formal presentation used for the first aria is not repeated. The auditioners will then make their request, and singers should proceed to perform the aria in a confident fashion. By no means should singers register anything on their face except pleasure at the chance to perform again. Auditioners often select what singers least expect, and a surprised expression, rolling of the eyes, a grimace on the face, or nervous giggling will read very badly.

If singers are dismissed, they should smile, say, "Thank you," collect the music from the accompanist with a smile, and leave. A second selection is customary at many auditions but, if it is not requested, singers should not show any dismay or disappointment. The auditioners may have heard all they needed to hear in the first selection, or they may be short on time.

If the auditioners want to engage singers in conversation, singers should answer their questions pleasantly and cogently, letting their personality show through. In conversation it is possible to give the auditioners the clear idea that the singer is someone the company would find easy and pleasant to work with. It is unwise to talk too much or to volunteer too much information. The auditioners generally are trying to carry out an efficient procedure, and they will appreciate a professional attitude.

Finally, for the sake of their own sanity, singers should do their best to forget auditions as soon as they are completed. At the beginning of one's career, as we have pointed out, very few auditions will yield immediate results. Dwelling on an audition and waiting by the phone hoping to be offered a role when a singer has been one of 100 people heard is not productive use of time. If one out of ten auditions is successful, a singer is doing very well.

When approached in this way, the audition can become a successful career tool for any singer—one that the singer can control, rather than one that terrorizes and controls the singer.

NOTES

1. Several excellent books are: Joan Dornemann, *Complete Preparation: A Guide to Auditioning For Opera* (New York: Excalibur Books, 1992); Michael Shurtleff, *Audition* (New York: Bantam, 1978); David Craig, *On Performing* (New York: McGraw-Hill, 1987) (this contains a great deal of additional wisdom for singer-actors of all varieties; and Joan Finchly, *Audition* (New York: Prentice-Hall, 1984). Fred Silver has written an extremely useful book entitled *Auditioning for the Musical Theater* (New York: Newmarket, 1986), which will also be of help to opera singers. Books by Wesley Balk and Eloise Ristad already mentioned in earlier chapters also contain a great deal of helpful advice on dealing with auditions and contests.

2. A useful reference is *A Singer's Guide to the Professional Opera Companies* published periodically by Opera America (777 14th Street NW, Suite 520, Washington, D.C., 20005), which lists audition dates and requirements. Opera America also publishes a comprehensive guide to the upcoming seasons of its member companies. Although many of these productions will already have been cast when this guide is published, it provides valuable information concerning the number of productions each company mounts per year, and a fair guide to the repertoire they seek to perform. The latest annual edition of *Musical America* (available in most libraries) also lists opera companies throughout the United States.

3. A useful (but somewhat outdated) guide to New York accompanists and coaches can be found in Richard Owens' *The Professional Singer's Guide to New York* (Dallas: AIMS Publications, 1984).

4. See the third line analysis of the opening to this aria in Chapter 6.

5. Another exception can be noted. A soprano who is a superb interpreter of "O mio babbino caro" and can really show every side of Lauretta—manipulating, winsome, girlish, yet worldly-wise—will get the auditioners' attention even after all other competitors have sung this aria, but the singer must be *very* good indeed to make this kind of impression.

6. Those who are interested will find a brief description of the system presented in Richard Owens' useful manual: *Towards a Career in Europe,* available through the American Institute of Musical Studies in Dallas, Texas (1983). Two recent publications that will be helpful for singers who want to audition in Germany are: *A Singer's Guide to Auditioning in Unified Germany* by Kenneth Posey (Singer's Guide, P.O. Box 10966, San Angelo, Texas, 76909) (1990), and *Kein' Angst Baby!* by Gail Sullivan and Dorothy Maddison (Kein' Angst Baby! P.O. Box 675, Burtonsville, Maryland, 20866) (1991). This second publication has an extremely useful Fach list with essential and suggested arias for every voice type. In addition, the *Deutsches Bühnen Jahrbuch,* available in larger libraries, is the equivalent of *Musical America* with agent and theater addresses.

7. Note that, for European auditions, smaller sized (3" × 5") photos are used. The larger 8" × 10" are considered to be in bad taste. Singers who anticipate auditioning in Germany might get a supply of these smaller format photos when ordering 8" × 10" photos.

8. There are many other aspects of performer-management relations that go beyond the scope of this book. We would like to refer readers to two excellent practical guides to management, and to many of the aspects of career development mentioned in this chapter: *Getting It All Together* by Ann Summers-Dossena (Metuchen, N.J.: Scarecrow Press, 1985); and *The Performing Artist's Handbook* by Janice Papolos (New York: Writer's Digest Books, 1984). Richard Owens' *Towards a Career in Europe* and *The Professional Singer's Guide to New York* (Dallas: AIMS), mentioned above, are also helpful. The former will give you additional information about auditioning for European agents. See also the additional references for auditioning in Germany mentioned above in note 6.

CHAPTER 12

— ❧ —

Performing with the Third Line: Competitions and Recitals

Competitions are related to auditions, but they have a whole different set of purposes. In an audition singers gain exposure through applying for one or more specific roles, for one specific company, and through displaying their particular style and artistic orientation. In a competition singers are not necessarily auditioning for a role. Here the aim is to look for a broader kind of exposure; the spectrum is much wider than in an audition. Singers must cover much more territory with repertoire and display of vocal abilities. People from different backgrounds and with widely variant perspectives on singing will be listening.

However, judges in competitions are usually people involved in producing opera in one way or another. Therefore, singers are not only judged to see if they deserve the prize to be awarded. They are judged, officially or not, in terms of where they might fit within the judges' future plans for producing opera. Occasionally, people judging contests are not involved with opera production, such as agents, critics, voice teachers, or ex-singers, some of whom now teach. Even though these people may not cast productions, they may be in a position to recommend singers for something, and knowledge of good talent is always important as a credential within the profession.

Basically, then, entering contests is one of the ways to access a network of professionals. It is also very satisfying to win prizes. By winning singers will start to make money from singing, which is the goal of every artist. For this reason singers should apply to all those competitions that they feel ready for, even if they are not going to be hired for productions directly as a result.

There is a caveat in entering contests, however. Because contests are a highly visible form of exposure, one has to be extremely careful and know where to sing. Performance in a competition may leave strong positive marks on a singer's reputation if he or she has done well, or negative ones if the performance has not been good. Contests are particularly difficult for singers who have won other competitions. They are expected to do well from then on. If they don't, they *might* be given the benefit of the doubt by the judges, but they may suffer a loss of reputation as a result.

Some competitions do not just provide money—they may lead to entry-level positions with professional companies, sometimes in small roles or chorus work. This can be an advantage, or it can be exploitative. There are competitions that will bind a singer to accept this kind of employment. The organizers will say: "If you win, you will be obligated to work with us." In such cases, singers should be careful before entering the competition to be sure they are willing to go along with the conditions of the prize.

Many singers become unhappy about competitions and even resent the competition system, because of how expensive it is for singers to compete. The contest is usually only held in one city, and there may be very few prizes. Singers may be competing only with their own age group or vocal type, or the competition may be for the best singer of any age or type. It is possible that a 21-year-old baritone may be competing with hundreds of 32-year-old lyric sopranos for a single prize. This may seem like comparing apples and oranges—what is a generic high-quality singer, anyway?

Rather than rail against the inherent unfairness of the competition system, it makes sense to take contests for what they are and decide whether to compete or not. Some questions singers may ask themselves before deciding to enter contests are: "Do I find contests to be difficult or easy? Am I able to compete and perform my best under pressure? Who are the judges, and what might they be able to do for me if I make a good showing? What has happened to past winners of the particular contest? What career possibilities might be linked to winning?"

Part of the decision to compete will be based on planning. All singers have to budget their time and money and decide how much money to invest in themselves for the next twelve months. The budget will involve everything from vocal lessons to air fare for auditions and competitions. This money should be thought of as investment money. As a test, before spending this money, singers should be able to tell themselves: "If I go to this place, and I'm well prepared, I'm going to leave a good image, and it doesn't matter if I don't get the prize, because someone of importance is going to be listening to me." Under these circumstances, the contest may be an excellent investment.

Singing is a business. Deciding to enter a contest is a professional decision, not a question of, "What do I feel like doing next week?" It is rather a question of, "How do I plan my life for the next twelve months and the twelve months after that?" The rewards are certainly worth the effort in most cases. By winning even a small competition, a singer's name will be before the public. By winning a big competition, a singer's career may be immediately opened, and he or she is on the way. This may seem to be an overly dramatic way of putting things, but it does happen all the time. There are competitions throughout the world: in Spain, France, Germany, Austria, and the United States; these are attended by agents and general managers looking for new and inexpensive talent.

A singer's organization and budgeting may take other factors than the competition into consideration. It is wise for singers to ask themselves, particularly when a competition is far away, "What will I have to gain if I go to Vienna or Barcelona, besides the competition?" The answer may be: "To go to a school in the area and practice languages, or contact other opera companies in the area and audition as well." In short, singers should not spend an enormous amount of money just to go to a competition. They should plan well enough to be able to "piggyback" other career development activities onto the contest. As an added benefit, the singer's own personal development is enriched by traveling.

It is not hard to plan in advance, but singers must do some legwork. *Opera News; The New York Opera Newsletter* in Maplewood, New Jersey; and *Opera Guide* in Van Nuys, California, are some of the periodicals that publish competition notices for singers. Most useful of all, *Musical America* publishes lists of competitions for a given year. Singers interested in competing should get the phone numbers of all the institutions that run regular auditions and competitions, write to all of them, and ask to be placed on mailing lists for contest notices. If there are no mailing lists, singers should find out which is the right month of the year to call. Budgeting the costs of telephone calls and postage is also part of any singer's career investment strategy!

Singers may need to raise the money to get to the contest site. If the contest is important, it is not unreasonable to beg or borrow it. Another successful strategy is to hire a church basement and put on a recital for donations from friends, family, and supporters. This should be part of every singer's income strategy.

With regard to contest prizes, it is undoubtedly nice to have the money, but the real prize may not be the money. Even if a singer doesn't end up with a money prize, it is possible to end up with something more valuable: the exposure. An agent or conductor may be attending the competition and become interested in singers heard there whether they win the contest or not.

Singers should therefore think of contest experience as an exercise in dropping seeds, and make sure that the seeds they are dropping are good ones. Thus singers should prepare themselves, know that they are ready, and go. They don't go to win; they go for all those other reasons. Winners are, of course, better off. But if singers don't win yet the seeds they have planted in auditioning are good, one way or another, sooner or later, the experience will yield positive career results. Even if singers go to Europe, participate in auditions and contests all over, and come back empty-handed, they should not be unhappy or discouraged. The visit should be seen as an important source of personal enrichment in terms of background and knowledge of cultures, places, and languages.

A future Tosca can visit Castell Sant'Angelo in Rome or walk the streets of Verona and soak up the atmosphere. One can visit the Theater an der Wien and visualize the place where *Fidelio* was premiered. The opportunities to learn are limitless. A trip to Europe is also a wonderful chance to see opera. There are hundreds of opera performances every evening in Europe—often of nonstandard repertoire, or in experimental productions. Singers can greatly expand their knowledge of the art of opera performance in Europe.

Such a trip also provides an enormous store of connections. The next time the singer goes to Europe, he or she will already have made friends. On the next trip it may be possible to stay in their homes. This means that the next trip is going to be less expensive than the first. Singers should plan to spend substantial time and energy in networking and marketing themselves. The people they meet may know directors and agents and can likely provide introductions to them.

CLOTHING FOR COMPETITIONS

It is essential for singers to know for whom they are singing in a competition. In general, appearance will count somewhat more in a competition than in an audition. Singers should appear totally professional when competing. To this end it is an advantage to know the kind of mentality the judges and the people running the contest have. When singing on the West Coast in a daytime competition, singers might be fine wearing white shoes with a summer dress or a sports coat and tie. In New York, white shoes may not be acceptable, and a navy skirt or suit might be more appropriate. Europeans are more traditional than New Yorkers, and much more traditional than Californians. Final rounds of competition, if presented for the public, will often require well-fitting formal wear both in the United States and abroad.

In short, it is important to do the proper kind of research. Singers can find out from colleagues what they saw when competing. Research will provide information on the latest trend and yield answers to questions like: What do people wear? How do people behave? Do they talk to the judges? Do they say, "Good morning?" Do they announce themselves and the aria they will sing, or do they just walk on and begin? In different places, one will find different attitudes. As with auditions, arriving early will provide opportunities to answer these questions if all else fails.

As in auditions, clothing is important. However, a singer's clothing strategy should be slightly different for contests. It should be geared to leaving a strong image of the singer as an artist. As insurance, it might be wise to have two or three dresses ready if necessary. For example, a soprano may arrive to sing in a contest in a red dress and discover that the singer before her is also dressed in red. If she is prepared with another outfit, she can go and, in a minute, change into a different color. She does this not out of vanity, but because she wants to leave a different impression on the judges than did her predecessor. It is foolish to go to Europe and return saying, "Oh, I didn't bring the right clothing, and that's why I didn't win." After investing time and money to go all the way to Europe, it only makes sense for singers to have some clothing alternatives.

As we mentioned above, in the finals of some competitions singers may have to compete in formal clothing. So, on top of the two alternative outfits, singers must also bring a formal outfit. In the opera world, formal dress is almost a uniform. When traveling, it is a good idea always to have formal clothes along even if they aren't necessary for competition, because one never knows when there might be a reception or a formal party. The opportunity may arise to meet an important person, and the hosts say, "Well, the reception is black tie." If the singer must say, "Oh, I didn't bring my formal dress/tuxedo." The singer cannot attend, or feels out of place.

REPERTOIRE

We mentioned above that, in a contest, the range of what one is offering has to be much wider than in an audition. Singers are not singing just to get a role, but rather to demonstrate the complete spectrum of what they can do as an artist.

For example, in audition situations there are companies that do mostly chamber opera because of their size, or because of their artistic sensibilities. There are companies that do only bread-and-butter operas like *La Bohème*, *La Traviata*, and *Madama Butterfly*. When auditioning for them wise singers know exactly what repertoire to present: the tried and true standards. In a competition, by contrast, the singer might want to do a bravura coloratura piece from a Handel opera. No opera company may ever do the opera in the singer's lifetime, but the singer will be showing off his or her most polished singing, and that's the point.

Oftentimes singers have a choice for the starting piece in a competition as well as in an audition. In choosing this piece, they must employ a reasonable strategy. For the first piece singers must always sing what they can sing best. The rest of the strategy—the other pieces the singers choose to present—are derived from research. What information does the grapevine provide? Who is out there? Are they orchestra conductors who are accustomed to doing symphonic works? In that case singers might do a Mozart concert aria instead of an opera piece. It makes sense to find out what the people that sang last season, or in last year's competition, sang. What was the trend? Is Puccini in vogue this year? Is this a provincial town with a provincial mentality, or is it a very sophisticated audience? For the former, singers might choose all Verdi arias, but for the latter something by Schoenberg or Luciano Berio.

Some of the same cautions about mixing extremes in repertoire are also to be observed in competitions. A soprano still should not offer Adele's laughing song from *Die Fledermaus* and an aria by Brünnhilde in the same competition. People still need to file the singer in their heads, and on their audition papers. It is good to be adventuresome in competitions—adding lesser known works— but not putting together jarringly disconsonant repertoire. A good exercise might be to imagine planning a short recital, choosing material with a view toward balance.

In a contest singers have one additional freedom—length. In an audition the singer wants to show a great deal in the shortest time possible, but in a contest if there are no limits posted in the forms, then the time, in most cases, is up to the singer. Thus a mezzo-soprano can sing all of "Non più mesta" (from *La Cenerentola*) if she wishes. In an audition she would likely never sing something that long, unless she cut it quite a bit.

There are many examples of excellent competition pieces that would never be used in auditions because of their length, or because of the difficulty of the accompaniment. King Philip's Aria, "Ella giammai m'amo" from *Don Carlos* is a good example. In an audition it is too long, but in a competition it might make a dramatic impact. In an audition if a soprano sings Marguerite from *Faust,* she should start with the Jewel Song. In a competition, she may want to start from the King of Thule section, and do the whole *scena,* because she wants to show everything she can do: sustained line, dramatic ability, and coloratura.

THE RÉSUMÉ

A résumé for a competition will be slightly different from one for an audition. For a competition, if singers have won several prizes, it is advantageous to list them first, instead of starting off by listing repertoire as they would for an audition. If the competition is "teacher-oriented," singers may also wish to list their vocal instructors and coaches. The National Association of Teachers of Singing (NATS) often organizes competitions, and the judges might want to know where the singer was trained; however, in most competitions this information is not necessary (in Barcelona, they might not know who the current voice teachers in the San Francisco Bay Area are). Listing information such as height, weight, and color of eyes usually is not important because the competition is not geared toward casting the singer to do a role.

Age limits are a feature (many would say, an unfortunate feature) of many contests. Singers certainly do not need to list age on a résumé, unless the competition asks for birth certificates to make sure that singers are not over some declared age limit. It is hard to justify age limits in most cases, but there are a few areas for which age limits do make some sense. One is when an audition or competition leads directly to a training program that is designed to work with inexperienced singers. In this case, the school or program may want to start training as early as possible to guide singers through a comprehensive course of study. If age limits are thus related to teaching, they may be understandable. It is usually easier to mold singers in their twenties than those in their fifties. Some companies and competitions also state, as part of their declaration of principles, that they are going to benefit young singers. If contests uphold principles stated clearly in the by-laws of the sponsoring organization, there is not much room to complain.

USING THE THIRD LINE
IN COMPETITIONS

Winning contests is a matter of presenting a total package in performance—a good voice, secure vocal technique, good diction, and intelligent expression. It is often the last factor—expression—that makes the difference between the contestants.

Intelligent third line analysis of contest arias, carefully rehearsed, can always make a difference in the way contest material is received. Contestants presenting a contest aria in a vacuous manner give the impression that they have no idea what the music or words are about—this is deadly in competition.

In addition, as we mentioned above, even though the purpose of a contest is not to cast singers in productions, most judges will still be viewing contestants with this idea in mind. Thus, if singers can create a complete interpretation for the judges, they have a definite advantage over other contestants.

Contests are, however, more like recitals in their mode of musical presentation. In constructing a third line interpretation for use in a contest, singers should emphasize musical expression (phrasing, use of fermatas, use of tempo variations, dynamics), textual interpretation (word stress, effective use of vowels and consonants), eye focus, and facial expression, and they should keep body gestures to a minimum. A few effective gestures may be enough in this context.

As with auditions, focusing on the third line in contest singing may well help singers vocally by taking their mind off problems of vocal technique. Performing the third line can certainly create a more natural, relaxed performance—one that will put contest judges at ease, and give the singer a decided edge over other contestants.

RECITALS

Recitals are an important chance for a singer to perform in front of an audience and to become comfortable presenting material in public. They are an excellent vehicle for professional exposure whether done on a small scale for a local audience, or in a large space such as Carnegie Hall. The advantage of a recital over other singing opportunities is that singers can be in total control of the process. They are producer, director, and performer. There is no need to audition for anyone to do a recital.

Organizing a recital is an exciting but challenging task. There have been several publications that attempt to lay out a strategy for programming and planning a recital. Among the best are *The Art of the Song Recital* by Shirlee Emmons and Stanley Sontag,[1] and *The Art of Accompanying and Coaching* by Kurt Adler.[2] As these books point out, a recital is more than just singing—it involves producing a whole entertainment event. Planning must include arranging a location, publicity, a rehearsal schedule, and a program for the recital. All of these factors are essential for a successful experience both for the performers and the audience. Occasionally a singer can find organizations that have a regular recital series within which the singer can be programmed. Churches in large cities often do this. Such a series is an ideal venue since many of the logistics of the recital may be handled by others, leaving the singer free to concentrate on the musical aspects of the event.

Traditionally, programming for recitals in Europe has always differed from that done in the United States. In Europe opera arias would not be presented in a recital with piano accompaniment. The logic is that art songs or lieder were written with piano accompaniments. Because opera arias were written with orchestral accompaniment and as part of a whole score, using a piano reduction of an orchestral accompaniment is therefore unacceptable. In the United States the practice has been much more flexible. Opera arias are freely used in recital with piano accompaniment, and this practice is beginning to be more acceptable in Europe as well.

Our feeling is that if the singer's goal is to be an opera singer, the recital should include operatic arias. The recital is a professional tool. A rather arbitrary set of conventions should not deter singers from presenting themselves in the way they believe will represent their talent the best. Of course, singers who particularly like lieder, oratorio, and other forms of music might wish to program the recital so that the first half is nonoperatic and the second half operatic. But every chance to perform and feel more comfortable with operatic material should be exploited. The recital could be a training ground to experience how the material runs for an audience. Then, when singers have to go to an audition or competition, the aria will already have been tested in front of others. Singers must remember that, if it is their goal to make a living as a singer, it is essential to sing in public as often as possible.

Nonetheless, singers must still plan a recital so that it has variety and color. A common formula is to have four sections to the program, moving from the oldest music to the newest, or from the most uncommon to the most popular, each section sung in the same language. A recital consisting of all the soprano arias from Puccini operas would be dull for all but the most diehard Puccini fans, no matter how well presented. Like a painting, the recital material should balance lively numbers with softer, more *legato* pieces; dramatic arias with songs of simple charm. Above all, the pieces presented should show the singer's vocal talents off to their fullest. In short, the program must make sense. Making sense means always asking: "For whom am I singing? What material represents me the best? Am I doing something varied enough? Do I have enough contrasts to make the program interesting? Will this enhance my performance of repertoire for auditions, competitions, and staged productions?"

In planning recitals, singers should know the importance of contrast. The ways to achieve contrast are infinite, however. For an all-opera recital, the first half could be all Mozart and the second part Verdi and Puccini. A whole recital might be based on German or French opera. Alternatively, the first half could be French, and the second half Italian. In other words, formats should be chosen that look clear and logical when the audience views the program. The last number, or an encore, might be something very popular or a real blockbuster, high and loud, to encourage the audience to applaud for another encore. Opera is 400 years old: from Jacopo Peri to Philip Glass. That entire world of music is at the singer's disposal in a recital. There is no reason to waste or neglect such an enormous variety of material.

Most of all, the recital must be entertaining. It is sad to note that the art of the recital is dying because recitals are usually boring. One person standing by a piano for an hour and a half can make for a deadly evening if the program is dull. We live in the age of special visual effects and rapidly changing musical experiences. A recital doesn't have to look like a rock concert, but there are ways to introduce variety. One way is by adding other instruments—a flute or violin. A friend can be asked to join the singer for a series of duets. One enterprising soprano in Boston commissioned a one-act opera for three singers and piano from a local composer. The only limit for a recital program is the singer's imagination.

Above all, the recital should be planned with a sense of enjoyment. It is not necessary for the audience to frown and get serious just because they are going to face a recital. The singer should do everything possible to help the audience feel comfortable and enjoy the recital. Sometimes wearing clothing closer to what the audience is wearing will do the trick. Sometimes planning music that will be more accessible to the audience or music that is guaranteed to make them laugh will lighten the mood. The program needn't consist of Ariadne's Lament followed by Dido's Lament followed by "Parto, Parto" from Mozart's *Titus*. The audience will be bored silly by such a program.

It helps all of the profession if more artists really try to make their recital and concert program fun. They should avoid fostering the attitude in the audience: "Here comes the Opera Singer! We are miles away, and there is a wall of ice between us, and our job is to wait here and look serious until the high note at the end of the second half of the program!" As long as singers make opera and the presentation of opera materials formidable, distant, foreboding, and things that only "certain" people can appreciate, they are doing themselves a disservice. They are closing down opportunities to the public, who are, in the end, the people who pay them. If singers always remember that a recital is supposed to be entertaining, that they are entertainers, and that they are trying to do themselves some good as well as make the audience happy, then they probably will always hit the right note in planning recitals.

THE THIRD LINE AND MUSICAL
PRACTICE IN THE RECITAL

Many people consider a voice recital to be a species of chamber music. They mistakenly think that this is therefore a different way of making music from the way they do it when on the opera stage. Singers should never think that in a vocal recital they are going to sing with a different voice, a different volume, a different mode of expression, or a different mentality from that on the stage. By getting into this frame of mind, singers will be detracting from their operatic efforts.

A healthier concept of vocal chamber music is to think of it as music created in intimate rapport with a pianist or other instruments without benefit of a conductor. Singers are not singing in spite of the pianist, or *despite* the pianist. It is essential to practice the pieces in the recital with the piano or instrumentalists just as if working with conductor and orchestra. The key is for all to play with each other to achieve a strong musical *ensemble*. In other words, the singer is not just a "star" who uses an accompanist in order to keep the pitch going.

We add, parenthetically, that one of the great benefits in doing recitals is for singers to fine-tune their sense of musical ensemble. Every time singers present themselves in music, and specifically in opera, they are making music *with* somebody else—with colleagues and conductor, or just with a pianist. Recital preparation, if done correctly, will help to develop good musical habits and attitudes.

Thus one can see that the term *accompanist* for a recital is a slight misnomer. He or she is a musical colleague, not a supporter. In preparation as well as in performance, singers must develop a close working rapport with their fellow musicians. This is not just an attitude. The rapport between singers and their co-musicians will be felt by anyone listening to the performance. If there are directors or conductors listening, they are going to sense this immediately, and they will extrapolate in their own minds the way the singer might work with a full orchestra under their baton.

Third line preparation emphasizes this musical rapport. Clear annotation of the score to emphasize the interplay between voice and accompaniment is part of performance. If this is built into both study and practice for the recital, it will show clearly to any audience.

THE THIRD LINE AND THE RECITAL
AS THEATER

Many singers think that all the things they have learned (and which we have discussed in this book) about dramatic presentation in opera disappear when it comes to a recital. The recitalist is seen somehow as able to deliver the program with a deadpan expression and no body movement. The image of the soprano clutching a dead bird once more springs to mind as a model for some singers—nothing could be further from the truth. As a recitalist the singer is an entertainer, as we have said before. He or she must deliver a visual/theatrical performance, regardless of how short the program, or how intimate the environment. For this reason the presentation must follow all the rules of theatrical expression (including third line analysis) even when the singer is just standing in the crook of the grand piano.

Since a recital is a full-blown entertainment from start to finish, singers and their co-performers must do the work of a director and conductor. Nothing should be left to chance. Everyone involved must be sure that they know what is going to happen at each step. A thousand questions must be addressed: What will the musician(s) wear? Who enters first? Who bows first? Who bows second? When do the musicians bow together? Who exits first? Who acknowledges whom? How many times do the musicians acknowledge each other, and how many times will they smile at each other? Does the singer turn inward toward the piano when the piano has an interlude, or face the audience? All of this is part of the choreography of the recital. It *must* be planned. If these aspects of the performance are not prepared, the ragged quality of the event will speak ill of all the performers.

Often we think of a recital as something that doesn't have much in the way of visual form. This is a great mistake. A recital is a theatrical event with a very sparse structure, and that makes it quite difficult to stage. The performers, their instruments, and their clothing are the only things the audience has to look at. There is no lighting, there is no scenery, there are no props. The performers are *it*. Because of this, singers will be in trouble if they spend all their energy worrying about hitting high notes and fail to give these other elements proper consideration. Finally, almost everyone will schedule a dress rehearsal for a recital, but oftentimes the details of presentation and staging are not worked out until that very moment, if ever. Ideally, one should have two or more rehearsals in the recital hall to do this work.

Because there is so little to look at, clothing takes on great importance in recitals. Clothing should be coordinated with the program. Again, many questions must be addressed by the singer: "What am I wearing? What are the other musicians wearing? Are we going to change clothes in the intermission? Why are we going to change? Why *aren't* we going to change? Shall we rent lights? Should the lights change from piece to piece? Should we use props (a fan, a flower, a champagne glass, a chair)?"

Clothing can do a lot to enhance the music in a recital. If the recital consists of a single long song cycle, a singer might want to wear one outfit. However, if the first half of the recital is dedicated to lieder and the second to opera, it might be effective to change, not only because it is good to create as much variation as possible, but also because a different visual image emphasizes the characteristics of the different music. As with all questions of clothing, this primarily applies to women. Few men change their outfits during a recital. Changing from a black tuxedo to a white one in a classical recital is not very common, but changing ties to match the mood of a lighter section of the performance might work very well. Loosening a tie to tackle Porgy or taking a jacket off to sing Ralph Vaughan Williams' *Songs of Travel* might be something to consider.

Singers need to be sure of their taste in clothing, particularly when producing their own musical events. One might be an excellent singer without having a well-developed sense of visual presentation. When performing in an opera, the director and costume designer will tell singers what to wear. When in a recital, singers may need advice on clothing if they don't feel confident about their own sense of style. Even when singers do feel equipped, it is a small thing to get a second opinion from a knowledgeable costumer. Singers should ask someone who has an idea of what should be worn for a particular program, at a particular time of the year, or in a particular city. All these elements count. Singers don't want to look out of place by overdressing or underdressing. Dressing well will always enhance their professional image. The recital is also a place where singers can look wonderful even if their figure is not perfect. Beautiful flowing gowns in rich fabrics can make any woman look glamorous. Well-fitting formal wear can make any man look handsome.

Finally, singers should remember that they are also actors when presenting their songs. Here they can make full use of third line analysis. Singers will not use the whole stage in a recital, and gestures will be much more limited than they would be in a full performance, but facial expressions should reflect the music in a deep and profound manner. Eye focus should paint a picture for the audience, and vocal coloring and shading should be every bit as rich and full as on the stage—perhaps even more so. The techniques developed in writing the third line in the score should be used fully in presenting recital material.

One way to create a clearer dramatic context for the music on a recital is to introduce songs with a short explanation, some humor, or an anecdote. A singer's speaking voice is a welcome relief on a musical program. Such introductions will help break the ice. It will give the audience some sense of the singer as a human being, and will increase the intimacy of the event.

To end this discussion, we emphasize that all singers have to create their own opportunities to sing—by auditioning for performances for which they will be cast, by entering contests, and by giving vocal recitals and appearing in concert. Singers cannot limit their career training to the voice studio. It is essential to sing under real-life conditions in order to learn how to sing, and in order to know how it feels to sing in front of audiences. By going to auditions and competitions, singers are participating in events that have been organized specifically for singers. By giving recitals, singers are organizing their own singing opportunities. The best advice for all singers is to sing, sing, sing, whenever possible; to expose themselves; train—and get out there and do it. That's the key.

NOTES

1. Shirlee Emmons and Stanley Sontag, *The Art of the Song Recital* (New York: Schirmer Books, 1979).

2. Kurt Adler, *The Art of Accompanying and Coaching* (Minneapolis: Da Capo Press, 1965).

CHAPTER 13

———— 🐚 ————

Expanding the Third Line: Opera as an Art Form

By way of review, it is important for all opera performers to understand that opera is a total art form in which the creation of sounds and the creation of images combine to establish a total experience for the audience.

Opera as a word doesn't mean much of anything. It comes directly from the word *opus* which can be translated as "work." The vague definition of the word tells us a great deal about the difficulties of pinning down exact definitions, but it is also an encouragement not to adopt a strict, fixed definition. We believe that leaving the definition of opera open is a very healthy attitude. As soon as people begin to emphasize any single fixed notion of performing opera, they are doing a great disservice to the *art* of opera.

Art is revolutionary. It challenges the observer to reexamine his or her own perceptions. It should not be comfortable or invite complacency. Unfortunately, that is precisely what has taken place in much of the operatic world today. No composer ever thought of his operas as works that would be preserved under glass like some precious porcelain. Even in their own lifetimes, composers modified and changed their operas to fit different tastes, political realities, and production problems. As artists, these composers knew that rigidity in creation and performance was the kiss of death for their creativity.

Artists create to express, not necessarily to please. Da Ponte and Mozart taunted the establishment of their day with sexual violence *(Don Giovanni)*, social revolution *(Le Nozze di Figaro)*, and unconventional marital philosophies *(Così fan tutte)*. Verdi and his librettists dealt with kept women *(La Traviata)* and ruling class rape *(Rigoletto)*. Still there is a tendency today to look at these works of art as "pleasing"-sound-making-recital-with-costume-"let's not make waves" affairs.

For the opera singer, art begins with the one little word "curtain." When the curtain goes up, there the singer is—exposed to the audience. Maybe the singer will not have to sing for several minutes. Maybe he or she will sing all sorts of things—recitative, ensemble numbers, little one-word snippets—which seem to have nothing to do with what most performers consider real singing. But there is no mistake about it. When the curtain goes up, all the singers on stage are performing opera. Therefore they must be ready to present themselves as the embodiment of their characters with all the insight they can muster—incorporating the historical and cultural sources, filtered and fixed in the opera score by the creators. The characterization then must be expressed and communicated through a solid, convincing, involved third line by the singers—the ultimate interpreters.

Singers who believe that there is only one correct way to effect that portrayal—through vocalism—will fail as artists in opera. The enactment of the characters they portray must be at the highest theatrical level, and it must be uniquely their own. This means that both vocal artistry and enactment must be personalized. Each singer must find a way to do this through study, through personal experience, and through developing sensitivity to the production, to fellow performers, and to the artistic staff and their desires. Moreover, singers must feel free enough to change and modify their performance each time it is done, through growth and professional maturation.

Today's performers are somewhat cursed by the ready availability of video and sound recordings. These create a false sense of a definitive performance. Sound recordings—even "live" ones—are not "real." They are engineered productions in which every imaginable electronic enhancement is used. Mistakes are erased, patches of rerecorded material are spliced in, weak voices are pumped up, and dynamic levels are modified.

Videotapes of live performances are more honest—but likewise far from definitive. They show close-up scenes which are never viewed by the audience, and musical balance between voice and orchestra which may be far from that heard in the opera house. They do have one great virtue for the singer, however. From them a singer can see readily how many glitches and errors occur in live performance—and also how little these small mistakes matter in the performance of a master artist.

To be an artist a singer must be able to perform great works, and in doing so must be able to add a personal touch—to interpret, to innovate, and to be comfortable tackling the work at the level of artistic distinction that it merits. There can be no room for narrowness or insecurity. However, innovation does not come out of thin air. One must know a great deal to be able to innovate. It is essential to be conscious of past traditions in order to build a base—a background for the singer's own particular contribution. One cannot *re-create* a score without understanding the original process of creation. The singer must come to understand what the original creators of the works wanted artists to present onstage, and this understanding is gained through intelligent research and regular exercise of performance skills. All singers must also be creators, but, to enter the realm of the creators, they must acquire enough knowledge to become humble. The most arrogant performers are often those who doubt or fail to understand the artistic or historical foundations of their art.

This is where the third line enters the creative process. In learning to create the third line, singers learn to analyze the intent of the composer and the librettist, and discover the opportunities they have provided for interpretation and innovation. The writing of the third line leads to a clear understanding of the implied stage directions the composer and librettist created through their particular setting of words and music. The rest is up to the singer—how those intentions are interpreted and how well the implied stage directions are executed is a matter of skill, training, and creativity. However, as we have reminded all readers several times, when fighting the composer and the librettist, the composer and librettist will always win and the singer will always lose.

In this book we have made much of the fact that opera performers must be actors as well as singers. There used to be a distinction in the theater between actors who sang and singers who acted. The tradition may have been started by W. S. Gilbert who, for his comic operas written with Arthur Sullivan, insisted on having actors who could sing. The distinction is less and less pronounced today. The musical theater of today requires thoroughly trained voices. Opera requires excellent actors. Without both singing and acting talent, today's operatic performances will not meet modern standards.

We believe that opera performers must tell themselves from the outset: "I am a performer who sings, and I must be flexible enough to tackle a very wide repertoire of music and acting which will at times require me to go further in musical realization, and at other times further in acting." This is what we like to call a *performing spirit*. It is a very healthy attitude to develop.

A singer equipped with a performing spirit, who trains accordingly, will be able to do anything required onstage. In performing a Gilbert and Sullivan opera, such a singer will research and understand the requirements of the form and emphasize the acting. Since the singing requirements in this repertoire are not so demanding, the singer might be willing to take a few liberties in vocal execution for comic effect.

On the other hand, with the performing spirit, the same singer will be able to attend closely to the vocal aspects of the performance when doing a relatively demanding, but (usually, although not always) static role, such as the Queen of the Night in *Die Zauberflöte*. In the *bel canto* repertoire, stage action might be greatly reduced, since the story line is basically secondary to the singing. Even here, however, with the performing spirit to serve as a guide, singers may be able to discover their own techniques for making singing visually radiant, and a static expression still can be expressively successful.

As singers' careers progress, they may decide to specialize in one particular area of opera or musical theater. It is wise to remember, however, that the more one specializes, the more career possibilities are narrowed. A fine actor with an underdeveloped voice must be certain that there will be companies where he or she can be employed with some regularity before committing to a career in this business. Similarly, a nonacting singer had better ascertain that there are sufficient employment opportunities for someone without believable acting skills. Such a person should not try to do Violetta in *La Traviata,* for example, no matter how spectacular her coloratura singing, unless she can make her a totally believable character on stage.

PRACTICAL REALITIES

To develop a career as an artist, every singer must perform. It is one of the realities of opera that training is very long and very expensive. Once the singer is ready, the market is very narrow. Even though the number of regional opera companies in the United States is growing fast, the number of singers fighting for jobs is also growing very fast. Moreover, the regional opera companies may have only three or four productions a year. This will not provide anyone with year-round employment.

Thus singers must face from the outset the reality that they must have a solid economic base to fall back on to support developing a career. It is essential to have another source of income that will not distract from preparation as a singer. This may be a flexible job, or a spouse, parent, or sponsor. In any case an independent income is almost a requirement for developing a career.

This brings us to a parenthetical issue. There are all sorts of possibilities to make money in the field of opera, even if one is not singing extensively. The important principle is for singers to learn while they earn. Given the option of being a stage manager or being a waitress, singers should think twice before rejecting the stage manager position. It is a wonderful way for singers to meet people, keep their name before them, and learn the repertory.

If eventually singers can reach a plateau where they are making enough from singing to be content, this is a very fortunate state of affairs—as much the result of luck and patience as hard work. No one should ever get the idea that this comes automatically—it is the exception rather than the rule. Singers who do reach this point in their careers realize that they had to endure a number of very frustrating years until they reached this place. The profession is cruel and deceptive. One year it is possible to make enough from singing not to have to worry about economic problems. The next year, there may be a severe drop in income for no discernible reason.

Many singers have the idea that they can go to Europe if they cannot make a career for themselves in the United States. This opportunity—particularly in Germany—was greater in years past than today. It is still true that if they are the right singers, in the right place, at the right time, they will get hired. However, obtaining employment in German-speaking countries today is not particularly easy. Auditioning and waiting for results is at least a six-month process, and singers must be in residence in Europe the entire time. Prospective singers' German language skills should be excellent, and they should be able to exhibit considerable polish in their performing skills.

The largest obstacle to obtaining employment in Germany is the change in the supply of singers to fill available positions. Germany is becoming more and more self-sufficient in terms of singers. For political reasons German opera houses have had to open their doors to a flood of Eastern European singers, many of whom have been trained for years at state expense. This has paradoxically opened a small door in Eastern Europe for American singers to fill positions of Eastern singers who have left for the West, but it is not clear how long this state of affairs will last. (For those who do wish to pursue this course, we have recommended several good manuals on auditioning in Germany in the notes for Chapter 11.)

As an alternative to running off to Europe, singers should learn from the other performing arts where artists regularly organize themselves to perform when opportunities are scarce. They create co-ops or chamber groups, rent a hall, get sponsors, hire a pianist, or get together with a small instrumental ensemble and perform, experiment, and get experience, exposure, and self-confidence. Sometimes their efforts take off and create whole careers for them. Opera singers can also create their own possibilities and perform for the love of it rather than sitting around waiting for the doors of La Scala to open!

We have said all of these discouraging things to convince all singers reading this book of one basic fact: those singers who succeed in developing a career in opera are those who make sure that they are thoroughly prepared, complete performers, not just vocalists. Moreover, they are willing to make things happen for themselves rather than waiting for things to happen to them. Singers with these tools have a fighting chance of joining the limited group of artists that make their entire living as opera performers.

Singers cannot indulge themselves by thinking. "As long as I have impeccable high notes, I will be able to get the conductor to protect me from stage directors who want me to sing in strange positions." Neither should singers approach the issue thinking that because they are good actors, the director will serve as a shield from attacks by the conductor who cannot tolerate lapses in musicianship. Fighting one's way like this through a career is no fun. A far better attitude would be: "I'm so well equipped that it will be difficult for anybody to reject me or fault my performance."

Rehearsals can be hellish with performers who have gaps in their preparation. Instead of the cooperative, pleasant experience that they might be, they turn into battles full of fighting and trickery, as ill-prepared performers try to avoid the tasks they are given onstage. Nobody wants to reengage a person who will bring problems to the rehearsal process. At some point the general manager will say: "What can I do with this great voice if I have to play referee at every rehearsal? Instead of rehearsing, this artist is wasting valuable production time fighting with the director and the conductor, alienating his/her colleagues, or frustrating the costume designer."

In the opera world of today, aspiring singers should never model themselves on those few singers who became famous despite the fact that their product is not well rounded, and who manage to cover their deficiencies by throwing tantrums every time they face a challenging situation. An artist in today's opera world must be ready and available to work. Those singers who do become international stars can do as they like, but, even at this level, a reputation for flexibility and a cooperative performing spirit will never go unnoticed. Even though a performer's first task is to make the audience happy, all singers will find that cultivating a true performing spirit will make them happy too!

It is the total package that singers are able to present which will make them a marketable product. The voice is only one part of that package. Musicality and training in languages and style is another part. Acting ability and appearance on stage are yet another part. Finally, a reputation for preparedness and cooperativeness round out the entire package. It is also true that the marketable product of yesterday might not be a marketable product tomorrow. Opera is changing very quickly, and singers must be prepared so that they will always have something to offer, independent of current trends or fads. There is fierce competition as well. There are always good performers emerging to challenge the existing market.

It is amazing how few singers inform themselves about trends emerging in the business of opera. This is, we believe, still part of the ethic whereby singers train in a cloistered manner: seven years in the voice studio, seven weeks learning music theory and other musical matters, seven days learning acting technique, and seven minutes learning about the business of the profession.

In any other business, people buy trade publications, go to conventions, and keep a strong network in order to discover what is new in their field. Singers may glance at *Opera News* to see who is doing well, but that is about the extent of their "market research." *Opera News* is, moreover, somewhat deceiving because it reports mostly images of the past. It continues to promote the cult of the individual and rarely criticizes the museumlike approaches to opera that are only a thin slice of the reality of today's opera world. After all, *Opera News* is published by the Metropolitan Opera, one of the great musical museums in the world today.

In order to discover trends in the field today, it is an excellent idea to attend conventions like those sponsored by Opera America. In attending these conventions, singers can find out who is winning competitions, why certain people are being engaged for roles and others are not, and what production trends are favored for coming years. It is also possible to meet a large number of people in the profession who may be able to provide professional help. All of this will help singers become aware of the directions they should take in their careers, and allow them to develop a set of positive steps for improving their professional standing. This is certainly better than continually feeling that one is somehow always a "victim" of the system who doesn't get cast because directors don't like short legs, or dark hair, or because the company was bad, or because it only hires its favorites.

WHAT CAN YOU OFFER OPERA?

We hope that all singers reading this book love opera enough to dedicate themselves to serving the art form even if they do not become international stars. We hope that they prepare themselves so completely in all aspects of the profession that even when they retire they may continue making their living with opera as directors, teachers of singers, coaches, producers, chorus masters, stage managers, prompters, or in some other work that will preserve their contact with the art. We hope we have convinced singers that not all artists in the profession are singers. If singers have the performing spirit, no artistic role will be too small for them.

Regional opera houses are giving more and more employment opportunities for artists in all aspects of opera. This is a very encouraging state of affairs. Singers can be very happy forging a career at the regional level where opportunities to do challenging roles will be greater than on the international scene. Opera will not provide many opportunities unless singers do something themselves. Getting involved is essential. Singers with the worst feelings about themselves and the profession are those who sit and wait passively until something happens in their community, and then complain if they are not chosen for a role.

Our advice to such people is simple: Start your own activity. Start reading scores with pianists. Organize people who also like to do this, then find a place to perform. Approach sponsors, publicize your efforts, and make sure that the community responds. Singers may be surprised at what happens if they take this active approach. It is their life, and they are the ones most likely to make something good happen for their career. More than one opera company has been started by a singer who wanted a chance to sing.

REVOLUTIONIZE, WITH NO APOLOGIES!

We hope that some readers do become impresarios! The world will be richer for it. But they should remember some of the other lessons of this book. If they produce works that attempt to replicate opera of 40 years ago, their chances of furthering the progress of opera as an art form are slim. The only way for a company to survive is to sell tickets, and to do this opera must respond to the needs and the sophistication of contemporary audiences, keeping one eye on the audiences of tomorrow as well.

Opera composers, producers, and directors have always had their eye out for public taste. Verdi is an example. He had to fight with the censors all of his life. Why? Because his operas were so close to daily life. The politicians, the church, the social lions, the tastemakers of the day—all were touched by his work. He was not only the composer but also the conductor, producer, and director. He knew what audiences wanted, and how to deliver it to them. Opera fans know this, and still they think of his and other operatic works as precious works hermetically sealed under glass—isolated from the real world.

The directors of today who are challenging opera are criticized for their "radical" theatrical vision. In theatrical terms, in fact, their visions are actually not very radical at all. It is opera's extreme conservatism that makes them seem so. No matter how controversial they are, these directors have been willing to take artistic risks, and for this they should be highly praised. The other extreme is taxidermy, not creativity. Singers must be willing to take some risks as well. The performing spirit should make aspiring performers willing to be less conservative in their approach. Any director will pull singers back if they go too far, but few singers ever go far enough! Unfortunately, most singers are continually getting the message that, unless they are able to deliver a perfect vocal product at every turn, they mustn't sing at all. This stifles artistry.

The artistic conflict was summed up nicely by Wagner in *Die Meistersinger.* It is the conflict between the pedant, Beckmesser and the free-spirited Walther von Stoltzing. Beckmesser sits behind his curtain and ticks off every mistake that Walther makes as he sings. But Walther sings what he feels in his heart with no inhibitions. He sings what he feels is *right*. He triumphs artistically while Beckmesser slinks off.

In the end, what is needed may not be a revolution in opera, but at least an "evolution" in the profession. We have alluded several times to the fact that opera is the laughingstock of the other arts. Whenever singers speak of opera, they must apologize or make excuses. They are always saying things like, "Yes, I know opera is boring, unnatural, dated and affected, but what I do is different—really, it is!" By this time, no one believes them.

Singers must show the public that things really are changing. *Le Nozze di Figaro* is really fun if singers will let it be fun, and not a four-hour recital in eighteenth-century dress! Figaro, Susanna, the count, Marcellina, and Bartolo are enormously amusing characters. Singers want the audience to laugh and cry with them, and not say to itself: "Why are they standing there? Why are their arms open like an airplane about to land? Why are they looking at the conductor and not at each other during the ensembles?" This kills opera and forces justifications that shouldn't be required for an art that stands on its own merits.

Singers will succeed in making opera an artistically successful art form if they remember that they are performing for an audience, and that they must *communicate* with it at all costs. If singers feel comfortable onstage and with themselves, and are willing to give as much weight to acting as to singing without feeling guilty, this may come to pass. If singers are capable of expressing, of interpreting, or creating a theatrical event, they will succeed.

So often singers will consider their whole performance a failure if they miss one note. This is sad. Indeed there will probably be a few people in the audience who will make this a topic of conversation over a drink after the show.

But the singers for whom a small technical failure will become a tragedy are the singers who give nothing else to the performance beyond technical vocalism! If a singer does nothing but stand and sing, there is little else for the audience to comment on! If those same singers would act and perform, the audience, rather than saying "Oh, well, s/he messed up!" will exclaim, "Oh it was so engaging—such an experience. I think s/he messed up a note somewhere, but what a performer!"

In closing, let us say that the reason for going on at length about the need for change in artistic attitudes in opera is that performing conditions really are changing for the better. Singers are more concerned with artistic intent these days than with notes. They realize that composers were trying to affect audiences with emotions and expressions through music. They are seeing what the composer as dramatist wants of his artists. Composers never wanted singers to just stand onstage with a static expression on their faces, giving out a stunning vocal line with no emotional or artistic reflection on the composers' intent. They wanted artists who could interpret their work fully.

All singers have the possibility to become the kind of total artistic interpreters who can do justice to the music and the emotions of opera. They only have to train well, do adequate research, study the scores, formulate the third line for everything to be sung, develop the proper performing spirit, and have the courage to use full expression in reaching the audience. When singers do all of this with their whole being, they will discover the core of truth in performing: artistry is not something granted by the gods to a few fortunate souls—it is the natural outcome of attitudes and habits coupled with hard work and dedication, enthusiastically pursued.

APPENDIX

——————— ❧ ———————

Resources for Opera:
An Annotated Bibliography

The following is an annotated list of books, directories, and periodicals that readers may find useful as a starting point in understanding the inner structure of opera, in writing the third line, and in the development of a life and career as an interpreter of operatic material. We have generally excluded textbooks and writings on specific composers, librettists, operas, and singers.

BOOKS

Adler, Kurt, *The Art of Accompanying and Coaching* (Minneapolis: Da Capo Press, 1976). [Reprint of University of Minnesota Press edition originally published in 1965.]

> Adler's fine book on accompanying and coaching might be overlooked by singers, but it should be carefully studied. It provides invaluable advice on interpretation, diction, and recital programming.

Alexander, Fredrick Mathias, *The Resurrection of the Body,* edited by E. Maisel (New York: Dell, 1971).

> The Alexander technique explained in Alexander's own words.

Balk, Wesley, *Performing Power* (Minneapolis: University of Minnesota Press, 1985).

Balk, Wesley, *The Complete Singer Actor, 2nd edition* (Minneapolis: University of Minnesota Press, 1985).

Balk, Wesley, *The Radiant Performer* (Minneapolis: University of Minnesota Press, 1991).
> Wesley Balk's fine books have helped numerous singers develop their capacity to act, move, and realize their potential as performers. These books are manuals for exercising and expanding the capacities of singer/actors without reference to specific musical literature. Balk's holistic approach to singing and performing promotes total mental well-being and a positive self-image.

Barlow, Wilfred, *The Alexander Technique* (New York: Random House, 1973).
> A classic work explaining the Alexander technique for overall body balance useful to singers. See also Alexander's own writings on this, and also Frank P. Jones' study of the Alexander technique elsewhere in this bibliography.

Craig, David, *On Performing* (New York: McGraw-Hill, 1987).

Craig, David, *On Singing Onstage* (New York: Schirmer Books, 1978).
> Although David Craig's books are geared for popular singers and musical theater, they offer wonderful insights for classical singers as well. They instruct the singer step by step how to "sell" a song in audition and in public performance, through understanding the structure of the music and through complete dramatic analysis of the music and textual material.

Dornemann, Joan, with Maria Ciaccia, *Complete Preparation: A Guide to Auditioning for Opera* (New York: Excalibur Publications, 1992).
> Joan Dornemann is one of the world's best known operatic coaches. This book, drawn from her lectures, gives invaluable advice on preparation for auditioning, from musical preparation to clothing and mental attitude. It is an empowering book that will help all singers gain a strong sense of their own self-worth.

Emmons, Shirlee, and Stanley Sontag, *The Art of the Song Recital* (New York: Schirmer Books, 1979.
> This is the classic work on preparation for recitals. It takes the reader step by step through every phase of preparation. It should be in the library of every serious singer.

Finchley, Joan, *Audition* (New York: Prentice-Hall, 1984).
> A useful work aimed at auditioners for the spoken stage, but with ex-cellent insights about the dynamics of auditioning for anyone in the entertainment business.

Goldovsky, Boris, *Bringing Opera to Life* (New York: Appleton, Century, Crofts, 1968).

Goldovsky, Boris, *Bringing Soprano Arias to Life* (Metuchen: Scarecrow, 1991).
> Goldovsky's excellent books are highly recommended, and are close in spirit to *The Third Line*. These books emphasize interpretation and pro-vide many musical examples.

Green, Barry, and W. Timothy Gallwey, *The Inner Game of Music* (New York: Anchor Doubleday, 1986).
> Barry Green has adapted the techniques of sports coach Timothy Gall-wey to the music world. This book emphasizes creative visualization as a means to reducing tension in performance and complete empower-ment of the artist.

Hamilton, David, *The Metropolitan Opera Encyclopedia: A Comprehensive Guide to the World of Opera* (New York: Simon and Schuster, 1987).
> A fine compendium of material on operas, composers, librettists, sing-ers, opera houses, and cities where opera is performed, arranged ency-clopedically.

Highstein, Ellen, *Making Music in Looking Glass Land—A Guide to Survival and Business Skills for the Classical Performer* (New York: Concert Artists Guild, 1992).
> This excellent book deals extensively with the business of music. It pro-vides practical advice on self-promotion, management, programming, networking skills, financial dealings, and hundreds of other practical aspects of making a living in music.

Hines, Jerome, *Great Singers on Great Singing* (New York: Limelight Editions, 1987).
> Jerome Hines, the renowned basso, interviews forty famous singers on the subject of singing. Singers recount their training, their best vocal exercises, and techniques that help them through difficult literature. There is a great vocal wisdom in this volume for every singer.

Jacobi, Henri N., *Building Your Best Voice* (New York: Prentice-Hall, 1982).
> A sensible and sage approach to vocal development by a prominent teacher.

Jones, Frank P., *Body Awareness in Action: A Study of the Alexander Technique*
(New York: Shocken Books, 1976).
> An enlightening study of the Alexander technique as it is used to retrain
> body alignment. Of great potential use for every singer.

Kagen, Sergius, *On Studying Singing* (New York: Dover, 1960).
> A master teacher dispenses straight talk on vocal instruction. A realistic
> introduction to what one should expect in a course of adequate voice
> training.

Kerman, Joseph, *Opera as Drama* (Berkeley: University of California Press,
1988).
> The classic work on the interrelation of music, text, and narrative story
> in opera written by the dean of American opera scholars.

Kobbé, Gustave, *Complete Opera Book,* edited and revised by the Earl of Hare-
wood, ninth edition (New York: Bodley Head, Putnam, 1976).
> One of the best known general introductions to specific operas in stan-
> dard repertoire.

Lindenberger, Herbert, *Opera, The Extravagant Art* (Ithaca, NY: Cornell University Press, 1984).
> Herbert Lindenberger's insightful book seeks to define opera as a spe-
> cific aesthetic form. It stresses the integrity of the internal construction
> of words, music, and narrative structure. This work will be useful for
> any artist seeking to understand how opera relates to the other perform-
> ing arts.

Kivy, Peter, *Osmin's Rage* (New Brunswick, NJ: Rutgers University Press,
1989).
> A fascinating treatise on the development of the philosophy of expres-
> sion in music, from the enlightenment to the present. Although it is
> academic in tone, it is bound to fascinate anyone concerned with ques-
> tions of how music engages its audience.

Kloiber, Rudolf, *Handbuch der Oper* (2 volumes) (Kassel and Munich: Bären-
reiter Verlag and Deutscher Taschenbuch, 1985).
> This is the "Bible" of opera production in Germany. It contains all in-
> formation pertaining to the Fach system, and in fact has legal standing
> for employment of opera singers in Germany.

Lear, Evelyn, ed., *Selections from der Rosenkavalier: A Master Class with Evelyn
Lear* (New York: G. Schirmer, 1989).
> This selection of scenes from Strauss's *Der Rosenkavalier* has been an-
> notated by Miss Lear in "third line" fashion. The suggestions for inter-

pretation are excellent, taking into account music and text. Whether singers are interested in performing this opera or not, this volume is an excellent example of how to write interpretive directions into the score.

Martin, George, *The Opera Companion: A Guide for the Casual Operagoer* (New York: Dodd, 1979).

Martin, George, *The Companion to Twentieth Century Opera* (London: John Murray, 1989).

> Martin's compendia of plots, characters, and commentary on operas are useful starting points for investigating any opera one is interested in performing. The second volume has a series of extremely interesting lists of repertoire for the world's major opera houses dating back to before 1800.

McClosky, David Blair, and Barbara H. McClosky, *Voice in Song and Speech* (Boston: Boston Music Company, 1975).

McClosky, David Blair, *Your Voice at its Best* (Boston: The Boston Music Company, 1972).

> These two books deal with basic techniques for healthy, tension-free singing as expounded by the McClosky Institute in Boston. McClosky, before his death, was one of the best-known teachers of vocal therapy in America.

Mezzanote, Riccardo, ed., *The Simon and Schuster Book of the Opera* (New York: Simon and Schuster, 1977).

> An extremely useful one-volume compendium of summaries of operas with information on composers and librettists arranged chronologically.

Miller, Richard, *The Structure of Singing: System and Art in Vocal Technique* (New York: Schirmer Books, 1986).

> For singers interested in technical aspects of singing emphasizing acoustics and physiology, Miller's book is a vast storehouse of information. Drawing on the earlier work of Vennard, Garcia, and other classic vocal instructors, Miller provides not only explanations but also exercises to help singers maximize the efficiency of their vocal instrument.

Mordden, Ethan, *Opera Anecdotes* (Oxford: Oxford University Press, 1985).

> Every opera singer needs a supply of good stories about opera, and this amusing book is one of the best collections.

Owens, Richard, *Towards a Career in Europe* (Dallas, TX: American Institute of
Musical Studies, 1983).
> Although Owens book is somewhat out of date, it still contains invalu-
> able advice about auditioning in Germany. It comes with an updated
> list of names and addresses of agents.

Papolos, Janice, *The Performing Artist's Handbook* (New York: Writer's Digest
Books, 1984).
> Papolos's book, now unhappily out of print, is one of the best manuals
> on business aspects of performing. Papolos's background is as a classical
> singer, and this book has a great deal of information specifically for
> vocal artists. She provides a considerable amount of practical advice on
> self-promotion and getting and keeping work.

Posey, Kenneth, *A Singer's Guide to Auditioning in Unified Germany* (San Angelo, TX: Singer's Guide, 1990).
> Another fine practical guide to auditioning in Germany by a singer who
> has done the tour.

Ristad, Eloise, *A Soprano on Her Head* (Moab, Utah: Real People Press, 1982).
> This now classic work provides invaluable advice on how to get "un-
> stuck" from unproductive musical habits by adopting radically different
> attitudes and perspectives on performance.

Robinson, Paul, *Opera and Ideas from Mozart to Strauss* (Ithaca, NY: Cornell
University Press, 1986).
> An invaluable book for understanding the background and intellectual
> context of operatic literature.

Sadie, Stanley, ed., *The New Grove Dictionary of Music and Musicians* (Washington: Grove's Dictionaries of Music, 1980).
> Grove's is the primary reference work for music. Every serious musician
> should be intimately familiar with this multi-volume work as well as the
> earlier 1959 edition. It is perhaps too expensive for many individuals
> to own, but is available in most libraries.

Shurtleff, Michael, *Audition* (New York: Bantam, 1978).
> Another superb book on the audition process in the spoken theater by
> an expert.

Silver, Fred, *Auditioning for the Musical Theater* (New York: Viking Penguin,
1988).
> One of the finest books on auditioning for the musical theater ever
> written. Silver provides a set of techniques for analyzing music and text
> line-by-line for interpretation in performance, which is certain to enable

anyone to become more powerful in their presentation in audition or on stage.

Smith, Patrick, *A Year at the Met* (New York: Alfred Knopf, 1983).
Patrick Smith takes the reader on a month-by-month tour of the Metropolitan Opera season. Smith, now editor of *Opera News,* gives an unusually comprehensive view of the way all elements of opera production interrelate. This book is a wonderful antidote to the usual singer-centered view of the opera world.

Stapp, Marcie, *The Singer's Guide to Languages* (San Francisco: Teddy's Music Press, 1991).
This is one of the most useful books a singer can own. Although it must currently be obtained by mail, it is worth the effort. Well-known coach Marcie Stapp has provided a wealth of information about the four major languages of singing: Italian, German, French, and English, in one volume. Here the singer will find advice about singing diction, grammar, and strategies for translation. Her observations on diction, particularly comparative vowel sounds in different languages, are highly comprehensive. Stapp also provides such helpful information as exhaustive lists of irregular stems and verb endings for the languages covered—guaranteed to help a singer crack the most difficult translation problems.

Sullivan, Gail, and Dorothy Maddison, *Kein angst Baby!—A Guide to German Auditions in the 1990's* (Burtonsville, MD: privately published, 1991).
Gail Sullivan and Dorothy Maddison make auditioning in Germany sound easy. The useful Fach lists and suggestions for repertoire will be of help to any singer.

Summers-Dossena, Ann, *Getting it All Together: A Handbook for Performing Artists in Classical Music and Ballet, New Edition* (Oakville, Ontario, Canada: Mosaic Press, 1992).
Ms. Summers-Dossena is an artist manager, and her book on succeeding in the music business is very useful. Because of her background, the extensive coverage of management and its functions is of particular use.

DIRECTORIES

Deutsches Bühnen-Jahrbuch (Hamburg: Deutscher Bühnen-Jahrbuch)
This is the equivalent of *Musical America* for Germany. Since eighty percent of all opera is produced in German-speaking nations, this reference work may be of real use to those contemplating careers in Europe.

Musical America—International Directory of the Performing Arts (New York: K-III Communications).

> *Musical America* is the most complete guide to the classical music business in North America. Opera companies, orchestras, festivals, contests, instrumentalists, and singers are all listed. It is very expensive, but is available at most libraries. Every singer should have access to this invaluable directory.

Opera America, *Career Guide for Singers* (Washington, DC: Opera America).

> This directory lists all of the opera companies affiliated with Opera America, along with their hiring policies and information on obtaining auditions. Apprentice and internship programs are also listed along with major contests. This is an essential guide for every singer interested in developing a career.

Opera America Season Schedule of Performances (Washington, DC: Opera America).

> Published annually, this lists the productions and performance dates for all companies affiliated with Opera America. With this guide singers can assess the repertoire of different companies, the length and dates of their seasons, and likely times to request auditions.

PERIODICALS

Back Stage (New York: Back Stage).

> Although geared to the spoken stage, musical comedy, cabaret, dance, film, and commercials, *Back Stage,* published weekly, is the most widely read publication for the live performance industry. Each issue is full of audition opportunities, some of which may be of real interest to opera singers. Additionally, *Back Stage* contains advertising for training, photographers, recording engineers, and business services for entertainers. The publication is a vigorous campaigner for the rights of performers.

The New York Opera Newsletter (Maplewood, NJ: The New York Opera Newsletter, Inc.).

> This admirable monthly newsletter is published by singers for singers. It lists audition, training, and contest opportunities as well as many useful articles on the craft and business of singing. The newsletter may be of most use to those just starting their career, but it contains information of interest to anyone working in opera.

Opera (London: Opera)

> This British monthly contains news of opera in Great Britain and in Europe. It provides a somewhat different perspective on the opera business than is seen in American publications.

Opera Canada (Toronto: Publications STE 433)
> Published quarterly, this journal covers opera events in Canada and throughout North America.

Opera Monthly (New York: Opera Monthly).
> This excellent publication takes as its special mission the exploration of new and innovative trends in the opera world. It covers emerging artists, living composers, and new works. It is an excellent place to look for cutting edge ideas in the industry.

Opera News (New York: Metropolitan Opera Guild).
> Published by the Metropolitan Opera Guild, *Opera News* represents a more establishment tradition in opera. Nevertheless, it regularly publishes informative articles on opera history, on the backgrounds of specific operas, and on performers. The articles are invaluable for anyone wishing to increase the depth of his or her knowledge about opera. Additionally, information on upcoming radio and television broadcasts of opera is also printed in every issue. Many major training programs and contests also advertise in *Opera News*. It is also a good way for singers to keep tabs on their colleagues, because extensive reviews of past productions as well as the casts for upcoming productions throughout the country are provided.

Opera Quarterly (Durham, NC: Duke University Press).
> Opera needs at least one scholarly publication, and *Opera Quarterly* fulfills that purpose. Articles on a wide range of opera topics, from history to musicology, are written by persons in numerous scholarly fields, as well as by singers, directors, and others working professionally in opera production.

Index

~&~

A

Abbado, C., 28
Accompanists, 191
Adler, K., 212, 217 n.
Aida (Verdi, G.), 31, 67, 139
Alexander (technique), 16, 21
Ariadne auf Naxos (Strauss, R.), 195
Arias, 138
Auditions, 25, 28, 183

B

Backstage, 33
Baker, D.J., 138, 142 n.
Balk, W., 17, 18, 21, 23 n., 86, 88 n.,
    111, 203 n.
Ballo in Maschera, Un (Verdi, G.), 163,
    185
Barber, S., 70. *See also Vanessa*
Barbiere di Siviglia, II (Rossini, G.), 66,
    112, 126, 148
Bellini, V., 90. *See also Norma*
Berg, A., 73. *See also Lulu*
Berio, L., 210
Bizet, G., 121. *See also Carmen*
Bohème, La (Puccini, G.), 76, 163, 170,
    195

Boito, A., 41
Bomarzo (Ginastera, A.), 22
Britten, B., 193

C

Career, 4, 139
Carmen (Bizet, G.), 26, 70–71, 83,
    121, 129, 158, 163, 188
Cavalleria Rusticana (Mascagni, P.), 87
Cavalli, F., 54
Cenerentola, La (Rossini, G.), 210
Chaplin, C., 88
Coaches, 12, 20, 112, 118, 138, 139,
    143
Competitions, 205
Composer, 34, 40
Conductor, 30, 53, 75, 89, 92, 93, 118,
    135, 139, 140, 174, 185, 190, 191,
    193, 214
Consul, the (Menotti, G. C.), 17, 149
Contes d'Hoffmann, Les (Offenbach, J.),
    47, 82, 83, 185
Contours, 119
Cosi fan Tutte (Mozart, W. A.), 41, 148,
    196
Craig, D., 203 n.

D

Da Ponte, L., 41, 103 n., 91, 119
Debussy C. A., 48. *See also Pelléas et Mélisande*
Director, stage director, 30, 64, 74, 82, 88, 89, 92, 93, 101, 118, 126, 135, 138–140, 174, 185, 190, 191, 193, 214
Domingo, P., 28
Don Carlos (Verdi G.), 25, 31, 42, 66, 83, 210
Don Giovanni, (Mozart W. A.), 41, 49–50, 119, 141, 188
Dornemann, J., 203 n.
Dvorak, A., 158

E

Emmons, S., 212, 217 n.
Entführung aus dem Serail, Die (Mozart, W. A.), 26, 185
Eugene Onegin (Tchaikovsky, P. I.), 156
Euridice (Peri, J.), 43 n., 54
Expression, 63, 65, 83

F

Fach, 18
Falstaff (Verdi, G.), 47, 188
Faust (Gounod, C.), 210
Favola d'Orfeo, La (Monteverdi, C.), 43 n.
Feldenkreis (method), 21
Fille du Regiment, La (Donizetti, G.), 26
Finchly, J., 203 n.
Fledermaus, Die (Strauss, J.), 26, 210
Focus, 75
Forza del Destino, La (Verdi, G.), 163
Freischütz, Der (von Weber, C. M.), 26

G

Gallwey, W. T., 18, 21, 23 n.
Gesture, 69, 134
Gianni Schicchi (Puccini, G.), 148, 195
Ginastera, A., 22

Glass, P., 213
Goldovsky, B., 34, 92, 103 n.
Green, B., 18, 21, 23 n.

H

Handel, G. F., 3, 193
Hänsel und Gretel (Humperdinck, E.), 148
Hotel Eden (Mollicone, H.), 3

J

Joyner, J., 19

K

Kerman, J., 43 n.
Kivy, P., 41, 43 n.
Kloiber, R., 18, 23 n.
Krywosz, B., 7 n.
Kupfer, H., 28

L

L'elisir d'amore (Donizetti, G.), 68, 74, 197
Languages, 152
Lear, E., 166
Librettist, 40
Lucia di Lammermoor (Donizetti, G.), 52, 87
Lulu (Berg, A.), 189

M

Macbeth (Verdi, G.), 87
Madama Butterfly (Puccini, G.), 15
Maddison, D., 204 n.
Management, 200
Manon (Massenet, J.), 196
Massenet, J., 196
Menotti, G. C., 149
Messiah, The (Handel, G. F.), 55
Mollicone, H., 3

Monteverdi, C., 43 n., 158
Mordden, E., 61 n.
Movement, 63, 65
Mozart, W. A., 41, 50, 52–53, 61, 71,
    73, 82, 91, 92, 103 n., 119, 129,
    133, 153, 164, 193, 213. *See also Cosi
    fan Tutte; Don Giovanni; Entführung
    aus dem Serail; Nozze di Figaro, Le;
    Zauberflöte, Die*
Mujica Lainez, M., 22
Musical America, 207
Mussorgsky, M., 194

N

National Association of Teachers of
    Singing, 210
New York Opera Newsletter, the,
    182 n.
Norma (Bellini, V.), 32, 70
Nozze di Figaro, Le (Mozart, W. A.), 35,
    41, 71, 80, 129, 132, 152, 187

O

Offenbach, J., 82. *See also* Contes
    D'Hoffmann, Les
Opera America, 203 n.
Opera Guide, 207
Opera News, 138, 142 n., 207
Otello (Verdi, G.), 15, 124
Owens, R., 203 n., 204 n.

P

Papolos, J., 204 n.
Pelléas et Mélisande (Debussy, C. A.),
    48, 158
Peri, J., 213. *See also* Euridice
Physique du rol, 14
Ponnelle, J. P., 28
Porgy and Bess (Gershwin, G.), 15, 23,
    52, 87, 158
Posey, K., 204 n.
Puccini, G., 52, 53, 54, 55, 73, 76,
    164, 193, 194. *See also Bohème, La;
    Gianni Schicchi; Madama Butterfly;
    Tosca; Turandot*

R

Recitals, 205, 211
Rehearsals, 136
Relaxation, 19
Repertoire, 19, 193, 209
Repetitions, 112
Résumés, 197, 210
Rheingold, Das (Wagner, R.), 55
Rigoletto (Verdi, G.), 13, 92, 148, 161
Ristad, E., 18, 21, 23, 203 n.
Robinson, P., 43 n.
Romeo et Juliette (Gounod, C.), 161
Rosenkavalier, Der (Strauss R.), 55, 135,
    166 n.
Rossini, G., 61 n., 73, 112, 126. *See
    also Barbiere di Siviglia, Il;
    Cenerentola, La*
Rusalka (Dvorak, A.), 158

S

Salome (Strauss, R.), 135, 188
Schikaneder, E., 61 n.
Schoenberg, A., 210
Sellars, P., 28
Shurtleff, M., 203 n.
Silver, F., 203 n.
Simon Boccanegra (Verdi, G.), 94, 195
Sontag, S., 212, 217 n.
Sorochinsky Fair (Mussorgsky, M.), 194
Stage director, *See* Director
Stanislavsky, K., 69
Strauss, R., 54, 55, 135, 166 n., 191.
    See also Ariadne auf Naxos; Salome
Stravinsky, I., 191
Style, 52, 148, 158
Sullivan, G., 204 n.
Summers, D. A., 204 n.
Suzuki, T., 17

T

Tchaikovsky, P. I., 156
Titus, La Clemenza di (Tito) (Mozart,
    W. A.), 213
Tosca (Puccini, G.), 10, 26, 42, 54, 161
Traviata, La (Verdi, G.), 65, 161, 162,
    163
Tristan und Isolde (Wagner, R.), 47
Trovatore, Il (Verdi G.), 78, 162
Turandot (Puccini G.), 31, 53, 197

V

Vanessa (Barber, S.), 70, 158
Verdi, G., 40, 41, 61, 73, 90, 94, 124,
    158, 163, 164. *See also Aida; Ballo in
    maschera, Un; Don Carlos; Falstaff;
    Macbeth; Rigoletto; Simon Boccanegra;
    Traviata, La; Trovatore, II*
Voice: teacher, training, studio,
    technique, 5, 11, 20, 25, 51, 64, 66,
    86, 92, 143, 159, 167, 193, 210

W

Wagner, R., 54, 55, 73, 193. *See also
    Tristan und Isolde; Walküre, Die*
Walküre, Die (Wagner, R.), 14, 196

Z

Zauberflöte, Die (Mozart, W. A.), 14,
    26, 60, 65, 105, 133, 161

DATE DUE